THE SECOND TEAM

"The Second Team is a young man's coming of age story in one of the most troubled times in American history. This first-hand account of the war demonstrates Downing's resilience and steadfast devotion to his guiding principles, his continued devotion to serving his country, and how that carried him forward to a successful civilian career. I will be recommending it for our museum gift shop."

- Edward T. Luttenberger, Communications Director,
The National Vietnam War Museum

"Downing finds beauty amongst the awfulness of war in this tale of tragedy, sacrifice and rebirth. Described through the eyes of an 'everyman,' the reader is thrust into the height of the Vietnam conflict and immersed into the lives of master helo pilots delivering the Army war machine's ability to wage war. Downing's account is relatable to all who struggle with their place in the world when hope is seemingly lost while committing to a mission with a higher purpose."

- Lt Col Charles "Dutch" M. Holland,
United States Space Force

"For all those children who grew up without the dad who fathered them... his life given on foreign soil... this book is for you. James C. Downing, Jr. pulls back the curtain on a place and time during the Vietnam War, as a U.S. Army helicopter pilot, revealing the destruction, heroism, and even boredom, followed by heart pounding terror. Connect with him as he shares his experiences, dreams, fears, and perhaps, connect with the father you never knew."

-Dawn (Bradley) Kurschat, daughter of CPT Robert N. Bradley,
Medevac pilot, KIA March 1967

"As a former Air Force Forward Air Controller in Southeast Asia (SEA), I relived my year in SEA with Jim's detailed description of his experiences in war all taken from his personal journal. He shared his thoughts of war, devotion to country, and personal faith. Realizing that our missions were totally different, we shared the same guiding principles of devotion to God, country, and family. His detailed account brought back many memories of SEA."

-Lendy C. Edwards, Lt. Col., USAF Retired

"I loved this story of a boy who wanted to fly. That ambition eventually led to flying combat missions as a helicopter pilot in Vietnam. This is an intensely personal account of one man's journey of faith, fear, and accomplishment. Filled with rich detail taken from the author's personal journals, this book is a shared experience for Military Veterans, pilots, and anyone who has faced the challenge of following a dream."

-David E. Jeffcoat, U.S. Army Reserve, 1972-1978

"As a former slick pilot, I enjoyed Downing's account! He caught the essence of what it is like to go from hours of boring resupply missions to moments of stark fear as sheets of tracers arch up to strike your aircraft. You are reminded of the little things that made up one's life in a combat zone: leaky tents, sweat and dust, trying to sleep through artillery fire. His detailed account brought back many memories of Vietnam."

-Gene L. Peery, CW2 UH-1D Pilot, Vietnam 1967–1968

"As an infantryman in Vietnam I greatly appreciated our helicopter pilots; we saw lives saved by their actions, but this is the first time I discovered what their lives were like when they weren't saving ours. I was amazed and thrilled by what pilots went through to try and keep us safe and alive. Thank you so much James."

-Jim Intravia, SP-4, Charlie Company 2/1, 196th Infantry Brigade,
Americal Division, 1969-1970

"I was with the H Company Rangers attached to the First Cavalry in Vietnam, and in dense jungle, I saw pilots put their helicopters down where I doubt one could park a Volkswagen Bug, because we called! They made those birds do things far beyond what the "book" said they could do."

-Michael Riggs, H Company Rangers, First Calvary, Vietnam

As a young boy I was mesmerized by the stories of fighter pilots in the Second World War from both the European and Pacific theaters of conflict. I would find myself experiencing the drama and sheer delight of the marvels of powered flight whether from an aircraft carrier or a hastily constructed field. As a much older "boy" and a minister of the Gospel I have the added blessing of knowing "Sonny" not only as an authentic Christ-follower, a brother in the faith, and long-time Tuesday morning breakfast and Bible-discussion companion but as a skilled helicopter pilot and careful journalist taking me back to my favorite boyhood past-time and introducing me to the reality of air war in Vietnam and the grace of God that was abundant there. My life is forever enriched by knowing Sonny and his story!"

-Reverend Douglas Martin, Fort Worth, Texas

"This is a captivating book that I could not put down. It describes a young boy's passion for flying and his journey in life as he fights his way through obstacles to achieve his dream of serving his country, his God and finding the right woman to marry and raise a family. In his detailed diary he describes his struggles, failures and successes. He tells of how his training and faith in God carried him through it all. The description of his day to day, almost incommunicable experiences of the war in Vietnam, is done with such clarity that you feel you are there living it with him from harrowing helicopter rescues, resupply missions to white knuckle combat missions and crashes. It describes the making of an American hero! The book is a tribute to the unsung heroes of logistics! It is a must-read!"

-James W. Ireland, Colonel, U.S. Army Retired 1968-1994,
Veterans of Foreign Wars Post 2894, Chesapeake, VA.

"I remember my Uncle Sonny taking my brother, sister and I on a plane ride out of Albert Whitted Airport around 1963 before he went into the U.S. Military. In his book you will read of his life experiences and dangerous encounters as a helicopter pilot in Vietnam. I was 8 at the time. He would occasionally come home on leave and play his recordings of the Smothers Brothers and others who had entertained the troops while he was in the military. If you enjoy reading interesting autobiographies and military facts of the Vietnam War, this is a riveting read from his own personal journal account."

-Cheryl Mellish, Niece, Med Tech

" The Second Team gives a highly detailed account about the unique experience of flying in combat. It also captures all the other things that occur in an austere environment far from home and emotional roller coaster of highs and lows that come with pulling troops off hot LZs one minute and worrying about stocking the mess hall in between sorties. I highly recommend this book for anyone who wants a glimpse into the realities of combat flying."

- Lt. Col. Donald C. Lowe, USAF Ret. AC-130 EWO and U-28 CSO

" Downing meticulously records missions, daily events, and personalities that mould the life of 'The Second Team'. Unusual specificity pervades this man's narrative and imbues it with authenticity. Vicariously, we ride on missions with Downing as he maneuvers the Slick that clips treetops, punctures green canopy, descends, hovers, unloads ammo, recovers the wounded airlifting rifle men and medics. Then, he laboriously ascends the hot LZ and exits the valley of the shadow now alive with green tracers (NVA)-another day in the life of an Air Assault Pilot. As a Marine platoon commander ground pounding between Con Thien - Khe Sanh in 1967 in support of 9th Marines, I daily observed chopper resupply and emergency medevacs. The helicopter was the ubiquitous presence in Vietnam. Downing comprehends and communicates this overwhelming presence to us."

-William Hogue, Captain USMC, Ret.

"To understand more about yourself and about your nation, you must know the stories that have built what you think you know. James Downing's book, The Second Team, will give you exceptional insight into the shaping experiences of his time in Vietnam, will inspire you with the journey of his faith through loss and challenge, and will give you greater understanding about a generation whose voices became muted upon returning home from service after one of America's most debated and complex conflicts. You'll discover there's more to your history when you read his."

-Julie Lyles Carr, Best-selling author of *Raising an Original*

The Second Team

A Vietnam Pilot's Journal Account of Faith, Freedom and Flying

To Wayne & Janette Duke
08/23/2023

by

James C. Downing Jr.

The Second Team
A Vietnam Pilot's Journal Account of Faith, Freedom, and Flying

This book is available at special discounts when purchased in quantity for use as premiums, promotions, fundraisers, or educational purposes. For inquiries and details, contact the publisher through encodableimpact.com

Published by Encodable Impact Publishing, LLC
Madisonville, LA
www.encodableimpact.com

Cover and Interior Design by Rebecca Coda
Editing by Rick Jetter

The cover picture was taken by Ranjith Aligal and Chinook on front cover by Daniel Klein via unsplash.com. Flag on cover by Relentless via pixabay.com. Chapter icons by Freepik (Military Fill) via flaticon.com. The Second Team logo designed by Rebecca Coda via Canva. Photos by James C. Downing Jr.

Library of Congress Control Number: 2021940913
Paperback ISBN: 978-7374099-0-8
EBook ISBN: 378-1-7374099-1-5

To the brave soldiers of the 1st Cavalry Division with whom I proudly served I dedicate this book to your acts of heroism and valor.

To the memory of my dear friend, Captain Robert Neal Bradley, who gave his life in Vietnam while trying to save others, I will always remember your friendship and honor your legacy.

To the Creator of the Universe who has guided my life through Providence and preserved my life.

To my mother who gave me life and nurtured me in my early years.

To my wife, Carol, who has given me true love, peace, and our children James III, Rebecca, and John. I was never genuinely happy or fulfilled until I found you. You have been and always will be the mainstay of our family. To me, you are one of God's greatest gifts.

To my family and friends who helped shape my early life, I am eternally grateful.

Contents

Foreword

By Julie Lyles Carr

A nation explains who it is by its wars. By its stories of valor. By its explanations of the values that make it worth sending its finest young people to the shores of distant lands, to the bloody fronts opposite an enemy, of the causes it believes are worth fighting and dying for. The early wars of our nation, from the Revolutionary War to the homefront Civil War both define and mythologize how we see ourselves as a people.

The Greatest Generation has told its stories. Young men sent to battle, young women learning to be riveters, victory gardens set to bloom. The generation that fought the battles of World War II, those who encountered the enemy at the front and those who battled the challenges at home, their stories have filled our collective ethos for over eighty years now.

Then there was the Korean War. My uncle served in that fight. As a child, I knew that he had served as a soldier, but the details around his war were murkier. While I often saw grainy newsreels of the Blitz and storming the beach at Normandy from World War II in my history class in school, there didn't seem to be as much material when it came to Korea.

And the mysteries that swirled around the Vietnam War, the conflict that was birthed just two years after the end of the Korean War, its edges were banked in a leaden fog.

An extended family member of mine who flew missions in the conflict doesn't tell his stories from Vietnam. They are too dark to him, too hard to tell. The scant details that were taught in my high school history class primarily focused on the protests, the political upheaval, the hot-potato juggling of the war from President Kennedy's dabbling fingers to President Johnson's broad mitts, to the clumsy and distracted grasp of President Nixon, until the war's end under President Ford. But collectively we don't seem to remember that the first American soldier was killed in 1959 in the Vietnam conflict, that our time there, in warfare, would expand to over 19 years. It's a war that doesn't fit tidily in a defined box, with clear provocations and the valiant defeat of the enemy. The soldiers of the Vietnam War are the people of my parents' generation, the generation who were raised by the Greatest Generation. And yet their voices haven't had the same foothold.

I grew up with numerous Vietnam vets. My dad's career as a rocket scientist kept us living near some of the largest Air Force bases in the nation, as the initiatives around the Space Shuttle program required test pilots, dry lake beds, and all things aerospace. My parents' friends and business colleagues represented every military division. But I didn't really know I was growing up around those who had recently come back from combat. The wounds of what they had experienced there, of the hostile homecomings they faced when returning to the United States, didn't make for easy storytelling.

The tenor of the stories that are out there don't have the same ring as those of the Greatest Generation, the seeming nobleness of that conflict. The best we've come up with as a moniker for those who spent their late teens and young adulthood in the throes of the Vietnam conflict is the Baby Boomer Generation. That seems hardly adequate a name for a generation that was attempting to live up to the reputation of their parents' generation while forging their way through social upheavals and a debated nationalism. We had become a society that wouldn't accept simple containerized stories anymore. But we also seemed to resent the frayed edges that lapped over the edge of the box. James Downing was part of my growing up years, a consistent, friendly presence in my home church. To be honest, I didn't really know about his history in Vietnam. He was one of the dads, part of the military families that we lived amongst because of my dad's career. He, his wife Carol, and their kids, were part of our traveling band of church families, a small collective that were assigned to similar locales through the years.

While I didn't know about James's wartime experiences, I did know he was curious. Smart. Funny. I appreciated his faith, his consistency in serving in the church congregations we were part of. He and his family took care of others, lingered long after services to chat, and always had some new research to share, whether on your handwriting style, a Bible geographical site, or interesting facts about your birthday.

It was years later, after I had moved away and married and had kids, and James and Carol had moved on from their military days, that I learned more of his story. I discovered his accomplishments as a pilot. I found out about his time overseas. Those stories helped me know him more.

And now, he has written it down. For me. For you. And for a coming generation that needs to know how to walk and fight and navigate strong opposing opinions and do your best, even when the crowds don't applaud.

His story has helped me understand more about a portion of our national history that has been muted for many years.

I don't expect the history around the Vietnam War to somehow spiffy itself up and be told with a singular voice. I'd rather hear several voices anyway, in their times of harmony, their clashing notes, and their minor chords. Thankfully, James has added his song to the chronicle, along with telling of the forces that drove him, the losses he suffered, and the influences he would not allow to drive his life anymore after his combat experience. Yes, this is a book on his military experience. And it is also more. It gives a portrait of the life of a soldier, of opportunities, of an escape from a harsh past, of the grit required to build a new life, and then to rebuild it again.

If you want to know the story of this nation, then breathe in James's story. Yes, it is about the war he fought. But more importantly, it is about the men and women who fight those wars, even when those conflicts are complex, even when childhoods have been difficult, even when homecomings are complicated. We are, after all, the stories we tell ourselves, and this is one you need to know.

Introduction

The primary thrust of *The Second Team* is my eye-witness account as a 24-year-old 1st Cavalry Division combat helicopter pilot and soldier during the Vietnam War. I saw, firsthand, that young helicopter pilots in the Vietnam War were both brave in combat and fearful of the possibility of death, that each mission could bring. This is my coming-of-age story, whereas a young man I was reaffirmed by my faith in God, became a decorated U.S Army combat pilot in the Vietnam War, and was transformed by the duty and patriotism of the United States Military. I am proud of my story, proud of my military service and grateful for those that shaped me into who I am today. It is with great honor that I stand shoulder to shoulder and salute the brave men and women, in every branch of the military. All Combat Veterans have sacrificed and served to ensure our American freedom, today.

When reminiscing about my time in Vietnam, I now understand, with clarity, that I was being transformed just as metal that is forged with fire. As a young pilot in the U.S. Army facing another tour abroad, my uncertain future in 1966 was viewed as an unfolding mystery and a giant leap of faith. As an older man, it has become easier to calmly reflect on my earlier life and the protection and guidance that Providence had afforded me. As the years progressed, faith became my sight. I now know it was my relationship with God that made all the difference in my personal protection, in building my family, in the purpose of my existence and the security of my well-being today.

Back then, I had much to overcome and to prove to myself. I was wrestling with a troubled upbringing and I simply desired to become, "my own man." During my trauma-filled youth, I was afflicted by severe and harsh punishment. By today's standards, I experienced physical and emotional child abuse right up until the time I was a teenager. I wanted to escape the pain of my life to become a person of peace and of honor. I desired to know what kind of mettle that I, myself, was made of. My test, my crucible, would be proven as a pilot of the U.S. Army.

During many of the combat missions I was terrified. As a pilot, it was a struggle to be brave, grow in faith, and earn my own place of respect in the sun. I was set free from all the emotional scarring of my youth simply by increasing my vantage point and seeing the world more peacefully from on high. Flying lifted me above the troubles of the world. I was independent, happy, and free to act on my own dreams for the future. One of my true loves was aviation. Duty to my country was my focus and becoming a world-class pilot was my aim. I was entrenched in mastering the art of helicopter flight and tactical warfare. My goal was to be known as an honorable man of valor and duty.

Not every soldier experienced the Vietnam War from my perspective. Today, many still suffer from post-traumatic stress disorder (PTSD) and daily relive the darkest side of humanity, still questioning, "Why did this happen?" or "Why was I there?". Watching dear friends killed in combat leave behind Gold Star Families may make one question whether there even is a God. Wars are not fair, nor have they ever been, they are results of conflict that involve guilty and innocent human beings. Understandably, feelings of anger, resentment and regret still plague many Veterans from every war. I have spoken with many Vietnam Veterans and each person holds their own heroic story and very personal perspective based on their own beliefs and experiences. I respect them for that. Their stories, too, deserve to be heard. To every Vietnam Veteran, perspective matters, and you are deserving of honor, recognition, and respect. Your feelings are legitimate, and it is my prayer that somehow my story will offer you connection, comfort, and peace. I entered the war as a man of faith in God because I had already experienced my own great awakening through my own childhood tragedy at a tender early age of 11 years. In this journal account, I speak to my personal testimony of faith in some of the gravest of situations and how my personal relationship with God helped me navigate dangerous combat missions and, by God's Grace, survive to tell my story.

To all those contemplating military service or have already started your career, my hope is that my God-fearing path may give you the courage to do what is right and to live your purpose through your military experience, even amidst adversity. For anyone who has experienced trauma, trials or temptations, my aim is that you experience hope for a bright future filled with happiness and connectedness. I personally believe God wants everyone to answer His call and accept the Grace He has in store for you, in a home, in the great beyond. Our life experiences are interconnected and the stories you share with others bind us together with a greater calling. You have great purpose on this earth and your personal narrative has the power to make all the difference.

In this manuscript you will experience the various emotions and senses that were lived through the eyewitness account of my combat tour of duty with the 1st Cavalry Division during the Vietnam War. The vision of publishing *The Second Team* for the public was dreamed about over fifty-three years ago. Time has rapidly slipped away since my last combat mission in Vietnam but, when I close my eyes, I can still relive the memories as if I were still there. I have seen death, blood, love, grace, sacrifice and hard work. When God breathes Providence, time has a way of standing still. Vietnam changed me, forever.

The day of my graduation from the U.S. Army Helicopter Flight Training Program was the same day my personal journal began, with daily handwritten notes from mundane moments to earth-shaking accounts into my 8 ½ X 11-inch spiral notebooks. For the most part, the dated entries included in this book are preserved as my original written words, thoughts, aspirations, innermost feelings, and military events encountered. Beginning with that first journal entry in 1964, I dutifully recorded daily entries until separated from the U.S. Army three years later in June 1967. Early in my first tour in Korea in 1964, I bought a Petri Camera with two lenses from the local Post Exchange (PX). From that time onward I took color slides and photographs to capture the events of my foreign service while I served in the 1st Cavalry Division in both Korea and in Vietnam. In retrospect, that camera is one of my most prized purchases ever made. Each still image is a memory and a piece of history frozen in time, laced with every emotion fathomable.

Aviation remained my one true love, yes, but then I met the love of my life, Carol, and in 1967 following my tour in Vietnam, we were married. Throughout my journal account sections, I hope that you will see the evolution and maturation experienced through the eyes of a helicopter pilot, son, brother, husband, and patriot. Most importantly, I found peace and honor as a faithful man of God with a loving wife, whom I absolutely adore, who bore me children that I love and cherish so much. I am truly a blessed man even considering what I experienced and what I saw during combat, war, conflict, and bloodshed.

I was able to build a fulfilling career in aviation that evolved from helicopters to jet aircraft where I finally worked as a Global Sustainment Engineer for a wide variety of world-class Lockheed

Martin aircraft platforms. I saw the first F-16 come off the assembly line at General Dynamics and walked the first assembly line for the F-35's at Lockheed Martin. I witnessed the evolution of aircraft and warfare, generation after generation. My retirement from Lockheed Martin in Fort Worth, Texas, came about on August 19th, 2016. Shortly after retirement from Lockheed Martin on my birthday, at age 73, I began deeply reminiscing about my combat tour in Vietnam as a period that was in the crucible, just as "metal is refined by fire."

Six months into my retirement, I was encouraged by my daughter, Rebecca, to type out my long, dormant, handwritten, personal journal account, into sections that mean more to me than labeling this book as "chapters," throughout. She inspired me to share my story with the purpose of comforting fellow Veterans, giving hope to those who have lost faith and to preserve my historical account of Vietnam which has never been seen before. Since I was retired, I had time on my hands and there was nothing holding me back from sharing my personal journal accounts with you. So it began, my tedious "labor of love" process of transcribing daily journal entries handwritten over fifty years ago—some with smeared pencil or pen and some more clearly decipherable. *The Second Team* is intended to serve as both a partial autobiography and historical eyewitness account of my time served in the U.S. Army from 1 July 1963 to 14 June 1967 when I was honorably discharged.

I began scanning and digitizing my photographs, maps, and other illustrations. Now, these treasured artifacts can be accessed by all. You will find my personal pictures embedded throughout this book and more photos may be viewed on my personal website. As the years passed, I wished I could remember the names of every infantryman, pilot, and crew—many of the names are not captured in this journal.

However, I feel blessed to be able to close my eyes each night and still recall most of their faces.

To add context to this coming-of-age story, I have included earlier portions of my life based on stories from my mother and other older family members, along with my earliest recollections of growing up. I share my inner dialogue as a child, as well as my afterthoughts as a grown man. The guiding principles that have always been most important in my life are my faith in God and Jesus, the love of my family and friends, the love of my country, and my love of aviation. For me faith has always been the belief in the power of an unseen realm that has always been ruled by the Supreme Creator of the universe, the Lord.

It has taken me more than fifty-three years to find the right time to share my personal journal account with you. The war in Vietnam was a very controversial issue at that time. That time-period coincided with the new-age hippie movement, which was is stark contrast to the traditional conservative values and morality standards that many of us live by today. We were often called "baby killers" and Vietnam Veterans did not get their deserved recognition. Some were brave pioneers of helicopter warfare, including my one account of the war, willing to die in combat for the freedom and patriotic duty for all Americans.

After Vietnam, I quietly moved on living my life of integrity and conservative values, not yet ready to tell my story . . . until now.

The influence of many good people, personal experiences, and God's Providence were already part of the fabric woven into my inner being before my tour of duty ever began. Vietnam gave me a glimpse of the divine, the experience of death and darkness, the peace of everlasting life, and the supernatural light of hope. Faith was the catalyst for my daily walk, freedom was the epicenter of my duty as an American soldier and flying fueled my happiness and healing. My wish is that you will connect with my words, somehow, and cherish the historical events of my story.

So now faith, hope, and love abide, these three; but the greatest of these is love.

-1 Corinthians 13:13

The Early Years

I do not recall the first time that I gazed into the sky and saw my first airplane. I had no premonition that Providence would be guiding my life down a different path than my ancestors had followed. But from early childhood, I felt that I was destined to become the first aircraft pilot in our family heritage. I was born, James Cranford Downing Jr., in north Florida during World War II on Orville Wright's birthday. I was born six years before Orville Wright died in 1948.

In 1939, President Franklin Delano Roosevelt issued a presidential proclamation, which designated Orville Wright's birthday as "National Aviation Day." Since I was named after my father, it was a Southern custom to refer to the son as "Sonny." Thus, my family and friends know me as "Sonny" while my father was called by our middle name "Cranford."

We traced our family roots back to the times of the American Revolutionary War. My great-grandfather had migrated from South Carolina to north Florida and homesteaded land there before the Civil War even began. We were deeply rooted in the Southern culture. Back then, the law was sparse and people were self-sufficient in protecting and defending themselves. Early in life, I began to trust my own feelings and my own perceptions of this fascinating world. As my awareness increased, I came to the realization that I was born into an extremely strict and demanding Christian Restoration Movement heritage of American pioneers. Punishment was very harsh for children compared to my schoolmates and much harsher by modern standards. I resented my terrible treatment especially from my domineering father. I was a sensitive child and I kept most of my deepest feelings to myself and simply endured the abuse just to get by.

My early life was affected by ever changing circumstances and family turmoil. In April of 1947, my family moved from High Springs, Florida, to St. Petersburg, Florida. My parents bought a house on Haines Road near Harris School. In March of 1949, my father suffered a severe heart attack and nearly died. My only living grandfather, Tom Downing, died ten months later in January 1950. There were many other family problems that continued to impact my early life and trauma—the losses that I still remember. It was during this time that the irreconcilable emotional trauma led to the divorce of my own parents, but, yet, they served to strengthen my future life as a husband and father.

The impact of World War II was still on everyone's minds during my early years. My father's brother, Uncle Vernon, served in the U.S. Army during that war. I was fascinated when Uncle Vernon told me stories about his experiences in the U.S. Army. His wife, Aunt Carrie, could not bear children and I enjoyed spending a good deal of time with them. They were exceedingly kind to me. He taught me how to hunt, to fish, and to shoot at an early age. Uncle Vernon was my first mentor who had an impact on my life, he was more of a father figure to me than my biological one. I loved and respected both Uncle Vernon and Aunt Carrie. To this day I still reflect upon them as role models of how parents really should be.

Spared for a Greater Purpose

When I was 11 years old, my family lived on Haines Road in St. Petersburg, Florida. My father was a locomotive engineer with the Atlantic Coast Line Railroad. The day after school let out in June 1954, my dad took me on a fishing trip to visit my father's brother. Uncle Lonnie was a farmer and lived out in the country not far from Wilcox, Florida. His home was located only a mile or two from the Suwannee River. At that time, Uncle Lonnie was engaged in harvesting a money crop of watermelons. However, the purpose of that trip was to go fishing.

My father brought our 77-year-old neighbor, Mr. Irvin Brubaker, with us. He was my father's good friend who lived across from us on Haines Road. That summer day we set out for an overnight fishing trip. We loaded our 12-foot rowboat, a green seven horsepower Elgin outboard motor, fishing gear, a two-gallon gas can (a mixture of gas and oil), and other provisions in the bed of our dark green 1950's Ford truck. The next day, we had good luck catching Black Bass. I remember the excitement of reeling in the line to produce my first catch of the day, I was grinning ear to ear with pride. In the late afternoon, we loaded our dressed fish, fishing gear, and watermelons into the back of the truck and headed south on Highway 19 for the three-and-a-half-hour trip home. I was sitting in the middle seat between my dad and Mr. Brubaker.

Sometime shortly after dark, I dozed off from our long day in the sun with my legs crossed behind the floor-shift lever. We were traveling near Palm Harbor just north of Clearwater, Florida. The instant I heard tires screech and felt the impact of metal, I was jolted awake like I had been hit by a bolt of lightning. I felt excruciating pain in my face and in my left leg. I could smell acid from the ruptured battery, steam from the crushed radiator, gasoline from broken gas lines, hot oil from the cracked engine oil pan, and I felt the engine heat seeping in from the area of the punctured firewall. As I came to my senses, I noticed that my father and Mr. Brubaker were already out of the truck. I could see flashing red and blue lights from a state trooper's cruiser. Outside I heard the trooper bellow in a deep assertive tone, "We have to get the boy out . . . this truck may catch fire!"

I could sense the fear in the state trooper's commanding tone, his voice emitted imminent danger. Hearing this filled me with stark terror. I realized that my left leg was pinned between the frame of the bench seat and the floor-mounted gear shift lever as the cab was crumpled by the violent impact with the other car. My left leg was crushed by the gear shift lever. The thought of burning to death made me even more afraid. Two state troopers entered the truck from both the driver's and passenger's door and sat in the seat to rescue me. I could hear their groans and smell their sweat as they planted their feet squarely on the bent fire wall and pushed back with all their might. Their quick action bent the tubes of the steel frame of the bench seat enough to free my leg. To my amazement, I was rescued. I exhaled a sigh of relief through the pain and terror, I was simply glad that I was still alive. But, this wouldn't be the last time.

One of the state troopers picked me up in his arms and gently laid me down on a blanket in the grass on the shoulder of the highway while we waited for an ambulance. I noticed that when the trooper picked me up that both bones below the knee of my left leg were almost protruding through the skin. Instantly, I knew that my leg was severely broken. A kind, nearby woman rendered aid by immobilizing my numb left leg as she tried to console me through her tender voice: "The ambulance is coming for you, brave boy, you are going to make it.

Hang in there," she whispered. I was in such deep shock and traumatized to the point of silence for the first time in my life. Adrenaline must have kicked in because, I did not feel much pain. Even at that young age, I was experiencing pain while at the same time spiritually awakening to the value of a human life, and the power and magnitude that came with surviving.

The cause of that tragedy was due to a drunk driver. A man had been drinking heavily in a bar at an intersection only one mile further south on Highway 19. He left the bar and was heading north in a grey 1950's model Desoto Sedan. We were heading south at 55 mph. Then, for whatever reason, the drunk driver made an abrupt left turn without stopping for oncoming traffic. Without any time for my father to react, our truck broadsided the Desoto. Witnesses reported that they heard the crash as far as one or two miles away. The impaired driver was thrown outside the Desoto and was lying on the ground near the truck driver's door. He was gravely injured and had suffered many internal injuries and a broken thigh bone. His injuries were so severe that he was not expected to live.

My father was a large man who weighed over 200 pounds. He happened to be wearing a jungle helmet which prevented severe head injuries. Back in 1954, seat belts were not yet installed in either cars or trucks. During the abrupt stop, the momentum caused my father's body to lunge forward. The steering wheel impacted his chest with such a force that the steering column was bent forward. His chest was badly bruised but none of his ribs were broken, thank God. He also had a deep cut on his left knee. Our passenger, Mr. Brubaker, suffered head lacerations and both of his arms were broken. At the time I didn't realize it, but during the crash, my lower face was propelled against the metal radio speaker grill on the dashboard. Later, I saw that the speaker grill had been bent by the sheer force of my face.

It was not long after the crash that the ambulances arrived at the scene. With emergency lights flashing, we were quickly transported to the emergency room at Morton Plant Hospital in Clearwater, Florida. After my bleeding facial injuries were treated, I was taken to surgery to have my leg set. When I awoke from ether, I was taken to a room, and I then saw that I was wearing a white cast up to my hip on my left leg. When my mother arrived from St. Petersburg, she was a great comfort to me as she held my hand, kissed me on the forehead and reassured me that she would nurse me back to health. What I did not understand at the time was that learning to endure pain would become a necessary part of my future military experience.

Tragic End of a Fishing Trip

Photo scanned from the Clearwater Sun, June 13, 1954.

My stay in the hospital lasted ten days since my leg needed to be reset after the swelling had gone down. After a few days, I began picking at the itching scabs on my face. My mother visited me every day and that soothed my physical and emotional pain. Our local minister, Jack Frost, also visited me and prayed over my recovery. It made me feel good to know that he cared and wanted to be an encouragement to me. I overheard him tell my mom that God must have "big plans" for me since He spared my life.

The wife of the Desoto driver also visited me one time while in the hospital. As a boy at the age of 11, I saw her crying as she looked at my injured young body lying there in the hospital bed. Without saying anything, I sensed how deeply she was sorry that her husband was drunk and that he was the cause of so much pain and suffering. I could feel her sadness and wanted her to feel comforted just as my mom had comforted me. I gestured to her as she gazed my way. With a tissue in one hand, I grabbed her other hand and assured her that everything would be okay. The resilient 11-year-old boy in me was simply happy to be alive after experiencing that awful pain and trauma. This early experience would affect the rest of my life.

That incident resulted in my first life changing epiphany. I realized that I could just as easily have been killed in that truck crash. But, I wasn't. I knew God spared me for a reason. From my Bible classes and the fiery sermons from the fundamentalist preachers, I realized that I was lost. I believed that God had spared my life for some greater purpose. It was at that time that I made a solemn covenant with God and vowed to be a faithful servant forever. As Providence continued to guide my life, months later, we received a large cash settlement from the accident insurance claim. After my leg had healed, my parents used part of the settlement as a down payment on a large two-story house in the northeast section of St. Petersburg. Our house was located on 10th Avenue only a few blocks away from Tampa Bay. We moved into our new house in December of 1955. We were blessed with a new home for my family out of this tragic accident. I had learned firsthand that good things could come out of a bad situation. I was grateful and resolved to become right with God. I wanted to live out the "big" plans that I knew God had in store for me just as Mr. Frost had shared with my mother.

Providence at Work

Over the course of the next year, I continued in much thought and Bible reading, and listened and learned intently at church. A few months later we had a new minister in our congregation, Harry Payne Sr. Mr. Payne was an accomplished Bible scholar, and he was also an instructor at Florida Christian College in Tampa, Florida, which was re-named Florida College in June of 1963. Florida College always had reflected conservative Christian values and teachings. The Payne family resided in the minister's residence and he commuted to the college in Tampa. Mr. Payne continued as our minister for the next few years. I learned a great deal from his in-depth teaching every Sunday. We became lifelong friends. Mr. Payne lived to the age of 102 years.

Providence appeared to be at work to continue my religious education. Our congregation also had a close association with the other instructors at Florida College. Although I never attended Florida College, I did profit from the Bible studies that were taught there. Often other instructors were invited to speak in our congregation and I benefited from their in-depth teachings even at age eleven. Their academia style teachings and their character examples convinced me to pursue becoming a serious Biblical scholar.

In May of 1955, after I was baptized by our minister, Harry Payne Sr. I believed that my baptism was the fulfilment of the covenant that I had entered with God. Afterwards, I felt that my covenant with God was sealed with that act of obedience to the Gospel. It felt wonderful.

Injury, however, does not always lead to profit, as I would soon enough learn the hard way, in times of war. I learned many lessons as I watched the mystery of life unfold around me as a U.S. Army combat helicopter pilot in Vietnam. Some things are still hard for me to understand. I experienced the loss of many of my friends and wonder why they perished when I didn't. But God's promises can lead to Providence, as Harry Payne Sr. would enter my life again, for another momentous day, many years later.

A Friendship That Shaped Me

I met George Artman Jr. when I transferred to Mirror Lake Junior High School. George was a few months older than I was and lived only four blocks from me. In a short amount of time we became close friends. I learned that his mother and father were divorced. His father was a Colonel in the U.S. Army. That friendship and his military presence fostered many more stories about the U.S. Army that piqued my interest in considering joining the military. George had a fascinating collection of miniature lead soldiers. We often used them to strategize and fight mock battles.

George had been taught by his mother to be a cultured gentleman. His mother, Julie, was in the upper St. Petersburg society and employed by the most fashionable department store in St. Petersburg as the Fashion Coordinator. She was well-known in the local area and I liked her very much. George was highly intelligent, and he had an extensive vocabulary and manners far superior from what I had been taught during my rough upbringing. I was the adventurous one with many practical mechanical skills. I could fix bicycles, build model airplanes, use power tools, and mow lawns. I could tell that George looked up to me for my ingenuity and tinkering abilities. I think that George admired my strengths, but I know I admired his. Most of the time, we just enjoyed each other's companionship. I remember the good times like the time my father bought me a used Cushman Eagle Motor Scooter when I was fourteen years old and repaired and painted it like new. George and I rode to high school together on it, we were best friends and cool for the times. When I close my eyes, those were memories that shaped my desire to become a true gentleman—someone who wished to be "painted like new" for my future wife to be, who was, at that time, of course, yet unknown.

George and I learned much from each other as we were growing up. His life influenced the trajectory of my life and, hopefully, vice versa. After I joined the U.S. Army, our lives drifted apart. I always thought that George was destined to follow in his father's career footsteps and join the military, but he didn't. For a short time George even attended a military school, but that was not for him. He went on to college and became a high school history teacher. Looking back, I never would have believed that it was I who was to serve in the U.S. Army, rather than George. I'm grateful for the time I spent with George and his family and the traits that they instilled in me. What seems to be a small influence of my life as a 14-year old boy, actually, forever forged a strong heart in the man that I became in both combat and in love.

Imparting a Love of Flying

I was drawn to another individual who would have a profound influence on the direction of my aviation career. In 1955, when I was 13 years old, H. Lano Mosley, his wife Mildred and his young family moved from Georgia to St. Petersburg, Florida. We worshiped at the same congregation that I had attended since I was four years old. Over the next several years, Mr. Mosley became another mentor who had impact on the direction of my life. He was one of my favorite Bible class teachers at church when I was a teenager. He fathered three daughters but had no sons. His oldest daughter, Sandra, was a year younger than I, and at the time, I had a huge crush on her. Like her mother, she was a lovely and genuinely fine young lady. I looked up to her dad and he seemed to approve of me even as a young teenage boy. Even though we never formally dated, we attended many teen events together and spent time together as a bonded group of young Christians right up to the time we went our separate ways in college.

About the time I met Mr. Mosley, I became extremely interested in aviation. I avidly read aviation books and articles, built flying airplane models and watched aviation programs and movies. I rode my bicycle to the local Bay Shore Park near our home on Sunday afternoons just to observe the model airplane enthusiasts fly their sophisticated model aircraft. Over the course of the next few years, I gained a good working knowledge of aircraft aerodynamics as my hobby evolved into an emerging passion.

Mr. Mosley was a B-17 pilot in WWII. As I was growing up and gaining more knowledge of aviation, I loved to hear his flying stories and always had many questions to ask. He was a man of influence and I greatly admired him; he continued to fly after the war and often flew himself and others on frequent business trips. He also was in a flying club and I vividly remember when he took me on my very first airplane ride in a Cessna 172 at Albert Whitted Airport in St. Petersburg, Florida. The front passenger seat was folded down as I stepped on the right main landing gear and crawled into the back seat and securely buckled my seat belt. There were four of us onboard for that flight. Both windows were open as Mr. Mosley shouted "clear" as he engaged the starter, I could see the propeller start to turn, I heard the whirling sound of the accelerating engine and I could smell the hot engine exhaust as it drifted in through the windows toward us. The reality of my dreams of flying was primed and ready for take-off!

There was no control tower at the Albert Whitted Airport, so we cautiously proceeded on the taxiway to the prevailing runway where other aircraft were taking off and landing. On the apron at the end of the runway, Mr. Mosley completed the pre-takeoff checklist. I could hear the RPM drop as he checked each of the two individual magnetos. With the check list complete, the windows were closed as he maneuvered the aircraft into a tight right 360-degree turn with the rudder pedal to check for any other approaching aircraft in the pattern. Everything looked all clear as we taxied onto the active runway. As I heard the engine rev up: I felt invigorated and alive as the throttle was pushed to the firewall and the surge of power accelerated the aircraft steadily down the runway. At about 70 knots, he eased back on the control yoke and – we were flying! We flew over Tampa Bay and St. Petersburg for about an hour. From that vantage point I could feel every ounce of trauma flow out of my body and found myself at peace. Everything felt right and I was convinced that flying was my future. Towards the end of the flight, we entered the downwind leg of the airport for the landing pattern and he made descending right turns onto the crosswind and during the final leg we lined up on the runway where he made a flawless landing.

I knew then that flying would become part of my future. That was the first occasion that I experienced, for myself, ascending into the sky and then gazing down on the beautiful green earth. During my first flight, my friend and mentor had imparted to me his love of flying. Without speaking a word, he had taught me more uplifting lessons in life in that one experience, than my own father had taught me over the course of many years. I had caught the flying bug and it made me smile just thinking about that day. For the next few years, I longed for a flying career of my own. From that day forward, I was focused on a career in aviation and hoped it would be one of the military flight programs I dreamed of.

After I graduated from high school, Sandy went on to attend Florida College and I attended Saint Petersburg Junior College. Our paths ultimately diverged when I enlisted in the U.S. Army and Sandy went on to meet a good young man while attending college. During my first U.S. Army duty assignment with the 1st Cavalry Division in Korea, she married. I was happy for her and her family as I would be for anyone. She was an example of the kind of girl that I envisioned I would later marry, someday, because she set the bar high as an honorable and good person. I was grateful for the example that she set as a faithful Christian woman and that her family set as generous and good people. Even though Sandy was not the one for me, she was the caliber of person I wanted to marry, someday. Her family showed me what it was like to live in happiness free from trauma and familial toxicity. They shaped my perception of what a family should be, and ultimately, through them, God showed me what I longed for. I trusted that He would, indeed, find a place for me in love and family.

The Child is the Father of The Man

Thinking back, I encountered a spiritual awakening the night I was helplessly trapped in our green Ford pickup truck. But I became acutely aware of my spiritual evolution about the time that I started college. My younger sister, Harriett, was known and referred to as the "smart child" in our family. She was a straight "A" student and the valedictorian of her high school class. She had many intellectual friends and spoke with esoteric verbiage and philosophically deep ideas. I liked this about her and genuinely enjoyed discussing topics of profound importance, such as how the universe was created, the true meaning of life, other religions, philosophy, and the Egyptian, Roman, and Greek classics. We were both young, searching minds, trying to evolve to a higher state of awareness as we were uncovering the mysteries of our existence. We were determined to understand the "intelligent design" of the universe. Harriet and I were good companions as siblings and especially liked to drive to the beach and watch the majesty of the sun going down over the Gulf of Mexico.

It was awe-inspiring to me to see the glowing hues of the dark amber, crimson, and ginger disk disappear below the horizon. These sunsets with my sister connected me to the Divine as I felt the majesty of the Creator. It was then that I pondered upon and began to formulate even more personal goals in life.

The Child is the Father of the Man

My heart leaps up when I behold
A rainbow in the sky:
So was it when my life began;
So is it now I am a man;
So be it when I shall grow old, or let me die!
The Child is father of the Man;
And I could wish my days to be
Bound each to each by natural piety.
--William Wordsworth

The awakened emotions I experienced as a child have stayed with me in my final years of adulthood. To this day as a Veteran, Christian and grandfather, I still reminisce about the people that God put in my path to influence my beliefs and desires. As a child, I wanted to become kind like my Uncle Vernon and Aunt Carrie. I wanted to become a respected military professional like George Artman, Sr. I wanted to become an accomplished pilot like Mr. Mosley. My hope was that I would, someday, find a kind and gentle Christian mate, like Sandy, to marry. I wanted to become intellectually philosophical like my sister, Harriet. I wanted to live a life free from the trauma and toxicity of my upbringing. Above all else, I wanted to seek truth and wisdom and I wanted to know God. As with the speed of life, it took time for all my dreams to finally coalesce into reality. I was prepared to work hard and take the necessary risks to live out my purpose. Many people on my Providential path helped awaken the good in me. I still experience these things today.

The Making of an Army Pilot

My dreams did not happen overnight, nor did they come without determination and grit. My sights were fixed on going to flight school and joining the military. I was making headway with my college classes, but I needed income to save up enough money for flight school. I decided during my early college years, to purchase a second hand 1955 Ford Sedan and a trailer and start my own emerging lawn business. I sweated buckets under the burning sun during the humid Florida summer of 1962 and worked to ensure that every customer was satisfied with the quality of my work. The tinkering and mechanical ability from my early years came in handy as I spent a lot of time keeping my lawn equipment and car running. I was bringing in money, but I needed a steadier income if I were ever going make it as a military pilot.

A year and a half passed by and I was still cutting grass. After completing some college pre-engineering and drafting courses, I started looking for a drafting position. I decided to apply where my brother, Harry, worked at a mechanical engineering design company that designed electric power plants. I was hired as an entry level draftsman. That was my first real job and it sure beat being in the hot sun outside sweating all day long. Once again, Providence came into play and God opened a new door with impeccable timing. It made me feel happy to be hired for my own talents and to finally have a steady income so I could afford flying lessons. I wondered where my so-called-God-given talent would get me in the future. I strived hard to master everything. I believed that God would provide a pathway for me.

Flight School

I was almost 20 years old when I began flight training at Albert Whitted Airport. I enjoyed flight training and it just felt right. I'll never forget my first flight toward obtaining my "Private Pilot Rating" in a Cessna 150, (tail number 7924E), on April 29th, 1962. I later soloed in that same airplane on May 27th of that same year. I studied hard and did well on the "Private Pilot Written Exam". And finally with beaming pride, I passed my Private Pilot Check Ride on February 11th, 1963. This was a transformational period in my life as I added a new skillset as a man, was independent of my parents, and was free to think and do all that I aspired.

As the result of continued Providential timing, the man of many talents, Mr. Mosley, became part owner of the same fixed-base flying operation where I received fixed-wing flying lessons. The flight operations had recently purchased two Brantly B-2 Helicopters to satisfy the increasing demand for helicopter training. Mr. Mosley wanted to help me succeed as a future U.S. Army helicopter pilot. At that time, the FAA only required fifteen hours of helicopter instruction for fixed-wing pilots to qualify for a Rotor Craft Helicopter rating. Mr. Mosley negotiated with the flying school for a "fly now and pay later" arrangement. I began my helicopter training in April before I enlisted in the Army on 1 July 1963. I was inspired and determined to become a helicopter pilot even if I had to pay for it myself.

For me, flying a helicopter was a new fascination and a novel challenge that I added to my aviation wish list. My first ride and training in a helicopter began on April 13th, 1963 in a Brantly B-2, N5943X. Glenn T. Pryor was my instructor. I remember my instructor starting the loud piston engine, seeing the main rotors start to turn, and smelling the engine exhaust. He told me that I was a natural because it did not take me long to learn to hover. In the helicopter jargon, "I discovered the hover button." I quickly mastered the task of coordinating the cyclic control stick, the throttle as part of the collective pitch control, and the tail rotor control petals. It felt so natural to maneuver the helicopter into a stable three-foot hover. I realized for the first time, "If you can hover, then you can fly." Even Mr. Mosley had never flown a helicopter. The complexity of a helicopter made it the ultimate flying machine and I was determined to conquer it. I took responsibility for my own flying career and completed six helicopter flying lessons before I enlisted in the U.S. Army. A few weeks prior to joining the Army, I gave my lawn business to my friend, Ron Bastien. I traded in my 1955 Ford Sedan for a used baby blue 1959 Triumph TR- 3 Roadster.

Warrant Officer Candidate Barracks at Fort Rucker, Alabama 1964.

During my enlistment process for the U.S. Army Helicopter flight training, I visited the local U.S. Army Recruiting Office on Central Avenue and applied for the helicopter flight program. The Army Recruiter, Master Sergeant Fred Filardo, was intense. On two occasions, I made trips to Jacksonville, Florida in my TR-3 for testing and a flight physical at MacDill AFB in Tampa. The boy who once assembled model airplanes was accepted into the U.S. Army helicopter flight training school and drove with confidence in his new cool blue ride, with joy.

Officially Mister Downing

I gave notice to my employer and I officially joined the U.S. Army on 1 July 1963. Everyone at work wished me well and was proud of the next chapter in my life. I was issued a one-way bus ticket and rode to Jacksonville for induction processing followed by a train ride to Fort Jackson, South Carolina, for Basic Infantry Training. Maybe the best was yet to come?

Early in the U.S. Army enlistment induction process, I and the other recruits raised our right hands and took the oath of allegiance to the United States of America: "I swear to protect and defend the Constitution of the United States of America against all enemies foreign and domestic." My enlistment in the U.S. Army officially began and I felt exceedingly proud. I had made it! I was on my own. I completed ten weeks of grueling basic infantry training at Fort Jackson, SC and returned home prior to traveling to Fort Wolters, Texas. While I was home on leave, I completed my Civilian Helicopter Rating prior to leaving for flight school. My body had become stronger and I was in top physical shape as I reported for flight training at Fort Wolters, Texas.

My helicopter flight training was conducted in two phases. First, I completed the U.S. Army Primary Helicopter Course at Fort Wolters, Texas, and my follow-on Advanced Helicopter Flight Training at Fort Rucker, Alabama. I graduated from Flight School at Fort Rucker, Alabama, on 16 June 1964 and became a Warrant Officer. I was then officially addressed as "Mister Downing." It was on that same day when I recorded my very first personal journal entry.

Downing graduation photo, June 1964.

Personal Pilot to the Major General in Korea

Upon graduation, I received orders for my first assignment with the 1st Cavalry Division in Korea where I would serve as Major General Hugh M. Exton's (The 1st Calvary Division Commander and West Point graduate) personal pilot for several months. This was a great honor and a highly coveted first assignment for any new U.S. Army pilot.

On many occasions, he shared with me his World War II combat experiences including tours with the 2nd Armored Division and participation in the Normandy landings. His military decorations included three Silver Stars, the Bronze Star, the Legion of Merit, the Air Medal, and the Purple Heart. Because most of his assignments were with field artillery units, the General spent many hours in Korea as the only passenger in my Hiller OH-23D Raven helicopter as we traveled each day to destinations from Seoul to the Demilitarized Zone (DMZ). The trips that would take hours by ground transportation would only take several minutes by helicopter. At that time, he had been serving in the U.S. Army longer than I had been living. I was honored to be his personal pilot and was afforded many hours of flight and personal mentorship as a soldier.

Major General Hugh Exton Korea 1964.

The tour in Korea provided the experience that prepared me for what lay ahead in Vietnam. It was a formative period of my life as a soldier. In addition to learning to be an effective soldier, I also learned a great deal about U.S. Army history and tactics as the General related to me in his long Army career on our many flights together.

James Downing Commanding General's Pilot, Stanton Field Korea 1964.

I greatly admired him and as we came to know each other better, he treated me more like a son. The General took the time to help me become a better soldier and; inadvertently, I became a student of Korean War history. Many of the famous battle areas were located within our division area. I located many of those battle sites and I pointed them out to the General as we flew over them. The study of the history of the Korean War was one interest that we had in common. We visited many of those sites together. Eerie feelings always came over me as I was standing by the General's side on those battle locations where thousands of United Nations (UN) and Chinese soldiers had perished together a decade earlier. As the armistice agreement had halted combat operations the DMZ became the official boundary that the 1st Cavalry Division was defending. Not many new Warrant Officers would be able to say that they had a two-star General as a friend and mentor. We were even on a first name basis. He called me "Jim" and I called him "Sir". General Exton was also a spiritual man and frequently on Sunday mornings we would travel to one of the many chapels that were scattered over the vast 1st Cavalry Division area to attend Protestant religious services.

I highly respected all aspects of General Exton's life and continuously learned from him. We were immensely proud in defending Freedom's Frontier on the DMZ. At that time, it had been just 11 years after the armistice agreement that had marked the end of the hostilities of the Korean War on 27 July 1953. I carefully observed and absorbed all the combat tactics and strategies as General Exton revamped the 1st Cavalry Division's strategic defensives positions on the border with North Korea.

The various units of the 1st Cavalry Division in Korea were often engaged in tactical demonstrations and deployment drills in manning our defensive battle positions. Our mission on Freedom's Frontier was the first line of defense from an enemy invasion from the north. A response with "speed and violence" were the guiding principles of the General's war strategies. Periodically various teams with umpires performed mock battles south of the Imajin River. For me, those combat training exercises became a dress rehearsal for the war in Vietnam.

While serving in Korea we experienced a change of command

ceremony. I observed and took photos as Major General Hugh M. Exton surrendered the 1st Cavalry Division Colors and in turn received the Colors of the 2nd Infantry Division. Many times, I had seen the 1st Cavalry Division Colors on display standing next to General Exton's desk at our headquarters at Camp Howze. The change of command ceremony occurred at the Recreation Center (RC) #1 on the morning of Thursday 1 July 1965. In another sad ceremony that afternoon, the covered 1st Cavalry Division Colors were prepared for shipment back to the United States. We all had tears in our eyes as we observed the 1st Cavalry Division Colors depart by helicopter. The motto for the 1st Cavalry Division was; "America's First Team" and the motto for the 2nd Infantry Division was; "Second to None."

After the change of command ceremony had concluded, I noted that my good friend, General Exton's, Aid de Camp, Captain John Chutter, was the first person I had heard proudly say, "Second to One." From that time on, many of our soldiers while saluting a superior officer would proudly state: "Second to One, Sir." I was enormously proud of the fact that I served in the 1st Cavalry Division on Freedom's Frontier in Korea.

By a strange coincidence on that same day, I had served in the U.S. Army for exactly two years. I had no idea at that time that I would, again, serve in the 1st Cavalry Division in Vietnam beginning in August of 1966. My tour in Korea would be the subject of another interesting story for another time.

Rotary Wing "Q" Course Flight Instructor

After my tour of duty in Korea, I was assigned to Fort Rucker, Alabama as a Rotary Wing Qualification Course ("Q" Course) flight Instructor for Bell OH-13 Helicopters. Our mission was to transition

U.S. Army fixed wing pilots into helicopter pilots. The training as a flight instructor vastly improved all aspects of my flying skills and it was an extremely rewarding time for me. I reveled in this new assignment and I was deeply happy to be living out my childhood dream.

I graduated in the upper third of my Class of 64-3W. I received orders for Korea as my first assignment after graduating from flight school at Fort Rucker, Alabama. I was assigned as the 1st Cavalry Division Commander's (Major General Hugh McClellan Exton) pilot. That was a great honor and a rewarding experience. The General and I ran that division. He always praised my ability and faithfulness as his pilot. The General had presented me with a signed 8 X 10 photo and a 1st Cavalry Division Plaque when he departed Korea which is still part of my prized Army collection of mementos. I learned a great deal about the Army and combat tactics from General Exton by being loyal and true to my country.

As a flight instructor I learned how to fly at an entirely new level. I was taught by the experts to explain through precision and detail how to both accomplish and to demonstrate each flight maneuver to a student. As I came to realize later, that training was to become a vital survival skill for my combat tour later in Vietnam.

At that time, pilots who were graduates of a U.S. Army Military Flight School had the opportunity to take a fifty-question exam on the Federal Air Regulations (FARs) to receive their civil certification. After a class training period at Shell Field on Monday 25 October 1965, I drove to Cairns Field at Fort Rucker and took the Federal Aviation Administration (FAA) Commercial Helicopter Written Exam. The FAA maintained a Regional Office there. I easily passed the test and received my FAA Commercial Helicopter Rating. That certification was required as a prerequisite for many civilian helicopter positions. Taking the exam and obtaining a FAA Commercial Helicopter Rating served me well. When I returned home from Korea, I was very proud of my assignment at Fort Rucker as an IP (instructor pilot). After my tour as an IP, I was proud that I had been selected to fly heavy lift helicopters. My flying career for my country and the Lord was just beginning.

Ozark Alabama

After my first overseas tour and returning home, I resumed attending the same church congregation in Ozark, Alabama. I had made many good friends when I attended church during flight school and it was comforting to see them all again. It felt good to be in the States driving my powder blue TR-3. Surely, I could find a good woman to start dating. Life and flying were good, exceptionally good. Being a flight instructor had exceeded my expectations and having a church family to come home to, gave me a sense of belonging.

A few months later, I was promoted to Chief Warrant Officer (CWO-2). I frequently made trips to my home in St. Petersburg, Florida, and had many good times with my family, friends, and my younger sisters. My sisters had set me up with many dates, but I had not yet found "Miss Right." If truth be told, my focus in life at that time was truly on flying . . . only flying.

It was in the church in Ozark, Alabama, when I was attending advanced helicopter training, that I first met 1st LT Robert Neil "Bob" Bradley and his wife, Virginia. They had one young daughter and Bob was a rated Army Aviator. He instructed some of our ground school classes when I was in flight school. The Bradley family often invited me into their home with true Southern hospitality. I viewed Bob as an older brother and mentor and aspired to have a family like his, someday. I wanted to be like Bob Bradley in every way. Bob and I would serve together in Korea a few months later as our Providential bond would become even stronger.

Orders for Chinook Transition

Months later in my tour at Fort Rucker as an instructor pilot, I received orders for flying a CH-47 Chinook Transition with a follow-on assignment to the 1st Cavalry Division in Vietnam. This would be the most complicated helicopter to learn to fly. My first flight in a CH-47 Chinook was on 20 June 1966 and this was my biggest feat, yet.

Flying the large Chinook cargo helicopter was a giant leap up from flying the small observation helicopters. My total accumulated flying time in the U.S. Army at that time was 1,515 flight hours. Arriving in Vietnam, at the age of 24, I was already an accomplished soldier and a U.S. Army Aviator with many stories to tell. My graduation date from CH-47 Class #66-8 was recorded as 29 July 1966 in my flight records. After having completed the CH-47 Transition Course, I was officially a Chinook pilot.

Prior to shipping out to Vietnam, I took home leave and drove my TR-3 the 325 miles to our family home in St. Petersburg, Florida. Two of my younger sisters were still living there. In preparation for the combat role in Vietnam, I was encouraged to dye my underwear olive drab as opposed to the brightness of a “tighty-whitey.” My mother also helped me dye my white “T” shirts and underwear in her washing machine. The mix for the dye was three parts forest green and one part black. I was determined to blend into my surroundings.

As I had done before, prior to shipping out to Korea, I stored my Powder Blue 1959 Triumph TR-3 in a back corner of my parent’s garage. Before I drained the radiator, disconnected the battery cables, and placed it up on blocks, I took one last trip to the beach with my sister, Harriett, in order the view the sunset over the Gulf of Mexico. I loved sunsets and sunrises and relished in them as much as I did when we were kids. As we watched the sun disappear over the horizon, I was reminded of God's majesty. With some apprehension I wondered if I would survive Vietnam and ever view another sunset at home. On the way home, I visited some of my closest friends for a final farewell. I also visited Mr. Mosley and thanked him again for all he had done for me.

After having bid a sad farewell to my family and friends, I departed on the long distant journey to a war in Vietnam. My mother had a very difficult time in letting me go. She told me, upon my return from Vietnam, that I had put many gray hairs in her head. I used to joke and say, "I joined the Army because they promised to send me 'a broad,' but they just kept sending me overseas." That didn't seem to lighten the mood, any. I still grinned, laughed and hugged her tightly, both knowing, that it might be our last time, forever.

The "father of the man" had now grown up and he was now preparing himself for the physical and mental transition to a combat tour of duty in the war in Vietnam. With determination, I set out on a long and uncertain journey into the future. Unfortunately, there was a major airline strike in progress at that time. After a few days of creative travel arrangements to head out west, I visited my older sister Clara and her family in Oregon. That was the last family contact that I had before shipping out. At the end of a short visit, I took a commuter flight to San Francisco and took a military bus to the Oakland Army Terminal for processing and to receive further instructions for my long journey to Vietnam.

My Arrival at An Khe

Our helicopter class became ingrained with the guiding influence of General Douglas MacArthur's famous 1962 speech at West Point from the time that we entered flight school.

> *Duty, Honor, Country: Those three hallowed words reverently dictate what you ought to be, what you can be, what you will be. They were your rallying points: to build courage when courage seems to fail; to regain faith when there seems to be little cause for faith; to create hope when hope becomes forlorn.*
>
> *--General Douglas MacArthur*

The words "Duty, Honor, Country" became part of the guiding aviation culture for all of us in Vietnam. I took those words to heart personally.

The Lost Day before Arriving in Vietnam

On Sunday, 21 August 1966, we finished our last-minute processing at the Oakland Army Terminal and we departed north on another military bus bound for Travis Air Force Base (AFB) at 1300 hours. Upon arrival at Travis AFB, we were issued Bachelor Officer Quarters (BOQ) rooms. I ate dinner in the officer's club and I returned to my BOQ room and retired early. I was awakened early the next morning and ate breakfast before departing the good old "U.S. of A."

on a U.S. Air Force C-141 Starlifter.Each passenger was issued a box lunch of a couple of meat sandwiches, potato chips, and a carton of milk before boarding the C-141 Starlifter. The dark green military passenger seats of that C-141 were configured to face each other. There were many other U.S. Army pilots on that flight. We boarded the C-141 and endured a long flight of 9 hours and 40 minutes to Wake Island, one of the most isolated U.S. airfields in the world located in the Marshall Islands as a sub-region of Micronesia. To break the monotony of sitting on such a long flight, I was permitted to frequently move about the cabin and to visit the flight deck during the flights to Vietnam. The stop was short as we fueled up, received more boxed lunches, and allowed time for the flight crew and passengers to use the latrine. We flew another 8 hours to Clark AFB in the Philippines. We rested on the ground four hours and then we proceeded on to Camp Holloway near Pleiku, Vietnam.

During the long flight we crossed the "International Dateline" and consequently lost the 22nd of August 1966. We simply missed out of an entire day. After the long and tiring flights, we arrived in Pleiku in the early afternoon on Tuesday, 23 August 1966. We all were experiencing extreme fatigue and jet lag. Upon arrival, we gathered up our baggage and received an in-country Code of Conduct briefing on how American Soldiers (the Ugly American Syndrome) were expected to conduct themselves while in Vietnam. This was to minimize loud, demeaning, thoughtless, arrogant, and ethnocentric behavior that often comes with typical tourism. They made it clear that we were on a military mission that required duty, honor, and country as our focus. Any violation of the U.S. Military Code of Conduct was subject to prosecution for war crimes. We were reminded to be gentleman-like in this primitive country of poverty, despair, and survival.

We were also required to exchange or convert our U.S. currency for Military Pay Certificates (MPCs). We called it "monopoly money." The MPC currency was used to prevent "American Greenbacks" from being infused into the corrupt Vietnamese black market economy. We were paid in MPCs while I was in Vietnam which was similar to what I had experienced in Korea. I was able to purchase things everywhere when I went to Vietnam with MPCs. I never had to change money into the local Dong currency. I also was briefed that no postage was required for personal letters sent back to the United States. All that we had to do was to write the word "Free" where a stamp would normally be placed. My mother ended up with a collection of my letters that were sent home from Vietnam. Rightly so, worrying about postage was a chore that was taken off of our plates. We had more to worry about.

After the initial general in-country briefing, some of us boarded a U.S. Army twin engine de Havilland CV-2 Caribou and were flown on to Camp Radcliffe at An Khe. There were mostly replacement U.S. Army pilots on board the Caribou. I recognized them by the Army wings on their shirts. The U.S. Army Chief Warrant Officer, who was at the controls, seemed to want to impress us with a short field landing. Ironically, his arrogance had led him to a hard landing that blew out the two tires on the right main landing gear. The aircraft then slid off the right side of the runway and came to an abrupt stop. The Caribou pilot was very embarrassed as he smiled, looked down, and shook his head. You could see his ego deflate and I vowed in that moment that I would not ever compromise the safety of others for the sake of showing off. After being tired and weary from the long journey itself, the jolt of that rough landing at An Khe and after collecting our gear, we still had to endure another welcoming 1st Cavalry Division briefing at the airstrip. We had more initial administrative processing and in-country briefings. The jet lag was nearly debilitating as I felt dead tired since I had arrived, all I wanted to do was just sleep. Instead, I remained alert and endured the introductions and briefing. The 1st Air Cavalry Division Commander was Major General John Norton. He served as the commander from May 1966 to March 1967. The troops referred to him as "Snortin' Norton" because he was always barking orders.

Camp Radcliffe

Camp Radcliffe was in An Khe, in the highland of the Binh Dinh province, where the 1st Cavalry Division was based. The construction of Camp Radcliffe had begun about a year or so earlier. When we flew in, I had noticed that the aircraft were parked in north to south rows on what was called the "golf course." The first group of 1st Cavalry Division members at An Khe were called the "First Team." The First Team's legendary exploits of the year before I arrived in Vietnam was later depicted in the movie *We Were Soldiers* (2002) starring Mel Gibson. A similar pilot account was documented in the book *Chickenhawk* by Robert Mason. I was part of the replacements for the First Team who were rotating back home after a year's tour of duty. As replacements, we were labeled "*The Second Team*."

Upon arrival, I was temporarily billeted at "A" Alpha Company of the 228th Assault Support Helicopter Battalion (ASHB). The four Chinook Company areas were positioned on the north end of the "golf course." Those four CH-47 helicopter companies were the heavy lift units of the 1st Cavalry Division. I was directed to our unit supply facility where I was issued a 38-caliber revolver, a chest protector, ammunition, and a survival knife with a sharpening stone, which was placed in a separate compartment in the sheath. Additionally, I had brought along my newly painted olive drab APH-4 Flight Helmet which was previously issued to me at Fort Rucker.

After supper in the wooden mess hall, I took a cold shower in a home-made company shower facility. I was issued bedding and a cot with a mosquito net in a nearby tent. After making my bed and stowing my gear, I sank into a very deep sleep on my first night in Vietnam. Peaceful sleep would soon become a rarity and I was lucky to start my life in Vietnam with anything that I could get.

Thankfully, the next day was a rest day and I could try and sleep off my jet lag. I was relieved not to embark on another long flight that day. I took care of more administrative matters as I eagerly anticipated beginning flying the Chinook in my new unit assignment. It had been over a month since my last Chinook flight at Fort Rucker and I yearned for my next flight.

Combat Flying Gear

Our issued Vietnam flying gear added personal protection for the pilots. My chest protector was clumsy and heavy with Velcro adjustment straps. Clearly, it was designed for protection and not for comfort. The required olive drab pilot chest protector design included a one quarter inch contoured steel plate that was bonded to a three-quarter inch ceramic layer. The chest protector was designed stop a 30-caliber round that was fired at a point-blank range. Even the Chinook pilot's seats were armor plated.

In Vietnam flight helmets were required to be painted olive drab to blend in with the dark green aircraft paint scheme, a white helmet would make a good target for "Charlies" (the enemy). The more experienced pilots advised me to always keep the clear helmet visor down in combat situations as added protection against shrapnel.

To complete my flying gear, I wore jungle fatigues, jungle boots, and Army issued flying gloves. The jungle boots were designed to dry out quickly from body heat after becoming wet. Everyone wore subdued olive drab underwear and jungle fatigues with black markings and insignias. Thankfully, I had already dyed my underwear while I was in my parent's home in Florida. Any remaining bright colored patches and insignias on my jungle fatigues had been blackened with a magic marker. The strategy for the subdued colors was to make it easier to hide from the enemy and snipers while we were on the ground. Everyone appeared like combat soldiers and carried weapons and extra ammunition when leaving the company area. On warm days, sleeves were normally rolled up past the elbows, but the normal standard operating procedure (SOP) was to roll the sleeves down during flight for added crash burn protection and at night as protection from mosquitoes. Hanging low on my side below my chest protector, I carried a 38-caliber revolver, extra ammunition, and a survival knife on an olive-green pistol belt. The primary purpose of the knife was to be able cut my seat belt, shoulder harness, or passengers and crew restraints if we became trapped during a crash. All this I learned not by choice, but by default. Later, my defaults would seem to be the norm.

During flights, I always rolled my sleeves down for additional flash fire burn protection. Only a small part of my face remained unprotected from a flash fire. After being issued my flying gear, my thoughts returned to the question of to which unit I would be assigned to. I was likely to be assigned to either the "A" or "B" Company of the 228th Assault Support Helicopter Battalion.

Settling In

After becoming familiar with the 228th battalion area, I was lucky enough to buy a small refrigerator for $90 from a nearby makeshift Post

Exchange. Some of the pilots who were already on station there for a while said that new refrigerators were hard to find because they sold out immediately as soon as they arrived. The PX consisted of merchandise that was stored in two parallel rows of Conex shipping containers. A walkway between the two rows were covered by tarps for sun and rain protection. When I first saw that a refrigerator was available, I snapped it up. It was a luxury to keep drinks and snacks cool from that humid jungle heat when generator power was available. It got miserably hot during the day in August, but it cooled down enough during the night to sleep comfortably without a fan. During the day, there were always patches of sweat adhering to my jungle fatigue uniform.

I began to expand my awareness of the immediate surroundings. We were cautioned about many poisonous snakes that were in the area. As a southern boy, I had an instilled fear of snakes, and being a grown man did not make that fear subside. There were different species of cobras and vipers in Vietnam. Of particular interest were bamboo vipers and cobras. There was one story going around camp of a king cobra that had been killed not far away from our company area. I saw the photograph of a six-foot man standing on a picnic table holding the head of the king cobra as high as he could reach with several feet of the snake still on the ground. It was not an encounter I ever wanted to have. The bamboo vipers and cobras were very deadly and it was known that local people died of snake bites while I was in Vietnam.

All meals in the 1st Cavalry Division, both in the field and in mess halls, were served on paper plates. Separate packets of plastic eating utensils, which also contained small packets of salt and pepper and a napkin, were readily available for eating food. I cherished seasonings when one might not think of how grateful they are in having them as options.

Another peculiar oddity of the Vietnam War was how human body fluids and waste were disposed of. The food and passing of these are described here because normal, human functions still needed to be maintained in what was going to be completely different in Vietnam.

Most latrines (crappers) were usually placed on the edge of a unit's perimeter at a distance from the living quarters. A typical Vietnam outhouse was characterized by the lower vertical portions of two fifty-five-gallon drums being cut off with a torch to a height of about 18 inches. Those modified drums were utilized to catch the human waste. A plywood platform with holes cut outs and sometimes even regular toilet seats were installed over the drums. Most outhouses were constructed with a basic wooden frame that were covered with rice paper. Normally, either a tin or a tarp for a roof was installed for rain protection. By design, there was an opening in the back of the outhouse large enough to slide out the waste drums.

When the waste had reached a prescribed fill level, a low-ranking soldier was assigned the duty of "burning crap." That process involved sliding the waste drums a safe distance away from the outhouse with a hooked steel bar. A quantity of JP-4 jet fuel would then be poured from a 5-gallon container into each drum. With the flick of a match, the contents of the drums would be set ablaze. As the waste contents burned, it produced dark smoke and a distinct stench that could not be mistaken. For urination only, a quantity of empty 2.75 rocket tubes were partially buried in the ground at a slant angle that reached a convenient height that would accommodate most soldiers.

There was one humorous story circulating about an inexperienced new young soldier. One day, his sergeant pointed to a 5 gallon can of JP-4 and said to him, "Go burn the crapper." As a rookie, he took these orders literally and he thoroughly doused the whole wooden structure with JP-4 and set fire to it. Needless to say, his sergeant was not happy with the results of that operation. I guess one could crap anywhere, but sometimes being civilized was what we needed within an uncivilized circumstance.

I quickly learned about our perimeter artillery defense strategy. Our artillery batteries (155-millimeter, "Mike Mike" Howitzers) were fired all night at suspected Viet Cong positions. The artillery firing strategy was employed as a deterrent against enemy attacks. It only took a short time for me to get used to the constant artillery firing. As I began to understand the standard operation procedures, it had become important to make the split-second decision as to whether the artillery fire was either "incoming" or "outgoing." Then, decisions were made.

I did not yet have much of an impression of the country because I had not seen much. For a pilot seeing things from the air, it provided the best visual orientation for me. However, I was becoming more accustomed to the sights, sounds, and the smells of the area as those sensory perceptions became locked into my subconscious mind. All things considered: I knew my Vietnam tour of duty would be abbreviated. I only had 290 days left until I was scheduled to separate from the U.S. Army. The normal Vietnam tour of duty was 365 days or 12 months.

Orienting Myself with My Surroundings

Sunsets and sunrises were beautiful and majestic to behold at An Khe that time of year. I could constantly feel the presence of the Creator of the universe from the movement of the heavens. The puffy white cumulus clouds, driven by the prevailing winds, were forming over the hilltops as the moist air was cooled as it was uplifted over the hillsides. Those conditions were foreboding and sometimes made flying conditions extremely dangerous, especially at night. The low clouds could instantly become a layer of thick ground fog. It was a known fact among helicopter pilots that it was exceedingly difficult to control a helicopter at a hover in thick ground fog without any visual ground references.

Low scud clouds formed during periods of heavy rains when the air became saturated with moisture. Most of the ground vehicles did not have tops installed and they were always covered with a layer of dust. The olive drab tents heated up by the sun during the day so it was better to stay outside in the shade unless it was raining. Lawn chairs and homemade picnic tables had been placed in the central areas.

Outgoing artillery had been firing a good deal of the time and especially at night. Helicopters were constantly flying in all directions. The smell of helicopter turbine engine exhaust permeated the air. Everyone seemed busy and I had many things to do. I carefully recorded everything in my journal. Being busy had helped keep our minds occupied. I was anxious to receive my unit assignment and to resume flying Chinooks. I wanted to know how it felt to fly combat missions to the various field locations.

On Thursday, 25 August 1966, the thunder of nearby outgoing artillery fire awakened me early that morning. It was cool the night before and I enjoyed a good night's sleep. I was still somewhat adjusting to the jet lag. I loitered around the area that morning and did not get much accomplished. Many of the troops played cards, some wrote letters, and some helped with the local battalion building projects. The ongoing building projects were systematically replacing the tents with semi-permanent wooden buildings as building materials became available. A few semi-permanent wooden buildings had been completed before I arrived. The First Team had already constructed the officers club, the mess hall, and a few other buildings. The construction of other wooden buildings had already been in progress. I arrived as many of the original First Team soldiers had completed their one-year tour of duty and they were rotating home. During this time frame, many replacement troops were arriving and there was a lull in combat activities as the arriving troops were being infused into the various 1st Cavalry Division units.

That afternoon, some of us were taken on a tour outside of our fenced in compound to the town of An Khe to do some sightseeing and local shopping. I bought a chair, a floor mat, and a few other things to make my living area in our tent more comfortable. Those accommodations were a far cry from my BOQ room with maid service at Fort Rucker. Considering we were now living in war conditions, I did not mind. But, some did. I had slept in tents before in Korea when we were on field deployments.

On the way to town, I was startled as we drove past "sin city". It was a fenced in and a guarded compound. There were many bars and brothels set up within the compound. Sex was referred to as "boom boom." The women who provided sexual favors were called "boom boom" girls. I saw mainly young, enlisted troops both drinking and busily engaged in the solicitation of the "boom boom" girls' favors. Most of the girls I observed were mature women who were not even attractive, in my estimation. Making money for themselves was clearly their only motivation.

All types of American soldiers had gone to war in Vietnam. Some of the troops were straight arrows who remained faithful to their religious beliefs or to their wives and girlfriends back home. However, many of the young troops that I encountered seemed to display questionable morals. When we returned from An Khe I wrote letters, did some reading, and reflected in my journal about how my life in Vietnam was rapidly changing. My personal hope was that some ultimate good would come from that conflict we were navigating there.

My First Flight Assignment

Friday, 26 August 1966 became a most significant day in my journey as a pilot. I was billeted at "A" Alpha Company. However, I was officially assigned to "C" Charlie Company that day. A game changing rumor was rapidly circulating that there was presently a shortage of Bell UH-1D (Slick) pilots for the 229th Assault Helicopter Battalion. Many of the brave First Team lift ship Slick pilots were rotating back to the U.S. after the completion of their pioneering First Team tour of duty in Vietnam.

Each of the four Chinook companies were required to temporarily supply three pilots to balance the total short-term pilot requirements. Three names were to be selected at random (that is literally drawn from a hat) for "Charlie Company." As destiny would have it, my name was drawn first. I felt a rush of excitement and I knew Providence had made its way into my life, yet again. That was an unexpected change of plans for me. As protocol would have it, I would be assigned for 60 days of temporary duty (TDY) with "A" Alpha Company of the 229th assault helicopter battalion, flying Bell UH-D assault helicopters.

A Change in Destiny

Without any prior warning, on Saturday, 27 August 1966, Providence changed what I considered was my destiny to only fly Chinooks. I would begin my tour in Vietnam as a Bell UH-1D Slick (aircraft that airlifts troops during combat assaults) pilot airlifting ground troops into combat. At first, the news came as a complete surprise, and I did not know what to think or how to react. After my mind started to process what had just transpired, I considered the fact that there was more danger involved in flying a Slick. This helicopter posed a much higher possibility of direct encounters of the enemy and in closer proximity. The landing zones (LZ's) had made the Slick mission inherently more dangerous than flying Chinooks. Sometime life is full of surprises and I viewed that as an opportunity to prove myself as an accomplished combat pilot. I also thought that maybe the diversification of my tour of duty would pass the time more rapidly with the versatility of mixed assignments.

Executing the Airmobile Concept

On April 19, 1961, Secretary of Defense Robert S. McNamara wrote Secretary of the Army, Elvis J. Starr, two memoranda on the subject of Army Aviation. The first directed to the Army to take a "bold new look" at land warfare mobility, conducting the examination "in an atmosphere divorced from traditional viewports and past policies." The second outlined six areas for examination and directed the Army

to "seriously consider fresh, new concepts, and give unorthodox ideas a hearing."
–Paul J. Fardink, Biography of Hamilton H. Howze

As a result of this memo, I would see firsthand how combat assaults were conducted under General Hamilton H. Howze Tactical Mobility Requirements Board, Airmobile Concept. That new concept integrated the helicopter into the U.S. Army combat role. I was previously exposed to General Howze's doctrine, while I was serving with the 1st Cavalry Division in Korea. At that time, General Howze was the 8th Army Commander in Korea. On several different occasions, I was present with General Exton as General Howze frequently spoke of the new Airmobile Concept during field exercises in Korea. I previously had been qualified in the UH-1D aircraft two years earlier, while I was in flight school at Fort Rucker, Alabama.

This would become my second tour of duty in the re-designated 1st Air Calvary Division. Two years prior, I had served in the 1st Armored Cavalry Division in Korea where our division was re-designated as the 2nd Infantry Division after the change of command ceremony in Korea. Prior to arriving to Vietnam, I personally had witnessed the historical evolution of the First Airmobile Division. The Bell Helicopter Corporation in Hurst, Texas, manufactured different versions of the UH-1 "Huey" helicopters.

When I arrived in Vietnam the UH-1B and C series helicopters were modified for the role of armed Gunships. UH-1D series helicopters had become the "workhorse" of the 1st Cavalry Division. The UH-1D Slicks transported the ground troops or infantry, which then, were disrespectfully referred to as "grunts," into the combat landing zones. The UH-1C armed Gunships, with 540 rotor heads, maintained the role of escorting the Slicks enroute to the combat zones. The UH-1C helicopter gunships in 1966 were typically armed with four M60 machine guns and 2.75-inch rocket pods. The machine guns were flex mounted, hydraulically driven, and were controlled by a "joystick" in the cockpit by an electro/optical sighting device that could be bore sighted. Several of the UH-1 helicopters were modified to carry 48 2.75 inch ballistic rockets. Those UH-1 aircraft were designed for the close air support role as Aerial Rocket Artillery (ARA). Additionally, Bell OH-13S helicopters were utilized as scout aircraft.

This made me think about my tour at Fort Rucker and after I had returned to the U.S. from Korea, I remembered visiting the Bell Helicopter factory in Hurst, Texas, near Fort Worth. A few other pilots and I had volunteered to ferry their "hot off the assembly line" brand new TH-13T Instrument Trainers, back to Fort Rucker. We arrived at the Bell Factory and were escorted to an office to sign for the aircraft. In the process of taking possession of the aircraft, we passed by "mahogany row" (the executive offices). I noticed an office with Hamilton Howze's name on it. I remembered him from my tour in Korea. At the time I thought that it was purely a coincidence that the U.S. Army would agree to order hundreds of Bell Helicopters. I wondered if it were a coincidence that General Howze retired from the U.S. Army and received a prestigious position of Executive Vice President with the Bell Helicopter Cooperation.

Alpha Company Serpent Seven

It seemed odd to me that I had not yet flown a single flight in Vietnam. I was assigned to "C" Charlie Company. I had been sleeping in Alpha Company, and I knew I would be going TDY to the 229th Assault Helicopter Battalion in the upcoming days. I had not yet participated in any flying activities and was anxiously anticipating the exciting and dangerous combat missions that would soon begin for me.

Saturday, 27 August 1966 began as another seemingly wasted day. I went downtown to An Khe to buy a footlocker to store some of my equipment since I would be away TDY for 60 days. I was becoming disgusted with some of the local people and the way they used the children outside of our compound to beg for money from every "GI." It was their learned way of life, and I no longer had a desire to go back downtown any time soon. It was disheartening to experience.

Time finally started to accelerate. That afternoon I was transported by Jeep to "A" Alpha Company of the 229th Assault Helicopter Battalion. Alpha Company was located on the south end of the "golf course". The Alpha Company of the 229th AHB code name was "Serpent." The seasoned pilots of the original "first deployed team" The First Team were referenced as "gung ho" and they were called "Tigers." At first, many of the young pilots did not seem to want a new Chinook pilot there. It seemed that everyone was apprehensive about me being the "new guy." I was away from my friends, feeling alone, and now experiencing a feeling of peer rejection. Their treatment and impression of me balled up in the pit of my stomach. It would take time and proven skill to alter their impression of me. What they were too cocky to understand at the time was that first impressions can often be deceiving.

As expected in U.S. Army protocol, I reported to the "A" Alpha Company Commander Major Jackson. My sleeping accommodations would be in a large old sagging squad tent called the "Continental Palace." The tent had a floor that was constructed from rough boards. The tent smelled musty and wreaked of mildew. One mismatched warped board was higher than the others and we were constantly tripping over it. The sides of the shaggy tent were propped open with bamboo poles for better air circulation during the hot August weather. Bamboo mats were placed on the sides of the tent to prevent the blowing torrential rain from coming inside. For insulation, an orange and white paneled nylon parachute was spread out and hung from the top of a tent pole. I placed my gear on a vacant cot with a mosquito net. Ash trays of fired artillery casings were strewn out on the floor. Storage shelves were crudely constructed out of wooden ammunition and rocket shipping containers. The showers at this location were hastily constructed shacks with water shower heads and faucets enclosed with rice paper. Water piping was attached to converted aircraft centerline tanks that were placed of platforms for gravity feed. The tanks would be refilled daily from the hoses of potable water trucks.

Pouring forms for the Continental Palace September 1966.

As soon as I arrived at the 229th AHB, I began hearing the exciting stories concerning the “The First Team” pilots and the 1st Cavalry Division’s first major historic battle at LZ X-Ray. Before we arrived in November 1965 the 1st Cavalry had taken many losses and they had suffered the tragedy of the battle for LZ X-Ray in the Ia Drang Valley. Their experiences of tragedy and loss of personal friends were still fresh in the minds of the First Team pilots.

The First Team had set the bar high for the rest of us replacement cavalrymen. We were to follow in the profoundly respected First Team pilots’ footsteps. I had only hoped that I could live up to the honor and courage of that unit. I, along with my fellow replacement pilots, would write the next chapter of the 1st Cavalry Division’s history in Vietnam as "*The Second Team*” pilots.

I soon learned that the mascot for alpha company “Serpent 7” was a 6-and-a-half-foot Golden Rock Python that was kept in a covered chicken wire pen in a prominent place in the “A” Company area. Evidently the year prior, the python was a mere 3 feet long when it was captured. But I hated snakes. The serpent and pen had a distinct strong musty smell. On my first evening at the 229th, we enjoyed a steak supper. After supper, the python keeper placed a whole live chicken into the pen with Serpent 7. The python had not eaten for awhile and Serpent 7 was hungry. Almost immediately the python came alive and grabbed the chicken with its mouth, encircled it with constricting coils, and quickly crushed the chicken to death. While this was all happening, some interested spectators were drinking beer as they watched for over a 2-hour period as the python broke the dead chicken’s bones and stretched the chicken into a streamlined and manageable size to swallow it. That chicken swallowing event was a live entertainment spectacle. I was not as engaged at the evening performance as all the others, I intermittently watched the event as I made up my bunk in the nearby "Continental Palace."

Later, my thoughts drifted back to my friends and family back home. I was isolated from my friends and did not know a single person in this unit. I felt lonely, but I had experienced similar feelings before when I served earlier with the 1st Armored Cavalry Division in Korea. As a young man, I still had much to prove to myself. I wanted to muster courage for the final combat role in Vietnam and I was anxious to get started. There was much to get used to in this new location.

Serpent 7 the Alpha Company Mascot 1966.

Flying was My Libation

Every night our friendly artillery, at Camp Radcliffe, pounded the surrounding hillsides. Not only could the loud artillery be heard, but the concussion shock waves of nearby muzzle blasts reverberated in my chest. Helicopter gunships ruled the day, and our friendly artillery ruled the night. The troops tried to be brave and sober during the day while at night many of them worshiped the goddess of libation. That reminded me of the sayings from my classmates during flight school:

"I am an Army aviator I will not drink,
But if I do, I will not get drunk,
But if I do, I will not get falling down drunk,
But if I do, I will fall on my face in order to cover up my wings."

As rumors rapidly spread, it soon become widely known that I did not drink alcohol at all. I had no desire. I was focused on the covenant I made with God as an 11-year-old boy and maintaining my core spiritual values. Often, I read my Bible during periods of down time when I was at home base. As a pilot and soldier in a war zone, I was committed to situational awareness and always staying alert because I wanted to survive. I perceived myself as a responsible person and I did not want to be caught unaware and unprepared in case of combat emergencies where lives were at stake. In warfare, one's personal beliefs are not nearly as important as how one reacts to the dangers of combat. I hoped their misconceptions of my first impressions would fade away as we got to know each other better.

I was always a morning person and most of the time, I retired early. However, about 2300 hours, I was awakened by the sound of gunfire. An enemy small arms attack was launched into the perimeter of our large compound. A few alert gunships quickly launched into the air one after the other as they headed directly for the "hot spot." The gunships trained their machine gun fire into the Viet Cong (VC) attack area. The red tracers lit up the night sky as the projectiles rained down death into the enemy ground target area. The seasoned gunship pilots always searched intently for muzzle flashes from the enemy weapons. The VCs were also referred to as "Charlie" otherwise known as our most fierce enemy. When "Charlie's" muzzle flashes could be seen, it usually proved deadly for the enemy. I could see the tracer fire and a few seconds later I could hear the reports of the machine gun fire. As a precaution, a rotation of gunships remained in the air during the rest of the night.

The artillery batteries fired flares continuously to keep the area illuminated against the darkness of the night. The gunships made another pass and fired rockets into the area. Some UH-1 ARA gunships augmented the aerial attack and fired loud rocket salvos into the same area. The aerial rocket artillery gunships were highly effective against mortars and other Viet Cong targets. After that brief enemy attack, all was quiet again. I was later informed the following morning that enemy bodies were found in the area where the gunships had attacked. This was a prime example of the game advantage for remaining sober.

Returning to My Home in the Sky

I slept late on Sunday, 28 August 1966. I ate breakfast and experienced more apprehension after the ground attack the night before. After some protesting from my Chinook unit, Alpha Company staff confirmed that due to pilot shortages that I would remain assigned to "A" Alpha Company for 60 days. Thus, I would begin my UH-1D checkout. During an initial unit flight check, a designated unit instructor pilot would fly with new pilots. When the IP was satisfied that the new pilot was proficient in the aircraft then he would be "signed off" and was then considered ready to fly combat missions. That was the same procedure that I had accomplished with new pilots toward the last half of my tour in Korea as the most experienced pilots in my unit.

It was now my turn in Vietnam to be the student. By Vietnam pilot standards, I was already an experienced pilot especially with my experience in Fort Rucker as a trained instructor pilot. I had the rank of CWO-2 and I had accumulated over 1,500 flight hours during the previous three years. I considered my previous experience as an IP at Fort Rucker and my tour in Korea as some of my best experience in preparation for a combat role in Vietnam. I always practiced the same flying techniques and procedures that I taught my students.

After being in country for about a week, it was finally my turn to fly. Like a "Homesick Angel," I wanted to get back to my home in the sky. I was delighted as I "strapped on" a UH-1D for the first time in over two years. My UH-1D local area check out with a unit IP was finally underway and my personal war in Vietnam was beginning. It was an emotional experience for me as I realized that I was about to take my very first flight in Vietnam. I immediately focused on my ingrained IP experience and was mentally prepared for that challenge.

It was the combat policy in Vietnam for two qualified pilots to fly in both the Bell UH-1 Iroquois and the Boeing CH-47 Chinook helicopters. The two-pilot crew concept was particularly important in the combat scenario for different reasons. Most of the flights were flown at airspeeds between 80 and 100 knots. Many of the flights were operated at treetop or nap-of-the-earth (NOE) flight levels. Trial and error had proven that it was exceedingly difficult for the enemy to hit helicopters that either maintained treetop levels or altitudes above 3,000 feet above the ground over the jungle. Flying at treetop levels could be incredibly stressful, dangerous, demanding, and it required the constant full attention of both pilots for the completion of the mission.

Normally, one pilot maintained the outside situational awareness and piloted the aircraft, while the other pilot monitored the instrument panel, warning lights, and the proximity of the other adjacent aircraft within a combat formation. One of the pilots would be designated as the aircraft commander. The task of manning the controls were swapped periodically to prevent pilot fatigue. Operating the radios could be a shared task. When entering landing zones or when taking ground fire, such things as electrical failures, hydraulic leaks, and flight control failures were more likely to occur. It was especially important when flying in close formation to avoid mid-air collisions. We often joked, "That could ruin your whole day." Logistically, the two-pilot crew could still complete the mission and return to base if one pilot became incapacitated, which frequently occurred.

Most 1st Cavalry UH-1D missions were operated in the configuration with the cargo bay doors open and rolled back. The cargo doors typically were rolled back for the door gunners to man the two standard M60 machine guns. The open cargo doors facilitated the rapid ingress and egress of combat troops, medical evacuations, and combat supplies. There was a modification of "hook shaped" cargo bay door stops, installed on the rear fuselage. That modification prevented the cargo doors from sliding and departing the aircraft in case the doors were either battle damaged or if the door rollers came off track while sliding.

It had been over two years since I had flown a UH-1 series aircraft as part of my flight training program at Fort Rucker, Alabama. On that first flight in Vietnam, the techniques that I employed with my previous students at Fort Rucker paid dividends. I used to say to my students; "Treat the aircraft like a lady." and "Be gentle with her." In preparation for my first hover from the ground, I increased enough collective pitch power to get the aircraft light on the skids. I then pulsed all the controls to get the feel of the aircraft before ever leaving the ground. I was confident that the helicopter was fully under control before slowly applying more collective pitch power and caressing her from the ground into a stable hover. The beginning of my first UH-1D flight in Vietnam on Sunday, 28 August 1966, proceeded much better than I expected. I felt safe and satisfied and was confident to continue.

I gently guided the UH-1D to a stable 3-feet hover and remained there for a while. Formally as an IP I used to say to my new helicopter students, "If you can hover, then you can fly." After having been satisfied with my hovering skills, we performed a few standard landing approaches and then I proceeded to the more difficult task of landing atop pinnacles on hilltops. Toward the end of the flight, I already felt confident and safe in the aircraft. Within a few more hours, I knew I would be doing very well.

It felt good to become one again with an old friend in that man-machine relationship. The UH-1D workhorse was sensitive to my control touch and was eager to respond to even my slightest flight control inputs. My lifelong desire for flying had reached a new level. If "The child is the father of the man," then my young flightless and dreaming child/father would have been immensely proud. Life was positive and good. After my debriefing, I was eagerly anticipating being scheduled for the next check-out flight.

During that first flight in Vietnam, I logged my first 1.5 hours with feelings of elation and confidence. Heading back to camp required facing the reality that many of my peers still found it difficult to accept me in that unit. Many were skeptical because of my spiritual beliefs as a Christian and even more so because I had elected sobriety. Even amidst rejection I maintained inner strength and confidence because of my close relationship with God. It was my personal belief that being a Christian and a good U.S. Army helicopter pilot were not mutually exclusive.

God has Greater Power than Human Weapons

On Monday, 29 August 1966, I did not have much personal activity. I spent some time organizing my sleeping area in our large squad tent that was endearingly called the "Continental Palace." I was not scheduled to fly that day, but I was on the schedule to fly the next day. I was anxious to finish my check out and to begin flying actual combat missions. I also noticed that the food in the mess hall was not that great; the food was much better in my previous Chinook unit.

Heavy rains began falling that evening. I was forced to move to a different sleeping area since all my gear became soaking wet. By my calculations from an improvised container, it appeared to be raining at a rate of about one inch per hour. I still felt somewhat isolated from my friends in my Chinook unit, but I planned to make new friends. I expected more flying activities. The rain stopped and, afterwards, it was cool and pleasant. All that I could hear was the sound of our generators cranking out electricity. Periodically our friendly artillery pieces fired outgoing projectiles into the darkness. I was beginning to get used to the sound of nightly artillery fire and the other activities in our company area. I lay in bed just thinking about my new circumstances.

I was glad that I would be flying Slicks even though they were considered more dangerous than flying gunships. I would not be pulling the trigger. I knew broken machinery could be replaced but not a human life. Although I was mentally prepared to kill if I had to, I hated the thought of hurling someone's soul into eternity and God's judgment. I did not want to carry that burden with me for life. The Communists tried to paint a glorious picture for their troops to encourage them to fight, yet by comparison, they possessed so little. Many troops on both sides had no idea why we were even fighting in that war so far from home.

Vietnam possessed a primitive beauty. It was a pity that this war was scaring the beautiful countryside with artillery and bomb craters. Beggars roamed the streets. Stores were cheaply made shacks. Women would willingly sell their bodies for two dollars and many of the troops ended up with bad strains of venereal disease. That was the very ugly side of the Vietnam War that I did not like. By contrast, I listened to the gentle rain and thought of how it cooled the earth and promoted the thriving new growth to quickly heal the scars of war that were inflicted on the earth. I saw lightning as it flashed across the sky from thunderstorms and seconds later, I heard the booming thunder which was louder than the firing of a large artillery piece. God, indeed, had greater power than human weapons.

Serpents High Potential

There was a visual sense of ruggedness reflected in our troops, to put it nicely. Personal appearance was on the bottom of the list compared to courage and performance. Many of the troops looked like "slobs" but no one seemed to care. Troops wore dirty jungle fatigues with the sleeves rolled up past their elbows. Jungle boots were not shined for weeks at a time. Many had not bathed for days at a time. When near some troops you could smell their acrid body odor of days of layered sweat. There was a fad in our company of growing non-regulation handlebar mustaches. One pilot was even growing a Fu Manchu style mustache. The young pilots appeared arrogant and quasi rebellious. They depended on raw courage as they followed their experienced leaders into combat. But whether experienced or not, everyone worked and played together. Despite some of their lack of hygiene and juvenile attributes, my perception of the Serpent Second Team was still one of high potential.

At night, our artillery batteries continued firing at suspected enemy targets. The artillery projectiles impacted on suspected enemy locations and left shell craters all over the jungle. That action was designed to keep "Charlie" constantly on the move. The bright muzzle flashes and the smell of smoke from burning gun powder became integral parts of our environment at An Khe. Thundering booms and the subsequent whirling noise could be heard as the fired artillery rounds bored their way overhead through the humid air on their way to suspected VC targets.

All around the compound were double rows of barbed wire fencing. Embedded in the barbed wires were Claymore fragmentation mines and flares that were set off by trip wires. These devices were placed as a first line of defense when "Charlie" tried to penetrate our perimeter defenses. Guard towers were placed every few hundred meters around the perimeter. Rows of sandbags were placed on the towers as protection from enemy ground fire. The towers were equipped with machine guns, searchlights, infrared Starlight scopes, and other electronic detection devices. Crews of gunships remained on alert and helicopters could be launched with only a few minutes' notice in case of any kind of mortar or ground attack against the compound. For added security, Vietnamese workers were not permitted to enter our compound. We were living and working in an area that could at any time become a combat zone.

Even though *The Second Team* Serpents needed further organization and coordination to become an effective team. The reality was they were soldiers willing to give up their lives in combat. They were becoming my team and I respected their skills and positions within the unit.

Flying Down to Hammond Field

Inside the aircraft there were a variety of both safety and crew protection features. Each UH-1D Slick was armed with two M-60 door guns that provided close range self-protection when entering landing zones. One of the most limiting conditions was the heavy weight of the aircraft due to the addition of armor plate, armored seats, and the door guns. The clumsy chest protectors and each pilot's flight gear reminded me of a knight mounting his horse. Pilots were vulnerable if the helicopter ever went down. Our unit's cavalry horse was the Bell UH-1D helicopter.

The flying conditions and density altitude (density of warm air) dictated how many troops or what weight of cargo could be safely carried. It varied depending on the conditions. The rule of thumb for experienced pilots was "if you can hover then you can fly." Individual pilot planning, judgment, and other techniques could also differentiate between experienced and inexperienced pilots in making this type of judgement. There were several techniques that I used to determine the load. I kept the airspeed on final approach above the translation lift speed (about 20 knots), made the approach straight to the ground without hovering, and increased (beeped up) the rotor speed to just below the red line value. Our motto was, "add five RPMs for your wife and for each child." More than once, I watched in horror as inexperienced pilots lost control of their aircraft in a landing zone, by not taking advantage of those techniques. Fixed wing pilots agree that two of the most useless things to flying safely were "the air above you and the runway behind you."

On Tuesday, 30 August 1966 I flew my second flight for 2.3 hours. We flew down to Phu Cat (Hammond Field) to practice power off auto-rotations as part of my UH-1D checkout requirements. The door guns were removed to lighten the aircraft and to prevent the possibility of unrecoverable hard landings. Once again, my previous instructor pilot training paid dividends. As an IP I performed hundreds of full touchdown power off auto-rotations at Fort Rucker. Now I was quickly getting the feel of the UH-1D and suddenly felt in control of the aircraft and safe. My full touchdown auto-rotations were executed flawlessly. That impressed my IP. On the return flight to An Khe, as we flew over the countryside, I saw that all over the valley hills they were scorched by artillery fire and bombs from airstrikes. That was a sobering feeling of sadness as I considered mankind should be working the land not destroying it.

James Downing and UH-1D 828 at Hammond Field September 1966.

As we flew by the An Khe Pass on Highway 19, I saw the wreckage of two aircraft. One was a C-130 and the other was an A-1 Skyraider. The crashes were most likely the result of low clouds obscuring the mountain top. Both aircraft were located not over 300 meters apart. Highway 19 twisted and turned along the side of the mountain and descended from the highlands down a wide valley on the way to the coastal plain at Quin Nhon. Vietnam reminded me of parts of Korea. I felt at home in the air in Vietnam. The only thing that that seemed different from Korea were the many tropical plants, like bamboo and banana trees and an enemy firing at us.

The local combat area extended from a few miles north from Quin Nhon to several miles north of the Bong Son area. Most of our combat flying missions in Slicks took place from the Phu Cat, Hammond Field area, up to Bong Son and the nearby LZ English. Most of my Vietnam narrative took place within that area. I marked most of the major landmarks clearly on my tactical map that I had pasted together. Little did I know on this first flight that this area would turn out to be an extremely dangerous area and primary focus of the 1st Cavalry Division during 1966 and 1967.

Down Time

Our unit was in the process of reorganizing after the infusion of many new replacement pilots from the United States. New combat strategies were being reformulated based on the experiences of the First Team. Most of the 1st Cavalry Division aviation units remained on the ground. A defensive posture was maintained but there were no new assigned offensive combat operational missions. I was sure that we would start up before long. I thought that I would like to participate in a few combat operations and then go back to accumulating flying time in Chinooks.

Wednesday, 31 August 1966 was another no-fly day. I took time to repair some of the leaks in the "Continental Palace." During heavy rains, the tent leaked like a sieve. I was beginning to get used to the local routine there. The heavy rains in Vietnam were remarkably similar to the monsoon rains that I experienced in Korea. I felt that I had a head start over the new Warrant Officers who had just graduated from flight school with Vietnam being their first assignment.

About that timeframe, I saw "Puff the Magic Dragon" or "Spooky" for the first time. I saw the armed C-47 airplane flying at night east of the Camp Radcliffe's perimeter. As the mini guns were fired I observed a red stream of tracers spraying the ground like a water hose. A few seconds later, I heard the "humming" reports of the rapid muzzle blasts which was coming from the aircraft. After that, I began calling the C-47 gunship "Puff the Tragic Wagon."

There was no flying activity for me again on Thursday, 1 September 1966 as a new month began. Our unit was waiting for word on what would transpire next. I patiently sat and watched it rain. My mind dwelled on familiar things back home. That evening in the officers' club a Lockheed representative provided a presentation on their Lockheed AH-56 Cheyenne Rigid Rotor helicopter that was under development. Lockheed was soliciting design feedback from Vietnam combat pilots. They were interested in understanding what could be incorporated into the AH-56 Cheyenne design that would make it better suited for combat situations. Many of our experienced pilots recommended that the tail rotor be positioned high enough to avoid striking the tail rotor on stumps as the aircraft flared into rough cut LZs.

Sadly, I found out later that the fast AH-56 Cheyenne would not even go into production. The less complex Bell AH-1 Cobra went into production instead of the Cheyenne. I longed to fly that fast and sleek AH-56 Cheyenne helicopter, but I never was given the chance. I never had the chance to fly the AH-1 Cobra either.

The conditions in the "Continental Palace" were about to improve. On Friday 2 September 1966, we scrounged a gas cement mixer, lumber for forms, sand, gravel, cement, nails, and other construction equipment. We worked most of the day building forms and pouring concrete for a new floor for the "Continental Palace." My former family building skills from my upbringing were an asset to the team effort. It felt good to be working hard together as part of a team. As soon as we finished pouring one section of concrete it started to rain. We would see the results the next day. There was still no word of resuming combat missions. It rained again that night and most of the pilots were partying in the officers' "O" Club. I enjoyed reading, reflecting and writing letters home.

I slept until about 0800 on Saturday and I got out of bed feeling terrible. I had come down with a fierce cold. My eyes watered, my nose ran, and I felt run down in general. A company briefing was held that morning. They anticipated starting a mission somewhere around 12 September 1966 in either Bong Son or Happy Valley. They were both identified as enemy hot spots. I suspected that the aircraft would remain on the ground for a few more days.

Taking advantage of the down time we poured more cement that day for the floor of the "Continental Palace." It would be nice to have a building to live in and to keep our belongings high and dry. That evening, there was a promotion party and everyone was gathering at the "O" Club. I sat quietly just trying to recover from my cold.

Every night, the artillery continually pounded away. By then, I thought that I should be accustomed to the sound. However, when I heard an unexpected boom out of the silence it was very startling. After I drifted back to sleep there was a brief time that I experienced pleasant and happy thoughts of my family, friends, and other familiar things I liked. Being unmarried and without a girlfriend, I pondered how wonderful life would be when I finally found the right girl after I returned home. I did not like the idea of falling in love and then receiving a "Dear John Letter" while away at war or even getting killed in Vietnam and creating a widow. I did not want to put some sweet girl through that experience. It would be wonderful to love and to share my innermost thoughts and a long life with a loving soul mate. I believed that my soul mate was out there somewhere.

That night, when I drifted off to sleep thoughts were pleasant, people were good and my dreams seemed real. My dreams were broken as the sound of those booming big guns pierced my peaceful solitude. I could hear the muzzle ballasts and fifty-pounds steel explosives hurled toward targets upwards of 15 miles away. Faint muffled explosions could be heard from nearby targets. I knew those explosions were raining down metal and intense heat that would kill all animal life in the immediate impact area. The reality of dangerous combat threats flooded my mind in full force.

The dangers of war and the hate from the enemy drew my mind back to my previous training and experiences in both basic training and in Korea. My consciousness invoked a primal instinct of "fight or flight." When facing dangerous conditions making quick, logical, and concise decisions was my number one priority. To survive combat as a pilot, many skills were needed. I knew my future encounters would require maintaining situational awareness, assessing threats, and making valid decisions instantaneously while there was still time to react.

By contrast, I listened to the gentle rain as it safely fell on our tent and on the surrounding grass. The rain cooled the earth and brought back foliage to the scarred countryside.

While pondering the philosophical aspect of life, that war seemed to me to be futile. Lives were continually lost on both sides every day for no ultimate purpose. The previous war in Korea did not end well and it left the country divided until this day. It seemed senseless.

Mortar Attacks and Combat Missions

Cannons to the right of them, cannons to the left of them, volley'ed and thundered.
--The Charge of the Light Brigade

I was sound asleep when at 2200 hours, startled, I jumped out of bed with a bewildering feeling as my heart was pounding in my chest. I looked northward toward the nearby "golf course" where all the aircraft were parked. Exploding mortar rounds flashed like flashbulbs and the sound of the explosions were rhythmically instantaneous. As with determining the distance from a storm from the flashing lightning to the resulting sound of thunder, I realized that we were well within the impact area for the "incoming" mortar fire. On Sunday, 4 September 1966, "Charlie" had unexpectedly torn us up with a surprise mortar attack.

As soon as I realized that the mortar rounds were impacting awfully close by, I sprang into combat reaction mode. I realized that I was not only caught with my pants down but with my pants off. I had been sound asleep in my olive drab t-shirt and underwear. Due to the urgency of the situation, I quickly put on my steel helmet, slipped on my shower shoes, grabbed my pistol, and ran outside of the tent. I was not prepared nor had ever been briefed on such an attack on the compound. Such a massive mortar attack had not happened before. My first reaction was to search for a bunker or another safe place of refuge. Not far from where I was standing, I saw a small enclosure surrounded by stacked rows of sandbags. As I entered the enclosure, I realized that I was the sole occupant. I cautiously crouched behind the sandbags and waited in that enclosure until the incoming mortar barrage ceased. I checked my watch and the mortar attack lasted about 30 minutes.

Immediately after taking the first mortar fire, the standby gun ships and aerial rocket artillery furiously launched and found the location of the mortar tube muzzle flashes. The dark sky filled with helicopters like fireflies. Our friendly artillery fired illumination flares that turned the dark night sky into daylight around our perimeter. I watched in awe as the spectacle unfolded. A combat assault force of Slicks airlifted infantry ground troops into the hot areas. Needless to say, our security forces remained on high alert the rest of that night.

Once the mortar attack ceased I went back to lie in bed. Just before drifting off to sleep, my senses told me that something was not right. Again, mortars resumed impacting nearby. After two or three projectiles impacted, I knew that they were incoming, again. As I jumped out of bed, someone yelled, "Incoming, put on your steel pots and get in the bunker." I was still clad in my olive drab underwear. I went outside and after a few quiet minutes I went back inside the tent to put on my boots and jungle fatigues. I was a little calmer this time and my heart stopped pounding. After the second mortar attack was over, we waited until 0200 hours and then I went back to bed, this time with all of my clothes on, hoping and praying that the mortar attacks had also retired for the night.

The Days Following the Mortar Attack

The next morning, when I looked closely into the sandbagged

enclosure where I took refuge the night before, I noticed that it was a bunker where Claymore mines were being stored. So, had the bunker taken a direct hit the night before - I would have been blown to bits. It appears the saying is true that, "God takes care of unsuspecting fools."

I was afraid that when "Charlie" found out that many aircraft were damaged and many people were killed or wounded, he would surely try to attack us again. However, "Charlie" paid a heavy price in dead bodies for that attack. In the aftermath of our gunship and combat assault counterattack, several mortars were captured and the field was littered with dead enemy bodies. I thought to myself, "Welcome to the war in Vietnam." It still seemed senseless to me.

"Charlie" hit several of our aircraft that night and one was a direct hit that ripped off a UH-1B tail boom. Many other helicopters sustained shrapnel punctures in the fuselage and rotor blades. The enemy mortar fire also struck one tent and killed two people and wounded twenty-eight others that night. Later that same day, four more troops died of their wounds. The enemy had drawn blood, yet I was spared. I experienced a mixed range of emotions watching the Grim Reaper take the lives of valiant soldiers while sparing others.

I slept until about 0730 and started a new week on Monday, 5 September 1966. That day I took many photos of the battle-damaged helicopters that were parked on the "golf course." After the mortar attack, there was an urgent demand for all the affected units to inspect their aircraft to determine which helicopters were still flyable. Inspections and battle damage repairs began that same morning. The attack also created a need to install sandbag revetments for each aircraft parking spot.

That next day, we poured more concrete for the floor of the

"Continental Palace." We anticipated that about one more day was needed for the cement floor to be completed. I worked outside all day in the blistering hot sun. I figured I'd be sunburned again. By the end of the day, we were all dog tired and hoped that "Charlie" would not mortar us again that night.

The cement mixer was "busted" on Tuesday, so we did not work on the "Continental Palace" floor. I worked on my personal area and built some shelves out of wooden shipping containers. The most exciting thing that happened that day was watching our python mascot, Serpent 7, eat a rat. I found myself studying his movements as he struck and coiled around the rat. The poor rat was quickly dispatched and was swallowed in about two minutes. This seemed to be a metaphor for me, our enemy was coiled up ready to strike at any given time, and like the rat, we wondered how we would ever escape Vietnam alive.

That evening, I had an invigorating conversation with one of the young Warrant Officers. He was well read and very bright. We started talking about science and math and then the conversation evolved into a discussion about religion. As young men, we pondered our reason for being there and how we could personally make a difference in the future. We continued to visit even through the outgoing artillery that continued to pound away in the distance. It was fulfilling to make a like-minded connection and I was happy to end the evening on such a positive note. Emotionally I was exhausted and ready to call it a night. In light of the recent mortar attacks, it was harder to drift off to sleep. Each night I put my faith in God's plan and prayed for our safety and an end to such a useless war. Prayer always seemed to ease my mind.

On Wednesday, 7 September 1966, the cement mixer was operational again and we finished pouring the floor to the

"Continental Palace." That act of teamwork helped draw our unit closer before we ever even flew our first mission together. We were consumed with pride for our communal accomplishment. That teamwork and bonding made us better soldiers. Completing the "Continental Palace" was the first time I felt that I was becoming an integral part of an accomplished fighting force. I was tired, yet proud of our unit and mostly I was proud of the soldier I that was becoming. I read some and then went to bed. I was at peace--at least for a little while, serpent and rat or not.

To broaden my horizon, my new pilot friends taught me to play Seven Card Stud Poker. I tried to learn some of the finer points of the game; but most of the time, I did not play, but watched the others and studied their body language and interactions.

On Thursday, 8 September 1966, there was more inaction. I slept late and read most of the day, something that didn't just pass the time away, but also seemed to calm me down. I learned to always be alert and responsive to the unexpected. I went to bed early again that night while anticipating a period of peaceful sleep. I was awakened in the early morning about 0300 hours to pounding rain and water leaking through the seams of the "Continental Palace." We jumped up and hastily fixed the leaks. Sleep, in Vietnam, was never going to be continuous.

My First Combat Assault Mission

With great anticipation, after lunch, I flew my third flight and first combat assault. I was pleasantly surprised that it only took two flights to be checked out. Since I was on temporary duty I would not be designated as an aircraft commander. Sometimes I was paired with experienced pilots and sometimes with less experienced pilots.

That day we were scheduled to airlift elements of the 5th of the Seventh Cavalry infantry troops into two defensive landing zones around our compound. It was my first combat assault mission. The troops boarded our aircraft on the "golf course." Our unit was to augment "B" Bravo Company. Our mission call sign that day was "Yankee Clipper." Since we were the fourth aircraft in the formation, we were designated "Yankee Clipper Orange Four." The commander of any unit or the leader of the assault was designated with the suffix, six. Thus, everyone knew who was in charge. The leader designated, "Yankee Clipper Six" as our designated leader for that mission.

The only radio traffic during a mission was to inform the leader of how much fuel was on board and when we were ready for lift off. We were going to land in a one ship LZ. For the economy of radio transmissions, the Yankee Clipper Six leader would key the radio and say "One ship LZ. Go trail with fifteen second intervals."

Everyone understood that we would take off in single file at 15 second intervals and that we would land in the LZ one ship at a time. On each assault, UH-1C gunships flew cover for the Slicks that were unarmed. The LZs that we were heading to that day were not considered hot LZs and we did not take any fire upon landing. For the most part, that mission could have been better organized. It seemed to me to be more like a "Chinese fire drill." However, it was a good training exercise, no one got hurt, and it gave me more perspective on what to expect on future real combat assaults.

Both LZs were small and covered by tall elephant grass. We came to a hover and our infantry troops quickly jumped off the skids. As I learned from my first tour in Korea it takes more power to hover over tall grass. In a normal hover condition, the downward thrust from the rotor system compacts the air under the helicopter in what is called the "ground effect." Hovering over tall grass defused the ground effect, requiring more power. If there was not enough power to hover over the tall grass then we ran the risk of sinking to the ground and crushing the troops under the helicopter.

By increasing the rotor speed to just below the red line, it provided more available inertia in the rotor system if more power was needed to get out of a bad situation. Helicopter pilots had a saying: "You don't want to run out of pitch, power, and ideas all at the same time." In the flights that day, we did not have any problems hovering. We were at a hover for only a few seconds. The troops always quickly egressed the aircraft and headed for cover. As soon as the last troop was off the aircraft, we quickly added power, started forward motion, accelerated with the noise down, and got airborne to reduce the time that we could take ground fire. Like Road Runner cartoons, "beep beep . . ." and we were gone.

We used designated Ultra High Frequency (UHF) and low frequency unit Frequency Modulated (FM) radio frequencies to monitor that mission. Prior to the mission, we lumped up (refueled) the aircraft to 1250 pounds of JP-4 from fuel bladders in the refueling area. At each hot refueling station, the fuel was pumped from bladders by a small gasoline engine. The flow rate was slow compared to the high flow rate from a high-pressure refueling truck.

We left about 1400 hours and did not get back until 1930 hours. We logged 2.3 hours of flight time that day. It felt good to be flying again. On the way home, the view of a waterfall on a mountain side added to the beauty of that treacherous countryside. Shifting my mind from the gravity of war to the peace and goodness that still existed, I found that focusing on the calming effect of nature helped me endure the darkness of war.

Operation Grasshopper was in force at that time. After the recent mortar attacks, aircraft were dispersed so "Charlie's" mortar fire could not concentrate into a single kill area. Dispersal ensured that some of the aircraft would always remain flyable. We placed our helicopter on Mustang row and were met by a three-quarter ton truck that drove us back to operations for debrief.

After a late supper of cold ham, I smiled with delight as I reflected on how my day first combat assault flight had been a success. Not only did I like challenging missions I ended up being good at them too. Combat flying was similar to the exercises and techniques I taught my students at Fort Rucker. Part of the training was to instruct them how to land and take off from tight and difficult confined areas.

My previous experiences in Korea and as an IP continued to pay dividends in Vietnam. As I started to wind down from my first combat mission, I reflected on my inborn urge for literary accomplishments. I thought that it was important to keep a journal of my time in the U.S. Army and dutifully continued to write entries every single day. I loved being a soldier. My previous assignments in Korea with the 1st Armored Cavalry and then being in Vietnam were chances of a lifetime that I felt compelled to document, knowing then, that someday, it would become primary source contribution to history.

Strategies and Routines as a Combat Pilot

The poor infantry troops were often wet and tired during the rainy season. The ground troops were the ones who had the real hardship in the Vietnam War. While isolated on patrol, they cautiously worked their way through the jungle with its swamps, leaches, snakes, insects, booby traps, and ambushes set up by the enemy. I noticed that the combat strategy in Vietnam was vastly different from the defense strategy of the 1st Cavalry Division that I experienced in Korea.

Correspondingly, our infantry troops in Vietnam carried a variety of equipment and offensive and defensive weapons that could be airlifted by helicopters. One critically important member of each combat unit was the radio operator. The radio was the lifeline of support for the Vietnam ground troops.

It did not take me long to understand the term “Broken Arrow” and the purpose of the 1st Cavalry Division Ready Reaction Force (RRF). Any ground unit that was in imminent danger of being overrun by the enemy could make a Broken Arrow distress radio transmission and our standby RRF would respond to the emergency call. We all knew of the impact of that emergency code phrase and we had to be able to respond quickly on short notice.

As part of our 1st Cavalry Division Airmobile Concept strategy, a unit of well-armed ground troops and helicopters remained in reserve and they would be co-located in a forward combat area. Our first RRF area was located at Hammond Field in the Phu Cat Valley. A prescribed number of ground troops, usually seven or eight, would remain in the immediate area of their preassigned lift helicopter. We were prepared to start up our aircraft with troops on board and launch in formation within two or three minutes. A designated RRF standby command and control "Charlie, Charlie" commander would coordinate the mission from a designated Slick. Escort gunships and Chinook helicopters were normally on standby as part of an RRF.

Typically, a rotation of three or four infantry companies were involved in combat assaults and other patrol activities. Ground troop units in field positions or on patrol were replaced every few days. Aircrews who flew long hours during combat missions would also have a turn to rotate for down time and rest. The returning troops and helicopter aircrews would then become the RRF and would be given time to rest from the constant grueling direct contact with the enemy.

The standard weapon for the ground troops was the M-16 Rifle. The M-16 had an exceedingly high muzzle velocity with severe shocking power projectiles. A squad and platoon usually carried an array of other weapons. It was easy to notice that infantry troops, armed with 7.62-millimeter (mm) M-60 machine guns with bipod legs mounted near the muzzle, frequently boarded our UH-1D helicopter. Some of the troops had brass belts of machine gun ammunition cross-draped from each shoulder. It was not uncommon to see soldiers with a variety of other weapons like 40 mm grenade launchers, shotguns, and hand grenades also board our aircraft.

The ground troops often wore a variety of personal equipment. Most of the soldiers wore jungle fatigues, jungle boots, flack vests and steel helmets that were covered by olive green canvas camouflage helmet covers with an olive-green elastic helmet band. Soldiers often placed small bottles of mosquito repellant, packs of cigarettes, and other personal items in their helmet bands. All soldiers wore two military identification "dog tags". A utility harness formed the outermost layer of each soldier's equipment. The utility harness was suspended from both shoulders and fastened around the soldier's waist. It was not unusual to see a canteen, a flashlight, ammunition pouches, field binoculars, hand grenades, a bayonet, maps, a machete, an entrenching shovel, and a medical bandage suspended from the utility harness. The equipment on the utility harness was strategically placed by each troop for immediate access when dropped off in a hot landing zone.

Each soldier also carried an olive-green backpack. Equipment in the backpack included a poncho, rations, and other personal items that would be needed after camp was made. I always felt sorry for the ground troops as they were the ones in real danger utilizing survival skills, they exhibited a special breed of bravery.

Relocating to Qui Nhon

On Saturday, 10 September 1966, we were informed early in the morning that we would be moving out later that day. I started packing and doing other last-minute things in preparation for our early evening departure. We flew out to our base camp at LZ Lane which was located a few miles north of Qui Nhon and near the coast. Qui Nhon was our base camp and Bong Son would be our forward operational area. I liked seeing the ocean and breathing the salt air even though this was the furthest thing from vacationing.

We unloaded our gear at LZ Lane and took off for Bong Son. Night was approaching and we were assigned the mission to fly chase for the "light ship." A light ship was a UH-1D equipped with an array of high intensity lighting that was installed in the cargo bay. The purpose of the mission was to circle around and illuminate the perimeter of the compound and to identify and report any enemy incursions. We also flew up and down the valley and roads trying to detect enemy movement. At the near completion of that long mission, the weather conditions started to deteriorate as our crew neared exhaustion. The lights started to get fuzzy as ground fog formed due to the drop in temperature. I had trouble keeping my eyes open as we landed at Bong Son and parked alongside the other aircraft. We ended the mission about 2400 hours after 3.3 hours of combat flying. I slept for a little while in the helicopter, but in the cramped conditions my muscles were sore the next morning. Upon awakening I swore that someone had beaten me from head to toe while I was sleeping.

We flew a resupply mission, pilot jargon for "hauling log", on Sunday, 11 September 1966, to some of the ground troops in the Bong Son area. One of the interesting characteristics of that war was that each ground troop base camp was supplied with a hot meal and cold beer every day. It was not uncommon to see our off-duty troops drinking beer early in the morning. The ground troops out on patrol in the jungle did not have that luxury. The chow that was prepared in rear area field mess kitchens was placed in olive drab insulated metal containers.

When on a resupply mission, our aircrew would often shut down to refuel and check our aircraft for damage between flights while the food containers were loaded on the helicopter. I discovered that a few of the field kitchens made fresh yeast rolls, daily. The field kitchens were always glad to feed the aircrews. Each time that I ate one of those comforting warm yeast rolls, I thought of my mother and my sisters, Harriett and Margaret Anne, who frequently baked them for dinner. Closing my eyes, for that moment, I sensed the familiar comfort of home. We logged 2.0 hours that day.

Our ship was down most of the day for a scheduled maintenance inspection, so we sat around swapping war stories of lessons learned while flying in Vietnam. We finally left that evening and arrived at LZ Lane near Qui Nhon after dark. I took a shower for the first time in two or three days. The shower felt wonderful even if it was cold.

Before retiring for the evening, I discovered that I had received several letters from home which was always a comfort to read. These small pleasures of life can keep a man going.

Flying into Hot Landing Zones

On Monday, 12 September 1966, we accomplished little flying. We took off from LZ Lane and flew to the forward area at Bong Son. We sat around waiting for our mission assignment. We flew two short missions that afternoon. Altogether, we only flew a total of 2.2 hours. I felt I was not getting much flight time and was hopeful that the pace would pick up soon. Writing five letters to the folks at home helped pass the time. There was some combat activity around Bong Son. Several aircraft were shot at, but thankfully no one was hurt. We flew back to LZ Lane and arrived after dark. I took another shower. In retrospect, boredom is a blessing in disguise.

I looked on the schedule board in the operations tent, but much to my regret, I was not scheduled to fly the next day, either. Wanting to put my combat skills to the test, I wanted to experience one of those big combat assaults. I would have to patiently wait my turn. That evening, I attended a briefing for a combat assault scheduled for the next day. Our company would airlift troops into three different LZs and then we would provide logistics support for other assaults. Our primary LZs were identified as Lee, Hood, and Jackson. I asked other pilots who experienced many combat assaults to share the strategy that they knew of, regarding combat assaults. They carefully explained in detail what to expect on the next day's missions.

Each LZ was carefully selected by a variety of techniques. High performance twin engine OV-1 Mohawks were equipped with side looking aerial radar (SLAR) pods for scanning the area to detect enemy movement. An OV-1 Mohawk equipped with infrared pods could pick up the heat signatures of the enemy. Recon helicopters would then fly over the area for visual confirmation. It was always a risk because there was a possibility that "Charlie" may be well concealed. The command-and-control commander and our air assault commander would recon the area and determine how the area would be assaulted and how many aircraft could land in the designated LZ at one time.

In preparation, the assault was always coordinated ahead of time and all the participants were briefed. The command-and-control commander would orchestrate the timing of the combined attack force. Normally the jets from U.S. Tactical Air Command (TACAIR) would bomb and strafe the LZ. Once the jets expended their allotted ordnance and exited the area the command-and-control commander would call for an artillery barrage. When the Slicks were on final approach into the LZ the command-and-control commander would call off the artillery attack. Lastly, the gunships lead the Slicks into the free fire LZ with guns and rockets blazing.

During the first wave, Slicks would land in the LZ and the UH-1D door gunners would pour machine gun fire into the nearby suspected high threat areas. As we approached the LZ, I could hear the sharp reports, feel the vibration, and smell gunpowder each time our door guns fired. As the first wave of troops set their feet on the ground in the LZ, all firing from the door guns ceased. Meanwhile, the escort gunships maintained right and left orbits away for the landing stream of the other approaching Slicks. I was told that the gunships were always ready to provide precision machine gun and rocket fire if an enemy threat was detected. Hopefully, that process would normally cause "Charlie" not to return fire at the landing force.

The veteran pilots further explained that the Viet Cong (VC) were rapidly learning that it was virtual suicide to fire at a gunship. "Charlie's" preferred strategy was to ambush patrols, to set booby traps, and to attack and over run the units on the ground at night. "Charlie" almost always used small arm and mortar fire in the night attacks. It was those night attacks that helicopter pilots feared the most. It was extremely dangerous to fly an emergency resupply mission into a LZ that was actively under attack. Sometimes it was a critical mission to drop off medical supplies, ammunition, and to air evacuate the critically wounded.

Flying in "V" Formation

I got up early on Tuesday, 13 September 1966, and to my surprise I was on the flying schedule board. Our crew was listed. We got up at 0500 hours with a crank time of 0620 hours. There would be a communications check (COM) to ensure that all aircraft were monitoring the same designated radio frequencies. We were to pull pitch at 0630 hours. Our assigned aircraft was 683 and our call sign was "Yellow Two." Our company call sign was recently changed from "Serpent" to "Hacksaw." Our group was composed of Yellow one, two, three, and four. Other groups were designated white, green, orange, red, and purple. The combined assault force was composed of a large twenty-four ship (gaggle) formation. We went out at 0600 hours to preflight check the aircraft. The crew chief had the aircraft prepared and the gunner had the cargo bay doors rolled back and the door guns ready for operations. Our aircraft looked lean and mean in the early sunrise.

Major Jackson's UH-1D had a distinct insignia painted on both the left and right pilot entry doors. The artwork displayed a coiled rattlesnake with white wings in front of a blue triangle. The coils of the serpent formed the number six. Thus, it was understood that the commander "Serpent 6" was the Alpha "A" Company Commander of the 229th AHB. Historically, units of the 1st Cavalry Division carried guidons to identify each unit down to the company level. Since the doors were interchangeable the doors could be easily installed on any Slick that Major Jackson flew. Like a Guidon, the insignia on the doors were understood to be our commander "Hacksaw Six."

Our assigned aircraft (683) had a tendency for the engine to hot start. The tail pipe temperature increased, but it remained within limits. After startup, we made the standard COM check of each aircraft. The old man, Hacksaw Six, started off. Yellow One to Yellow Two, Yellow Two to Yellow Three, and Yellow Three to Yellow Four. The other color flights continued the COM check and the last flight (Purple) responded back to Hacksaw Six completing the communication check. Thus, with no reported discrepancies, the flight of twenty-four ships was ready to launch and start our mission. Yellow was the first wave of four aircraft and our ship was number two. We were to fly a heavy left "V" formation. Two aircraft followed the leader at the head of the "V" with one aircraft following on the right side. I had dreamed of this since I was a boy and I wanted to prove that I was somebody of worth. Visions of family and friends, the American flag, and freedom were the catalysts of my ambition. Faith, hope, and love was my purpose. In that moment, I felt empowered to make a difference and thrive. The trauma of my youth dissipated as the excitement of what lay ahead consumed me. While we were flying, my total focus was solely on maintaining the situational awareness and flying that mission. I did not want boredom at that time, nor did I have time to be scared. I was excited to serve my country, now, in a bigger way, more than ever before.

We departed the Qui Nhon area and headed directly north to Bong Son. Each of the flights of 4 ships maintained the heavy left "V" formation. The flight to Bong Son took about 30 minutes. When we arrived, our infantry assault troops were lined up on an improvised tactical runway at Bong Son (Two Bits Control). Forward air controllers (FAC), "black hats" on the ground at Bong Son, provided field tactical air traffic control. We circled in and made a left base approach from the south. I watched as the first of the twenty-four aircraft landed at the far end of the runway.

It was 0700 hours when the other aircraft lined up in sequence behind them. We reduced the power to flight idle and conserve fuel. We remained on the ground for fifteen minutes while each ship took on six combat troops. Yellow One and our ship, Yellow Two, were the exception and were to take on seven combat troops. Seven fully equipped combat troops produced a critical load factor for the Slick. While on the ground, we remained at flight idle. At 0715 hours, we were set to go. Yellow One sent out a radio call, "Hacksaw aircraft return to operating RPM."

In preparation to execute that mission, I recalled the information that I gleaned from the mission briefing and from discussions with pilots that flew many previous combat assaults. Each flight of four was to maintain 30 second intervals. Since some of those LZs were suspected VC hot areas, the normal plan of attack was to be followed. The Air Force flying F-105 Thunderchiefs (Thuds) would drop their ordnance and strafe the LZ.

When the Thuds reported that they exited the LZ area, artillery fire pounded the LZ until two minutes before the first "Yellow Wave," (which included our aircraft) and determined precisely when they would arrive. When Hacksaw Six transmitted that the artillery fire had been lifted, Hacksaw Six-Yellow One would lead the Yellow flight as the first wave of Slicks into the LZ. Our gunship escort orbited on both sides of the LZ area to provide close area fire suppression support. The door gunners on the first flight of Slicks fired their M-60 machine guns into high threat areas in the LZ until the arriving troops were in the line of fire in the LZ. The first LZ to be assaulted was Lee, which only had room to land three ships at a time. The flight time to LZ Lee was fifteen minutes.

We took off and followed a river Southwest from Bong Son then turned north into a small valley. I noticed that a stream was running through the valley. Palm trees outlined the bank of the stream along its course. As we entered the valley, I could see the Air Force jets strafing our next LZ. We were then three minutes from landing.

Ahead of us, I saw that helicopter gunships were positioning themselves to provide protective cover for the vulnerable Slicks. We were then opposite the LZ. We turned on to a final approach into the LZ as I went through my final mental self-protection checklist: visor on my helmet down, seat belt and shoulder harness cinched down tight, inertia reel locked, beep up the rotor speed to just below the red line, and I prayed a silent prayer, "Dear God please protect us." We were then committed to whatever fate would bring. We would either become rats devoured by a python in seconds or spared by the good grace of the Lord.

The LZ was on the top of a hill. There was a bald spot with a tree line running down the side of it. As we came closer, I noticed tall elephant grass was covering the LZ. About a half of mile out from the

LZ, the gunship's escort started laying down suppressive fire. They rained down fire into suspected areas where "Charlie" might be hiding. Red tracers from the gunship's quad machine guns were pouring fire into the tree line. Rockets were fired and could be tracked by following their smoke trails into the target area. The rocket explosions could be seen as bright flashes with accompanying puffs of gray smoke arose from the ground.

Then the "pucker factor" set in as we prepared to land. There was a saying that I remember: "You can't do anything about the bullet that has your name written on it. But, always be aware of the bullets addressed 'to whom it may concern'." It was critical for pilots in high threat areas to maintain situational awareness especially at times when the aircraft were in close formation. More Vietnam pilots died as the result of mid-air collisions, pilot error, and maintenance malfunctions than from actual enemy fire. We also joked about another saying: "Only your laundry knows how scared you were."

We slowed down and adjusted our speed to maintain proper separation as we prepared to land. The other pilot was focusing on a suitable landing spot and I was intently tracking the proximity of the other aircraft in our flight and closely monitoring the gauges on the instrument panel. Our door gunners were concentrating on identifying and responding to any enemy fire. The first aircraft, our brave Hacksaw Six Yellow-One leader, was very vulnerable, but he landed shortly before our ship also touched down. My eyes were straining and my heart was pounding as I searched for threats and other possible unexpected dangers. Our door gunners started firing into the tree line. Right behind me, I heard the loud rapid reports of our two M-60 door guns and I viewed the stream of the red tracer's trajectory into the tree line.

As we came to a hover, we passed over a shell hole that was warm and still smoking from a recent explosion. Some of the bomb and shell holes exposed the earth and cut down trees and bushes. I could see through my chin bubble that the height of the elephant grass posed no threat and the troops would not have far to jump. By then, the area was ablaze with red tracer fire.

As the skids hit the ground, we gave the order to our door gunners for the troop to disembark and our gunners immediately motioned for the troops to get off the aircraft. If the troops were hesitant or would not exit the aircraft, the door gunners would push them out. We recounted a common expression: "Happiness is having strong door gunners."

We were on the ground for about five seconds and then we began a rapid nose down forward exit from the LZ. As we departed through the smoke, I could see the ground troops stooped over as they darted for cover. We applied full power and were climbing like a "home sick angel." I thought to myself, "So far, so good . . ." and we all exhaled a temporary sigh of relief.

We headed out to "D" Delta Company to pick up troops for the next assault into LZ Hood. That operation was expected to be about the same as the previous one. We shut down at Bong Son and waited for the remainder of the twenty-four aircraft to return. We loaded six more troops. The ground troops were laden with equipment, were dirty, and filled with apprehension. They were looking for any reassuring words from the pilots. In this moment, I felt like a combat pilot. I explained to the troops that the assault on LZ Lee was not that bad and that I did not expect that much trouble at LZ Hood. To this day, I don't know if that explanation made the infantry feel more at ease or not, but I hoped that it had helped a bit. I went on to explain that it was especially important for them, upon landing in the LZ, to exit the aircraft as soon as possible.

After dropping off the troops and pulling away, I watched our Yellow Two, which was ahead of us, go down. I saw in my peripheral vision Yellow Two beating blades against the landscape as it crashed into a gully. The aircraft was totaled, but luckily, the crew was not injured and they were quickly rescued. I knew God had heard my prayer of protection and provided solace. I also heard that near one of the LZs, a Slick aircraft was shot down. A gunship had escort orbited the downed Slick and provided cover until that crew was also rescued. Many of us had escaped the grip of the python that day.

About 0830 hours we headed out for the assault of LZ Hood. LZ Hood was smaller and only two aircraft could land at one time. We launched in flights of twos at fifteen second intervals. Like LZ Lee, the flying time to the LZ was about fifteen minutes. On final approach the gunships blasted the landing area. LZ Hood was a sharp pinnacle landing area. One of the rockets ripped up the foliage and exposed the red clay beneath it. We made an uneventful assault and upon landing, the troops were quickly out and gone. We headed back to Bong Son and refueled the aircraft and loaded another six troops for the assault on LZ Jackson. The assault of LZ Jackson went smoothly and the combat assaults were completed for that day. We then flew a few resupply log missions back into LZ Lee then we headed for our permanent base at An Khe.

At An Khe, our mission was to augment the 227th Battalion with their large airlift. We were in the Yellow Three position. We flew a few more missions out of An Khe and then returned to our base camp near Qui Nhon after a long and tiring day. That day we flew 9.3 hours, 7 of which were flying hours logged as combat assaults. This was quite a change from flying 2 hours or not being on the flight schedule at all.

That evening, our ship was on call as part of the RRF in case some unforeseen emergency arose. I felt confident flying the Slick during that day's activities and I could tell the other pilots gained respect of my piloting abilities. I experienced a strange feeling every time that I flew into an LZ. I never knew what to expect or what kind of opposition was lurking around every unexpected corner. I always tried to be cautious and carefully monitored the instruments to get the advanced warning of a malfunction that was the result of the aircraft being hit by ground fire. I felt proud to be established as a combat pilot and content knowing that it was all meant to be. My new-found confidence was God-given and it defeated the python that so badly wanted to gobble me up.

Yellow One Hacksaw Six

On Wednesday, 14 September 1966, we flew two more combat assaults near Bong Son. The first mission was to airlift Army of the Republic of Vietnam (ARVN) troops into a small peninsula that jutted out into the South China Sea. We flew in from the west to the east. Naval gunfire from an American Naval Cruiser offshore prepped the area. I could see the gray ships in the blue-green ocean a few miles from shore. We were scheduled to make two airlifts into that area as Yellow Two.

We came in high and slow to allow our gunship escort time to locate and prep the area. That area was a very rocky landscape with a few gardens scattered about the area. A maze of trenches made the area appear treacherous. As we approached the LZ, the gunships fired a pair of rockets that landed just short of the LZ. Adjusting the aiming point, they fired more rockets that impacted the landing area. We landed in a heavy left "V" formation and the ARVNs jumped out racing for cover.

After dropping the troops, we poured the coal to the engine, applied full power, and headed out for the safety of the open sea. We passed over the shoreline and viewed the sharp cliff and beautiful blue green water. That area reminded me of the Oregon coast. A small bay jutted inland through a narrow pass. White caps were breaking on the shore and boats were sailing out to sea to go fishing. Near the pass was a white beach with grass roofed huts and coconut palm trees. The scene was as stunning as any south sea island.

Native boats and fishing nets were drying in the sun on the beach. It was a beautiful scene, but I knew I could not let my guard down because it was still extremely dangerous. We drew some tracer fire from the village yet none of our ships were hit. That was a sad mistake for the enemy. The gunships fired rockets and machine gun fire into the area and after that there was no more hostile gun fire. We headed back and picked up the second wave of ARVN troops who were waiting in a cemetery. Since the enemy fire was suppressed, the second lift into the LZ was relatively easy.

We feared that the next LZ would be the "granddaddy" of them all. We were to assault a fortified enemy village which turned out to be three unfriendly villages. We were to fly in and land between two of the villages. We launched at 1300 hours. In keeping with the normal assault protocol, TAC air would attack first followed by an intense artillery barrage. Our unit, ARA, and gunship would provide close air support for the Slicks.

Our pickup zone was LZ Jackson that we had air assaulted the day before. We picked up six ground troops and waited for the other aircraft to arrive and form up. Our "Yellow Flight" formed up in a heavy left "V" formation. The other designated colored units formed up behind us. The LZ was large and there was no problem landing a flight of four aircraft. Our aircraft was designated Yellow Two and we would land in the first wave. We approached the LZ low and fast. One village lined the river on the right side and another village was on the left at the base of a mountain. ARA followed us in and fired rockets into the village. I could see explosions erupting everywhere.

Debris was flying into the air and I noticed out of my side window that a red stream of tracer fire was disappearing into the village's huts and trees. We stormed into the LZ with our door guns blazing. We landed in a nearby rice paddy field and went into and out of the LZ in about fifteen seconds flat. We broke left over the river and we joined up in formation with Yellow One. At that time, we could hear in our helmet headsets a transmission on the emergency UHF frequency guard frantically reporting that a gunship had just gone down nearby in the rice paddy.

Our fearless leader Yellow One-Hacksaw Six transmitted "Yellow Two follow me . . ." as he turned in the direction of the downed gunship. We intuitively knew that we were then on a rescue mission. We orbited the aircraft on the ground and monitored the area for any approaching enemy troops. Yellow One swooped down and landed adjacently to the downed gunship. The rotor system of the gunship was still winding down. I could not see any major damage to the gun ship and the crew was scrambling to accomplish the checklist for a downed aircraft.

The crew chief opened the quick access avionics bay and removed the UHF and FM radio modules black boxes. The gunner and crew chief quickly removed the four quad mounted M-60 machine guns. The rest of the crew secured maps and other onboard weapons and helped carry and place the equipment into Yellow One's cargo bay. The remainder of the downed crew followed and immediately boarded. With everything on the checklist completed, Yellow One pulled pitch and headed on a course across the rice paddy away from the enemy. We joined up as Yellow One headed back. Time after time Hacksaw Six demonstrated his bravery and especially when protecting and saving U.S. troops. He was a true leader and we greatly respected him.

As we departed the area, I noticed movement at the edge of the river. It was a scared water buffalo that was running full speed ahead and attempting to escape the noise and fire that was pouring into the village. All around the village, bomb and shell craters, scorched spots, downed palm trees, and mangled huts were evidence of the devastation of that recent combat assault. After the gunship crew rescue, we flew back together to Bong Son. We refueled, shut down and awaited further orders. I had been in Vietnam for less than a month and I already had become a seasoned combat pilot. My emotions were mixed as I was proud of my aviator skills and the teaming of my unit, but I was also internally troubled and burdened by the innocent souls that were lost in the villages.

Aircraft Recovery

The mission of a RRF was to be able to quickly respond to unexpected emergencies on short notice. A frequent mission of the RRF was to rescue the crew and to recover downed aircraft. Once an urgent call came in that an aircraft was down, Slicks loaded with a platoon size force of ground troop and an aircraft recovery crew departed within a few minutes. Helicopter gunships escorted the Slicks to the downed aircraft site. The ground troops would then secure a perimeter around the downed aircraft. The aircraft recovery crew would rig the aircraft for a sling load recovery. Once rigged, either a

Chinook or a Skycrane would hook up and lift the aircraft out of the area. Once the downed aircraft was in flight, the Slicks and gunships would then return to extract the ground troops and the aircraft recovery crew. We were ordered to fly to a forward base which happened to be Hammond Field near Phu Cat as part of an RRF. We flew aircraft 839 that day. That ship was a rugged patched up war bird that gracefully displayed her scars of war. That aircraft was probably damaged during the previous mortar attack on the "golf course." Yellow zinc chromate primer skin scab patches covered the many holes in her side. Two long torn gashes in her cargo door skins were stitched together with safety wire through even rows of small stop drilled holes on each side of the gash. That aircraft carried us safely through all that day's combat assaults. There was a problem with the malfunctioning standby generator and the aircraft was overdue for a scheduled inspection. However, her guns never jammed and we did not take any additional hits.

Each time that we shut down, the skillful gunner disassembled, cleaned, adjusted, and reassembled each of the 2 door guns with great precision and professionalism. Many of the door gunners were ground troops who extended their tour of duty in Vietnam to sit behind the M-60 machine gun in a helicopter and fire down at the enemy on the ground. After we refueled, parked, and shutdown at Hammond Field, I noticed a few Chinooks parked there. I would fully understand later that when I returned to my Chinook unit, the purpose of a RRF and the recovery of downed aircraft would be complete. One of those parked Chinooks later slung load and recovered the gun ship that was shot down in the rice paddy.

As we began to relax at Hammond Field, after that long day, I began to ponder and to evaluate my experiences thus far in Vietnam. I was sure that my experiences would have a direct influence over the rest of my life. I wanted to be brave and do my job well even though I was afraid each time we assaulted a dangerous LZ. I hoped I could be an influence for good.

Each LZ brought a separate challenge to be faced. People were getting killed or wounded every day and the plush green earth and the burning enemy villages were filled with dead bodies. Shell and bomb holes were visible everywhere. The earth could not fight back but it did slowly heal the scars with a new green growth of plants and trees. I voluntarily signed up with the U.S. Army, so I faithfully executed my duty. Wearily, after each encounter with destruction and carnage of each combat assault, I thought to myself, "Why?"

After parking the aircraft, we walked back to operations to debrief. As we headed that way, a gunner unexpectedly asked me, "How do you feel about killing women and children?" With mixed emotions stirring within me, I did not know what to say or how to respond. I felt a kindred bond with him and I knew that he was also wrestling with his own conscience after witnessing, firsthand, the day's carnage. He was the best door gunner that I had ever flown with in Vietnam. I remarked, "We were doing what we were tasked to do. But, didn't it feel good to help rescue the crew of the downed gun ship?" He nodded his head up and down. We walked the rest of the way to operations together in a silent kinship, united through empathy. We had logged 4.5 hours that day.

On Thursday, 15 September 1966, I woke up at 0600 hours. I slept in the chopper the night before and to my surprise I got a fairly good night's sleep--which I never thought would happen. I woke up feeling like a newborn skunk. I was dirty and unshaven. I made myself a cup of "C" ration hot chocolate and opened and heated up a can of beef steak and potatoes for breakfast. Nothing tastes awful when you are that hungry. We remained at Phu Cat until 1000 hours and then we flew back to our base near Qui Nhon. I took a well-earned shower and shaved. I did not like feeling grungy. Like my mother used to say, "Wear clean underwear in case you have to go to the hospital." I almost felt human again.

In keeping with the fad of the other pilots, I started growing a mustache. It was against U.S. Army regulations, but Hacksaw Six would jokingly say, "What are they going to do, send us to Vietnam?" I scrounged some ammo boxes and built a bunk with a place to store my gear. I did not know what was planned for the rest of the day.

Late in the evening, I was assigned to another aircraft and crew. Our aircraft and a few more were scheduled to fly to Hammond Field at Phu Cat. We were scheduled to augment the missions of other units. We took off after dark and headed north up the valley to in a loose formation. That flight as it turned out, terrified me.

Bad Weather and Dangerous Missions

I was flying with a young Warrant Officer on Thursday, 15 September 1966. He was the aircraft commander at the controls. As we slowly approached Hammond on final approach at about a 100-foot altitude, we flew into a heavy rainstorm with accompanying low scud clouds that immediately and dramatically reduced the horizontal flight visibility. He was flying in the left seat and I was in the right. The pilot at the controls peered into the darkness but could not see any ground references. A few seconds later, I could tell that he most likely was experiencing spatial disorientation or vertigo by what transpired next. I became concerned and afraid. My heart started pounding and I knew this could quickly become a life threating situation.

Instinctively, I immediately sensed that something was drastically wrong. On my side of the aircraft, I could see a tactical runway light as I looked through my right-side door window. Our aircraft was out of control. It was in a tail low attitude, drifting backward and to the right, and it was rapidly descending toward the ground. Immediate action was required to avoid a collision with the ground. Instantaneously, my IP and survival instincts kicked in. I took the controls and at the same time keyed the intercom button and said with a stern voice. "I have the aircraft." I applied forward cyclic stick input to level the aircraft and to return it to a slow forward speed. I pulled up hard on the collective pitch power lever to stop the rapid rate of descent toward the ground.

After what seemed like an eternity that lasted about five seconds, the aircraft leveled, and the rate of descent was checked as the rotor low RPM warning tone was blasting in my head set. We had drifted down to an altitude of about fifty feet, but now we were safely flying again. As the aircraft accelerated through translation lift, less power was required and the unloaded rotor system increased the rotor speed back into the normal operating range. The rotor speed returned to the set normal green operating range as I exhaled a sigh of relief.

As I was breathing a little easier, I keyed the intercom and said, "You have the aircraft." As he took the controls, I could tell that he was both terrified and that he was still spatially disoriented. He still could not see any ground references. I keyed the intercom again and said, "I have the aircraft and I will complete the mission." He was the aircraft commander, but he did not have any objections that I had taken over. That was the first time in a long time that I had come that close to destroying an aircraft. Luckily, my underwear did not speak of my fear and I seemed to have gained the unit's respect that night. I considered the mission a success and I felt I had officially become part of "*The Second Team*."

I keyed my mental channel to God and said, "Thank you Lord." After a few anxious minutes, we landed safely. It took a while for me to regain my composure as I thought of how badly that flight could have turned out. I remembered two phrases that I learned from my flight school days. One phrase was, "Always keep your situational awareness or the earth may rise up and smite thee." The other was, "Only your laundry knows how scared you were." We survived to log 1.8 hours.

Distressful Encounters

We flew resupply missions (hauled log) for Charging Bear of the

1st of the Fifth Cavalry unit on Friday, 16 September 1966. We flew 13.0 long hours that day. As I recall, that was the most I had ever flown in one single day. We started out before daylight and continued flying until 2200 hours that night.

I could no longer grumble about not getting enough flight time. We flew 5.5 hours on the first go and 7.5 hours on the next extended flight mission. We only stopped long enough to look over the aircraft and to gulp to down some "C" rations. I was hungry enough that I could eat the beans and franks ration, cold. I always kept a P-38 (a small can opener) on my dog tag chain which was around my neck for just such a stomach refuel occasion. Whenever we were low on helicopter fuel, we lumped up from fuel bladders without even shutting down.

During one of the log flights, I backhauled my first captured Viet Cong prisoner. He was blindfolded with his hands tied behind his back. He appeared beaten and he was afraid. To me, we were all sons and daughters of God and I only hoped by his life being spared that he too may come to know God like I did that day in my tragic car crash. Silently, I said a prayer on his behalf and turned him over to God. On another flight that same day, I witnessed an A-1 Skyraider, which could carry a huge amount of ordnance and destroy another unfriendly VC village near Bong Son. I had pledged an oath to protect and defend Americans and I was committed to the U.S. Army mission. I was relieved to know that God was much bigger than this python-rat war.

Later, I heard distress radio calls as helicopters were going down. While flying low level over villages, I could see the local people grieving over dead bodies that even included children. I was feeling their pain and grieved for them. It was very painful for me to witness such carnage against innocent farmers in such a beautiful country. I yearned to comfort them and to deliver peace.

After dark, while we were on our way back from the last mission of the day, we ran into yet another heavy rain with the accompanying low scud clouds. My fear index immediately reached a heightened level of concern. As I glanced over at the same young aircraft commander, I could tell that he was terrified. I monitored the altitude indicator and our forward airspeed. Thankfully, we soon broke out of the low clouds and we could both see the ground and the tactical lighting array. Those types of flying conditions were starting to sprout white hairs and make an old man out of me fast. After a long day of flying, we safely arrived back at Phu Cat at about 1930 hours.

I reflected on the horrible things of war that I had, again, witnessed that day. Seemingly wasteful death, destruction, and despair had swept over the land of the Vietnamese, many of whom were simple peaceful people. Every country is plagued with people that are ill-willed and dark, but each country also possesses innocent and loving citizens who cherish freedom, family, and prosperity. My biggest hope was that it would all soon be over and that it marked a change in history for peace and Godliness to prevail.

Viet Cong Insurgents

As you know, when I signed up for the U.S. Army, more anything, I wanted to fly. I loved America and freedom and wanted to serve and protect my country. As a newly enlisted soldier, I didn't understand the political war that was transpiring, I only knew that I was learning to fly and, on a mission to end Communism, for the Vietnamese people. For me, things seemed to be a humanitarian effort, at the time, and I was there to make my country proud. We understood the Viet Cong insurgents as the ones forging a civil war in pursuit of power and control of the people. The VCs were one of the powerfully negative forces during this time, not the Vietnamese people.

We backhauled from secure LZs some captured enemy prisoners and some of our dead troops in gray body bags. American fighting men had taken fire from the enemy in a state of valor protecting and defending the United States, from both foreign and domestic enemies. Throughout my time in the Army, each body bag that was loaded on my aircraft was met with dignity, prayer and respect. They served a purpose greater than themselves and they deserved to be remembered for their valor. The python can swallow any one of us at home on American soil or in Vietnam. Any mission is a mission of importance no matter where it happens.

We shut down on a marked landing pad in one village to unload the critical supplies. I could see that some of the VC villagers had been shot. One enemy VC troop was stretched out on the ground nearby with an exit wound in his side. His wife, friends, and relatives were standing around him wailing and crying. From their expressions they appeared angry and full of hatred. A U.S. soldier, with a M-16 in his hands, had just shot the VC soldier and he was staring down at him as the enemy's life-force was drifting away. The enemy's eyes soon glazed over as his life-force departed his body.

At the same time, the young GI was just as full of hatred and sorrow as he gently laid the palm of his hand on the still warm body bag of his friend who was shot dead by the VC soldier. The GI stood angrily cursing the grieving relatives as he said to them, "I should have killed all of you! You did not cry when he shot my buddy!" Such was the horror and the sorrow brought about by warfare. Only the Grim Reaper was happy that day.

The troops unloaded our cargo of hot food in insulated metal containers, beer, medical supplies, and ammunition. We then loaded the items that we were to backhaul. With tears in his eyes, the young soldier slung his M-16 on his shoulder and he helped load his friend's body bag into our cargo bay. The beads of rainwater on the gray body bag were dripping onto the cargo bay floor just as a tear of grief rolled down the side of the young GIs face.

A Temporary Assignment

Other ground troops assisted in the boarding of wounded soldiers and other important items until our helicopter was fully loaded. After restarting and returning to operational RPM, we did a quick hover check to make sure that we were not overloaded. As we were leaving, the young soldier waved to us and I waved back. I felt the weight of the world on my shoulders. After unloading our cargo at Hammond Field, we flew uneventfully back to our base near Qui Nhon. I later ate supper and took a shower. I hoped that I could sleep a bit that night even after seeing some haunting sights.

There were no observed weekends or holidays in war. However, occasionally in Vietnam, a cease fire truce was agreed upon. I slept until 0730 hours, ate breakfast and shaved on Saturday, 17 September 1966. That day, I was to be temporarily assigned to the 161st Assault Helicopter Company (AHC), call sign Sharks, which was based nearby on the top of a hill near Qui Nhon. They needed an extra pilot for a few missions. Since I was the temporary unit pilot, a Jeep dropped me off and I reported to the commander.

I was sure that I was being shifted around to man enough aircraft to support combat missions. I bought some stationary and other items from their well-stocked PX. One unexpected treat was a fine lunch with a fresh chilled tossed salad. We were served on a fancy table with a white tablecloth, silverware, and real glasses. In war, this was not only a rarity but a luxury. The 161st hired a staff of locals to accomplish the domestic duties. The food was excellent. That night, we would return to Phu Cat and I would sleep in a helicopter again. I only flew 0.3 hours that day.

Back to "A" Company Again

On Sunday, 18 September 1966, I flew log missions with the 161st AHC again. Some of the rated liaison officers were having trouble getting flight time and they flew with us that day. I was surprised to see two of my former students, Captain Maxwell and Captain Roberts who were in my "Q" Course classes when I was an IP back at Fort Rucker, Alabama. It was good to see them again and I felt more connected through our kinship. After a long and sleepless night, I was told that I would return to "A" Company of the 229th AHB. Our reunion was short lived but it also felt revitalizing and offered me hope.

Out of the blue, and totally apart from the war the question occurred to me, "What would I do after I got out of the Army"? I had no idea. That bridge would be crossed when I got to it. I dismissed the thought and went about my day. That day 2.2 hours were added to my flight time.

We were on duty that day as part of a RRF at Hammond Field on Monday, 19 September 1966. We stayed there about 12 hours, but we didn't fly any missions. I showered and went to bed. About 2100 hours we were alerted. We jumped up and manned our aircraft. However, the mission was called off and we went back to bed. We only logged 0.7 hours that day.

On Tuesday, 20 September 1966, we flew combat assaults all day long. In the mission briefing the LZs were identified as Pelham, Forest, Johnson, and Bragg. Our troop pickup would be from LZ Lee. All morning, we flew assaults and that afternoon, we made a troop extraction from LZ Box where a chopper had gone down.

Each time that we shut down at Bong Son, Two Bits Tower children crowded around us. They begged for food and money. They tried to sell fresh fruit and shoeshines. I possessed deep empathy and felt sorry for them and as a result, they always ended up with half of my food. Sometimes the children traded "C" rations for fresh fruit. I bought a large pineapple from one of them. Later, I carved the pineapple with my survival knife and shared it with my friends. It was sweet and was well worth the trade of rations.

Caution ran through our every action because the VC warfare trick was to encourage the children to walk up to our troops with a concealed hand grenade. They were trained to pull the pin and hold it out to our troops. The VC knew fully well that the explosion would also kill the child. I was always vigilant to determine what each child was carrying before even approaching. I hated the thought of having to shoot one of those innocent children to spare our troops.

We also carried sling loads in cargo nets from LZ Box. ARA and armed Chinook gunships "Guns-A-Go-Go" from the 228th ASHB had been blasting targets in the immediate area around LZ Box. That night, we made two combat assaults. The first airlift was to the top of a ridge line and the second airlift was into a rice paddy field. The troops that we airlifted were part of a RRF at Hammond Field from the 1st of the Fifth Cavalry.

When we started out, it was pitch black. The artillery fire suppression would come from a nearby artillery battery. Our flight routes were chosen to avoid the gun target line and thus prevent us from being hit by friendly artillery fire. Soon after we departed Hammond Field, we could see the muzzle flashes from the artillery and seconds later the flashes of the exploding artillery shells in the LZ.

As we approached the first LZ, it was illuminated by artillery flares. The flares were beautiful as they illuminated the area almost as bright as day. We made a steep approach in and dropped off the first wave of troops. One aircraft was in trouble. The aircraft reported a strange heavy vibration that was possibly caused by a hit to a main rotor blade from ground fire. The aircraft safely limped back and made it safely to Hammond Field.

During combat assaults, some villagers often brought their families and their livestock into the rice paddies to avoid being hit by our artillery fire. Our gunship escorts call signs were "Box Kite" and "Deadly Shark" from the 2nd of the Twelfth Unit. We were designated "Yellow Three." All went well that night and we all returned safely back to Hammond Field. During that long day we logged another 10.8 flight hours.

I had been in Vietnam for one month on Wednesday, 21 September 1966. That was another long flying day. We flew 12.5 hours. For the most part, we flew resupply log missions for "Golden Lion Four" from the 2nd of the Fifth Calvary. We flew multiple missions in and out of LZ Pelham and other LZ positions located nearby.

Infantry scout patrols had made contact with the enemy in that vicinity and several of our ground troops had been wounded. We had recently participated in combat assaults in that area and unloaded hot food, beer, medical supplies, and ammunition. As one would guess, the highest priority items were beer and ammunition. That afternoon, we witnessed an airstrike in progress south of LZ Pelham. The jets were diving into the area and dropping bombs. Following that spectacle, we hauled more log and flew in one more combat assault.

Distinguished Flying Cross

"C" Charlie Company of the 2nd of the Fifth Cavalry had been pinned down on the peak of a mountain. That unit had sustained several recent serious casualties. A fire fight was in progress and medical supplies and ammunition were urgently needed to keep the ground forces from being overrun during the night by an incredibly determined enemy. On that mission, we were on our own. In the darkness, a gunship escort would be of no benefit to us. Due to the close proximity of the enemy, a gunship pilot would not be able to distinguish the position of friendly troops from the enemies in the dense jungle. We all did not want to incur additional "friendly fire" casualties.

There was no clearing for a medical evacuation "Dust Off" helicopter to land. Our mission was to hover over the tall trees and to lower the urgently requested medical supplies and ammunition down by rope. The weather conditions made the accomplishment of the mission more difficult and dangerous. It was overcast and pitch black when we arrived over the coordinates of the LZ. As in a western movie, it was time for the cavalry to arrive just in the nick of time.

Since we were on an isolated single ship mission, we turned off our external navigation lights on the final approach so the enemy could not see us as we approached that dangerous location. We made contact with the unit on our FM radio and we requested that they pop handheld parachute flares in order for us to pinpoint their exact location. Immediately, we observed small hand-launched parachute flares rising above the dense canopy of the tall trees. The flares then drifted back down and were obscured by the dense foliage as they burned out. After pinpointing their exact location and focusing on that area, we turned on our bright landing searchlights to gain a clear visual reference for our precarious hover with our skids positioned just above the violently swaying branches of the tall trees. The accomplishment of that mission required the full concentration of both pilots. We were both on the controls in case one of us was hit. The young Warrant Officer that I was paired with was the designated aircraft commander. He was very brave and steady as a rock.

A nervous radio operator responded from the ground unit confirming that they could see our landing lights and that we were directly over their position. I knew that many VC were in the immediate area. I expected to take ground fire. As rapidly as we could, our crew chief and gunner carefully lowered the critical supplies by ropes from the cargo bay. We hovered there fearfully on top of the trees for an elapsed time of about fifteen minutes. Speed was of the essence since we wanted to minimize our exposure time to enemy ground fire.

When the critical resupply cargo was successfully unloaded, the ground troops could not thank us enough. They were appreciative knowing that they had a good chance to make it through the night. That made me feel much better and we had not fired a single shot. We wished the unit well and then we changed the FM radio frequency back to our own unit's radio frequency and began a hasty retreat. We applied a forward cyclic input and as soon as we cleared the trees and obstructions in our immediate flight path we turned off the landing light and headed back to base. I did not even want to think what would have happened if we were hit or if we had experienced an engine failure. Up to that point, it was the "hairiest" piece of flying that I had ever experienced.

When we both started breathing again and were exceptionally proud of the difficult resupply mission that was just accomplished. The medical supplies and ammunition would sustain them until the

Cavalry could arrive at daylight with gunship escorts. We radioed our unit and reported that the mission was complete and that we were returning to Hammond Field.

As if that emergency resupply mission was not dangerous enough, we experienced more rain and fog as we were landing at Hammond Field. We knew that we would lose visibility in the fog as we hovered close to the ground. We devised a new strategy. One pilot would watch for the ground to appear. The other pilot would monitor the artificial horizon, the airspeed indicator, and the instantaneous vertical velocity indicator. We would then proceed at a slow forward airspeed while maintaining a slow rate of descent. The most important parameter for survival was to keep the aircraft level. We thought that the worst that could happen was a hard landing resulting in bent skids. The process worked and thank the Lord that it did. We survived to fight another day. The ground visibility was so bad that we radioed for a ground vehicle to lead us to our parking area. In effect, we were flying in formation with a Jeep. No battle damage to the aircraft was found on the post-flight inspection. With my previous confidence built up, I felt that, finally, I was an integral part of that brave unit.

What we did not find out until later was that we were recommended for a Distinguished Flying Cross (DFC). Sometime later, the request was approved by the Division Commander and we were both awarded with DFCs. Our gunner and crew chief received Air Medals with a "V" device for valor. The Citation from the Distinguished Flying Cross Award read the following:

> *For extraordinary heroism while participation in aerial flight. Chief Warrant Officer Downing distinguished himself by heroism while serving as pilot of a helicopter on an emergency resupply mission in*

the Republic of Vietnam. Answering a request for volunteers to fly emergency supplies to an infantry company under heavy fire, Chief Warrant Officer Downing unhesitantly accepted the dangerous mission. Demonstrating outstanding flying ability, sound judgment, and unflinching determination, Chief Warrant Officer Downing successfully completed the mission while exposing himself to hostile fire and despite extremely poor flying conditions. Additionally, he was required to hover above tall trees while ammunition was lowered by rope, thus further exposing himself to enemy fire. Chief Warrant Officer Downing's courageous action is in keeping with the highest traditions of the military service and reflects great credit to himself, his unit, and the United States Army. By direction of the President, under the provisions of the Act of Congress, approved 2 July 1926.

A Little Time Off in Qui Nhon

After accomplishing the previous night mission, flying in the daylight was so much easier. Thursday, 22 September 1966 was a light day. We flew combat assaults for two hours that morning and then we returned to Bong Son. We made three airlifts into an area near LZ Pelham. We airlifted ARVN troops and American advisors. Many of the ARVN troops appeared afraid and were slow in exiting the aircraft. One United Nations officer had a braid on his uniform, carried a cane, and had a little mustache. He went around barking orders and banging people on the head with his cane. He was a United Nations Airborne Commander, he looked sharp, but he was very cocky. As usual, as we shut down at Bong Son after the missions, we were plagued by hungry children who were trying to sell all kinds of things. Many of the children seemed happy because this was the only life that they knew.

We mingled and traded stories with some of the pilots and ground troops. They were talking about 20-millimeter canons and 51 caliber machine guns that were captured in the area around LZ Pelham. That was in the same area that we had flown the emergency resupply mission the night before. It was a wonder that we did not receive fire from those heavy weapons. That afternoon, we flew a few routine combat assaults with "B" Bravo Company the call sign was "Clipper." We ended up with 5.0 hours of flight time that day.

On Friday, 23 September 1966, a few of us were given a day off. We were driven into Qui Nhon in a truck. After a long dusty ride, we arrived downtown. My first impression was that it reminded me of Seoul, Korea. The main streets were filled with restaurants and bars. Most of the bars blared loud music and were full of "Boom Boom" girls. The streets were full of new signs since the Americans had only been there a short time. The signs expressed trite sayings and many of the words were misspelled. The locals did not speak English very well, but they could pronounce the word "money" flawlessly. We were plagued by shoeshine boys, pimps, and other peddlers. One peculiar thing that I noticed was that many of the older Vietnamese women had blackened teeth. I was told that blackened teeth was caused by them chewing "Betel Nut." Betel Nut was a strong stimulant that gave them a buzz. As we passed by some of these women I would smile and say, "Give us that bright smile grandma."

The common expressions of the local people were, "Hey you!" and "You buy?" Some of the restaurant names were: Blue Angel, Golden Dragon, and Charlies which was interesting since we called the VC "Charlie". Some of the restaurants had green chicken wire cages out front and they had bright red and green signs. We ate at Charlies. The music was blaring and the food was not bad. I ordered steak, which was probably young water buffalo, and French fries. The young Warrant Officer's wife had recently given birth to twin girls. He proudly showed me a photograph of them while we were eating. I was happy for him. He genuinely loved his family.

We stayed one night in Qui Nhon in a secure American run billet. It was adequate and better than sleeping in a helicopter. I bought a few local paintings to ship back home as I had done when I was in Korea. I took a variety of photos of the local area. Basically, there was nothing there that I wanted. We stopped in at the United Service Organization or USO Club. The only perk was ice cream, television, and one American young woman (round eye) who worked there. I also rode a rickshaw for the first time in Qui Nhon. Everything there was too expensive. I returned to the billet on Saturday but I did not sleep well. I think it was too quiet and the bed was too comfortable. We ate breakfast at Charlies again, and this time it was not good at all. We had become accustomed to Army chow so I hoped that I would not get dysentery. We departed Qui Nhon and arrived back at our base camp at LZ Lane around noon. We ate lunch and the U.S. Army chow never tasted better.

Eating Ice Cream at the U.S.O Club in Qui Nhon 1966.

Witnessing the Worst Possible Scenario

I was still tired and slept part of the afternoon in the bunk that I built. I wrote letters, updated my journal, and rested. That night, someone fired a small arms rounds into the nearby hillside. The ground troops got jumpy and poured streams of tracer fire into the hill. I was startled when I suddenly woke up by what I thought was a fire fight. I was relieved that it was a false alarm and I went back to sleep. The next morning, the operations staff dragged me out of bed at 0430 hours on Sunday, 25 September 1966. We were scheduled to fly a command-and-control mission for Charging Bear. The purpose of command-and-control missions was to fly a battalion commander, who would be coordinating combat assault operations. An additional console of an array of portable FM radios were installed in the Slicks cargo bay. The commander was then able to monitor several different unit radio nets at one time. What I didn't realize was that the unit had other plans for us when we arrived. Our first mission was to fly back VC prisoners that were captured in a valley near LZ Pelham. They were blind-folded and their hands were tied behind their backs. They were soaking wet. They looked scared and were shivering from the early morning cold.

Mixed emotions were displayed by our ground troops before the VCs were loaded into our aircraft. One of our ground troops wanted to treat VC humanly while another, who was visibly terribly angry said, "Kill the SOBs." Other troops appeared unconcerned; they were simply doing their jobs. For a moment, I thought that the VC prisoners would be executed based on the demeanor of our angry soldier, but that time, the young soldier controlled his rage and lowered his M-16. During the course of that war, I came to learn that sometimes there was nothing more ruthless than a young U.S. soldier who had just witnessed a close friend being shot, maimed by an enemy, or killed by a booby trap. Many times, the young soldiers helplessly stood by as the ground soaked up the life blood of their dying comrades. I personally made it my mission to save as many of the wounded soldiers as possible. If the wounded could endure the flight to an aid station, then there was a good chance that they would survive.

The VC prisoners were captured in the vast network of tunnels that were dug in the area around LZ Pelham. A black special forces Sergeant, who was fluent in the Vietnamese language, was skillfully interrogating the VC prisoners. We evacuated the VC to Hammond Field. On a later flight, we backhauled weapons, dishes and other artifacts that were retrieved from the large tunnel network. All over the ground were VC safe conduct passes and other propaganda material. The immediate area was marked with bomb and shell craters. A number of poor scared peasant farmers huddled together on the ground in fear for their lives. It was difficult for me to witness.

Even more horrific, I witnessed a most gruesome event that I will never forget. Not much time had elapsed when we watched in horror as an Army lieutenant from the ground troops carelessly, without ducking, walked on an incline right into an adjacent Slick helicopter's main rotor blades that were spinning at full operating RPM. His head was split wide open in decapitation. It personally sickened me to observe his blood and brain matter being slung in all directions. I could feel the blood drain out of my own head as I willed my stomach not to spew. His lifeless body quickly slumped to the ground and he lay motionless. He was another senseless death and another victim of the Grim Reaper. Witnessing this took the horrors of war to a whole new level. I never got accustomed to seeing people die. I felt incredibly sad for that young and brave soldier. I had to reign in my emotions since we still had more missions to fly. That incident was another reminder for me of how quickly one's life could be tragically taken in a split second.

More rain and low clouds kept us on the ground part of the time. After the day's missions, we returned home. That day 6.4 sad and devastating hours were added to my flying time. That day's activity would provoke a serene and placid entry into my journal account.

Building Combat Flying Time

As my personal war continued, on Monday, 26 September 1966, we flew a command-and-control mission for Golden Lion. The weather was difficult. We needed to fly dangerously low below the clouds. I keyed the intercom and said to the door gunners, "Keep your eyes peeled. This is a hot zone." We followed a road that led us to LZ Bragg. Next, we flew low level and followed the river to our scheduled landing spot. We were very vulnerable to ground fire, but we landed safely. Before we arrived, they had installed the command-and-control radio console in another aircraft. They released us and we flew back home.

The weather was rapidly changing. It was cold, rainy, and damp. After experiencing the tragedies of recent events, I just wanted a short time to calm my nerves and to clear my mind of all the trauma that I had just witnessed. As circumstances of that day progressed, avoiding trauma was not in the cards for me as I witnessed some cattle near one LZ that were blown apart. It was a graphic scene that emotionally took me right back to the scene that I had just endured. As I flew over, I could see the cattle laying there rotting in a rice paddy field. Some of the cattle had gaping holes in them and others were fractured into two or three large pieces. It was obvious that the cattle were killed during an artillery attack prior to a combat assault of that village.

Back at our base camp, someone had caught another snake that was about 18 inches long. He paled in size compared to Serpent 7. Even though I hated snakes, hearing the news temporarily took my mind off the tragic scenes I had witnessed. From pythons to rotting cattle, those images created metaphors in my mind representing scenes from the past and have lingered with me in my life after the Army.

Republic of Korea Tiger Division

I was assigned to RRF duty that night. All of my gear was still in the aircraft and we were always ready to go on a moment's notice. We never knew what to anticipate. Day after day, we flew out in the morning and then returned in the evening. Danger lurked everywhere. It was hard not to get depressed. I loved flying, but I hated the distressing bloody carnage that I was experiencing, daily, in that war. Yet, I would do my duty until I could be separated from the Army in June 1967. Maybe we were not fighting for a greater purpose; maybe we were just playing a deadly game. For the most part, it seemed like a hunting trip. We hunted a deadly enemy, but we could only kill a few of them at a time.

The cost to kill each VC was enormously high. The perspective of the innocent peasant farmer was different. They watched the Americans burn down their houses and kill their livestock and they wondered how we were going to be their friends and help them. Even more so, the carnage wrought by the Republic of Korea (ROK) Tiger Division was even more brutal and treacherous when it engaged the enemy. If one of their troops was killed or wounded from a village fire, they killed everything that moved in their attack on that village. The VC and the villagers were terribly afraid of them. There was also treachery from the enemy. In one village, the Americans shared their "C" rations with the villagers and as the Americans turned to leave, they were shot in the back. One troop died and others were wounded. That act only resulted in severe retaliation in which many of the villagers were killed. It seemed like a lose-lose situation. A night or two before, Hammond Field was mortared, several troops were killed, and a few aircraft were destroyed. The war of attrition continued. I had slept in my helicopter at Hammond Field. Luckily, I was at my home base near Qui Nhon when the mortar attack occurred. I considered myself lucky to be out of the grasp of any serpent and distant from rotting cattle. I only logged 1.0 hour that day.

A Change of Pace

We flew more combat assault missions the next day on Tuesday. The LZs were: Thomas, Hooker, and Pope. As we were going into LZ Hooker, a gun ship received ground fire and a gunner was hit in the hand. On the second lift into LZ Thomas, we returned with a soldier who had suffered a broken leg. I suspect that his leg was broken when he jumped out of an aircraft into the LZ. He was in great pain and his leg was swollen. We promptly delivered him to the medical aid station. Once on that mission, I thought that we had been hit by ground fire. But after landing, we could not find a bullet hole. More likely, our rotor was down and caused a piece of debris to strike the belly of the aircraft. We then flew a mission to augment "B" Bravo Company.

When we returned home, a few of us went to the "O" Club to watch a movie and to my surprise, I saw a major at the bar drinking with friends. The major was my old company commander from my Korean tour. I briefly greeted him and we talked about our tour in Korea. In Korea, he was a harsh commander and not well liked. We saw a movie and later returned in a Jeep. Late in the evening, we were all hungry. One of our senior officers, a major, broke into the mess area. He cooked some eggs and made some grilled cheese sandwiches. We all had a good time during that spontaneous cookout and felt a little more relaxed for a change. We stayed up until midnight as I helped with the cleanup. Our crew logged 7.3 hours that day.

It felt good to sleep late on Wednesday since I was not scheduled to fly that day. We used the time to move into a larger tent with more room. The time off helped to clear my head. The next day, I was assigned more RRF duty. We flew to Hammond Field and sat around all day. While waiting on standby, someone accidently set off a tear gas canister. No one carried their gas masks, so we headed up wind. After we returned, I watched another movie at the "O" Club. I was not on the flying schedule on Friday, so I slept late and I wrote a few letters. That evening, I was again assigned for RRF duty and I remained available to fly on short notice. All was quiet and the aircraft remained on the ground. This journal account talks about my sleep patterns and meals, from time to time, not because I wish to repeat myself, but because it was some of the only peacefulness that I cycled through during the madness.

A new month began when I was awakened at 0300 hours on Saturday, 1 October 1966, in preparation for more combat assaults. We were scheduled to arrive at LZ Barbara at daylight. We accomplished two different airlifts into LZ Barbara. Intelligence had received information that many VC were in the area. A VC Sergeant, who had defected, provided the specific location of the other VC unit. The defector was to receive $1,000 dollars if that information turned out to be true. Although we received some ground fire from that location, it seemed light. Gunship attacks quickly put an end to the enemy ground fire. We returned to Hammond Field and remained there the rest of the day. We returned home and received a briefing for a big operation on the next day into LZ Garnet. We logged another 4.2 hours that day.

We got up at 0500 hours on Sunday. We were to arrive at LZ Garnet at 0700 hours. Our crank time was 0620 hours followed by a standard communications check. We lifted off at 0625 hours and we arrived at the LZ at 0700 hours. That LZ was designated as a free fire zone with no firing restrictions. The area was very rocky and that made it more difficult to land. We airlifted troops from "B", "C" and "D" companies of the 1st of the Seventh Cavalry. That also was the designation of General George Custer's unit. We made several airlifts into that LZ and we were finished by 0830 hours. We remained on the ground at Hammond Field on standby for the rest of the day.

Back at camp, we constructed some makeshift horseshoes out of steel rods and amused ourselves with a game. Some of the crews read, took naps, laid out in the sun or did whatever else they could find to do near the parked aircraft. We always tried to unwind and refocus our minds because at any moment we could be called into action. Just before dark, we made two airlifts of three colors which totaled twelve aircraft into an area right on the ocean. As we approached the valley, we could see a village that was on fire as the result of air and artillery strikes. The intense fires lit up the whole area. A destroyed village was the price to be paid for supporting the VC. That was their own rotting cattle. We logged 6.1 hours that day.

Monday, 3 October 1966, was one of those times of longing for home. We were all weary of the long days of flying combat assaults filled with the eyewitness of death. Our ship flew resupply missions most of the day. The missions appeared unorganized and not well planned. We were contour flying near the ground. I was at the controls in the right seat when I felt a thump on the left side of the aircraft. I looked over my shoulder and saw pine needles and small green pinecones floating in the cargo bay. I also noticed that pine needles and pinecones were also imbedded in the ammunition chute of the left door gun. I realized that I had struck a lone slender Australian pine tree of about one inch in diameter at the base. They were grown around my home in St. Petersburg, so I immediately recognized what it was and what I had just done. Suddenly, the mission became more exciting as the startled crew realized that we had struck a tree. The single tree was invisible on my side of the helicopter and the pilot on the left side did not see it coming either. We just clipped the soft branches at the top of the tree. I looked over my left shoulder and smiled at our left door gunner and said, "Sorry about that." He knew that I owed him a beer. All we could do was just laugh. But, I will never forget the look that I received from the door gunner as he reacted to the shock and blunder of what had just occurred. To our surprise, when we landed, we found no damage on the post flight inspection. I offered to help clean the door gun as I patted him on his back. He was very gracious and said, "I've got it sir." I think he could tell that I was exhausted. He was one of our best door gunners. We flew 6.0 hours that day.

Flying on the Edge of the Envelope

Early on Tuesday morning, we flew another combat assault. We assaulted a town near Xuan An. We airlifted six sorties of ARVN troops into that area. The ceiling was low and it forced us to fly dangerously low to about 700 feet above ground level (AGL). The LZ was near Hoi Hiep. The distance to the LZ was only about 12,000 meters. That was a sixteen ship "gaggle" with four colors. We received some ground fire from the nearby village to our left. We were "Orange Three" in the last formation.

As we were approaching the LZ, the Orange Flight began receiving ground fire. The VC were firing directly at our aircraft since we were positioned near the village. Tracer fire was coming at us, but the VC gunner aimed low and the tracers passed harmlessly under our aircraft. No other aircraft were hit. The vigilant gunship pilots immediately responded and attacked and silenced the gun that was firing at us. We made five more uneventful airlifts into that area and we were then released from the mission. That was the first time that our helicopter was targeted directly. We returned to Hammond Field and remained on standby. It rained constantly and we experienced a very soggy afternoon.

At Hammond Field, I watched as the military police (MP) herded a group of VC prisoners into a separate barbed wire enclosure. The VC were cold and wet. Armed guards stood around the area. One guard in a Jeep aimed a machine gun at them. I did not know or want to know what would happen to the VC prisoners. Sometimes, they were turned over to the ARVN troops. In one reported incident, the ARVN soldiers marched the VC down the road, made them kneel down, and promptly shot them with machine gun fire. Sometimes, it was hard for me to realize what opposing forces would do to each other and it brought back to mind the same scene of rotting cattle.

As helicopter pilots in Vietnam, we flew on the edge of the envelope. There was the ever-lurking possibility that we might "buy the farm" at any unsuspected time. For me, faith in God was comforting. I realized that I could be shot at any time either in the air or on the ground. To add to the anxiety, a mortar attack was expected that night. We were given permission to fire up our birds and return home. The clouds were so low that we flew home just above the trees. Sometimes we took great pride in just making it home in one piece. The lessons learned in flying low level in Korea were immensely helpful to me in Vietnam. We logged 3.1 hours that day.

On Wednesday, 5 October 1966, I heard an interesting story about an OH-13S Scout crew, call sign, Snoopy. The scout aircraft had a crew of a pilot and an armed observer with a M-16 Rifle. The scout aircraft was flying a recon mission over a village when it drew a lot of ground fire and the aircraft was hit many times. The pilot was wounded. The aircraft lost partial power and was not able to fly with both passengers. The pilot landed in the middle of a large rice paddy field. The observer applied first aid and patched up the pilot to stop the bleeding. The observer told the pilot to take off and radio for help. The observer then hit the ground and took cover behind a rice paddy dike. The pilot struggled to get his helicopter airborne and he immediately made a radio call for help on the emergency UHF channel. The observer was also a M-16 expert marksman. The observer managed to pick off several approaching VC. Shortly thereafter, a gunship and a Slick answered the emergency call for assistance. The gunship quickly dispatched the remainder of the VC who were by then in the open and approaching the observer. The Slick pilot swooped down and picked up the brave observer. The observer was credited with saving the pilot's life. The pilot and the observer were soon reunited back at Hammond Field. We added 2.3 routine hours for the day's activities.

We were not scheduled to fly on Thursday, so some of us went to Qui Nhon to do some shopping. It was raining and the three-quarter ton truck we were traveling in leaked. We went to the PX and downtown. I bought a guitar and ordered a pair of boots. We had a good time bargaining with the shop keepers. When we returned I played my new guitar and sang until they made us stop at 2300 hours. This was a nostalgic experience for me as I used to play and sing with my younger sister, Marilyn, when I visited on the weekends from Fort Rucker. I was never that good, but it brought me joy. That day was a pleasant distraction from the war.

We were on RFF duty on Friday, 7 October 1966, and we were deployed to LZ Crystal near the village of Phu My. At 1000 hours, we flew to Hammond Field and remained there until 1330 hours. We were released and we "pulled pitch" for LZ Lane near Qui Nhon. We only flew 1.3 hours that day. That evening, there was a promotion party for all the enlisted men who were to receive new stripes. We enjoyed the ceremony and the luxury of grilled steaks. Most of the troops took advantage of the celebration and had too much to drink. My libation was still aviation and flying.

Moving North

There were rumors that we might soon move our base camp further north. That relocation would take the war into new and unfought combat areas. For a short time, I felt at peace. I went to bed and dreamed that I was home. I slept late on Saturday, 8 October 1966. There was nothing scheduled for me on the operations board. Recently, it rained off and on all the time. The rain made flying a challenge, but it kept the air cool and settled the dust. Some of the officers made another trip into Qui Nhon to go swimming in the ocean. There were no scheduled activities again on Sunday.

That evening, one of our young officers briefed the crew about two nurses whom he was trying to impress. He promised the nurses that they could fly with us the next day. The crew was sitting in a Jeep discussing the pros and cons of the mission. The officer asked permission from Hacksaw Six to include the nurses in the flight schedule the next day. The commander's concern was, "What will I tell the General if one of the nurses gets hurt?" He thought for a minute and said, "No guts no glory." As it turned out, we might even have a nurse as a door gunner. On Monday, 10 October 1966, I was relieved to hear that the nurses would not be assigned to our aircraft. I worried for their safety and didn't want to be responsible if we were to take on the enemy. They were assigned to fly in other aircraft and they were limited to only flying into very secure areas. I heard later that when their aircraft was being refueled, that the fuel operator was startled. The refueling receptacles were near where the left door gunner sat. The refueling technician opened the fuel cap, inserted the fuel nozzle, and felt the fuel begin to flow. He glanced at the door gunner to see long flowing blond hair and a woman wearing lipstick. The technician was smiling as he did a "double take." It was truly a rare occasion to see an attractive American female or "round eye", as a door gunner on the battlefield.

Our assigned mission that day would be more dangerous. We hauled log all day for Charging Bear. The biggest laugh was when we were dispatched on a mission to only haul paper plates into a LZ which in my estimation that was a gross exercise in irresponsibility. We resupplied many LZs and ended up flying 9.3 hours. We arrived home after dark. As we gathered in the "O" Club, we were all amused and had a good laugh as the story of the nurse door gunner was recounted.

There was not much activity on Tuesday, 11 October 1966. A few of us went to Qui Nhon. We went to the PX first. Then, we went to a guarded beach and swam in the ocean. I even had a turn at water skiing behind a boat that was operated by the USO Club. It had been a long time since I water skied at home in Florida. The next stop was to pick up my new boots that I previously ordered. The boots would make interesting conversation pieces when I returned home. We stopped off at the USO Club and ate real ice cream with chocolate syrup and even went back later for an additional root beer float. As the ice-cold treats melted in all its sweetness it gave me a sense of small joy, that one might otherwise, easily, take for granted.

When we returned to our base camp, I received a package from home that included a book of instructions for playing a guitar. I goofed off with my friends and Lt. Ox even played his flute, squeaky notes and all. In addition, some of my developed photos also arrived. Even the rain ceased and the stars could be seen at night. It was refreshing and I was genuinely happy for the moments of joy that I had experienced that day. I thumbed through the guitar book and started strumming on my guitar. It was another relaxing day to be grateful for.

LT OX was playing the flute and fellow Warrant Officer playing my guitar.

We returned to Hammond Field for more RRF duty on Wednesday. All seemed quiet and we sat there waiting and killing time all day. I practiced more on my guitar until my fingertips started to get sore. I ate oranges and wrote letters. I heard more war stories from other crews as we waited on the ground. We only logged 0.8 hours.

It was told that Boxkite gunships from "D" Delta Company had captured about thirty VC near the coast. The gunships were herding them around and flushed out more VC from the bushes with machine gun fire. They only had three options to choose from; to surrender, die, or attempt at hiding. The VC decided to surrender, and the rumor was that it was because they were afraid of the "horse." When they saw the 1st Cavalry Division gun ship with a horse head insignia on it, they gave up. I personally think that they were more afraid of the machine guns and rockets that accompanied the "horse."

Operation Irving

I thought that in the near future, we would set up a new forward base camp further north on Thursday, 13 October 1966. The justification for the move was that it took longer and required more fuel to keep flying out of the Qui Nhon area. Our combat operations were to push further north. Our new operation's code name was "Irving." The purpose of "Operation Irving" was to rout out the enemy influence and weapons from the local villages in the Bong Son area. Paid informants would often provide information on enemy activities. Thus, suspect villages would be assaulted and our ground troops would carefully search the village for enemy soldiers, food supplies, and weapons caches. The villages that were caught harboring the enemy paid a dreadful price. We pulled RRF duty all night at Hammond Field. We departed at 0700 hours and flew back to LZ Lane. There was no flying that day and that evening I practiced on my guitar. I was getting better at it and my friends in the area were not complaining about my improving skills as much.

Friday, we experienced a new mission performing the duty of division courier. Our mission was to support the Signal Corps as they were delivering important and sometimes classified messages to various

LZs on routine single ship missions. We logged 6.2 hours.

Operation Irving was rapidly expanding. A surveillance OV-1 Mohawk aircraft had been detecting VC activity north of the Phu Cat mountain range not far from LZ Garnet and LZ Bloodstone. ARVN troops had captured or killed about 100 VC in that area. In addition, VC radar sets and guns were discovered. That usually indicated that the VC were massing en force there. The better trained ARVN airborne troops were "kicking Charlie's tail." Our ARVN brothers-in-arms were performing well.

We flew the single ship courier mission again on Saturday, 15 October 1966. Because of our experience the day before, our mission went smoothly. After returning to LZ Lane at Qui Nhon we logged 5.1 hours of flying time. For amusement that evening, we took Serpent 7 (our now seven foot long Golden Rock Python mascot) into the "O" Club. That incident threw the club into an uproar. One pilot, like me, who was afraid of snakes, drew his pistol and threatened to shoot Serpent 7. The snake handler quickly draped Serpent 7 around his neck and retreated outside. I had enough fun for that day and went to bed.

On Sunday, 16 October 1966, we ended up logging 8.2 hours of flight time. We started our day by flying log for Charging Bear of the 2nd of the 5th Cavalry. The next assignment was to fly in a twenty-four-ship combat assault mission into a LZ that was northwest of Hammond Field. That flight was easy and we did not take any hits from ground fire. Next, we were assigned to a two-ship emergency resupply mission for Charging Bear. The mission scheduler said that gunships would soon arrive to provide cover for us on that mission. When the mission scheduler mentioned a gunship escort, we knew that we were going into another hot area. I think that when the VC saw the two gunships, they were afraid of the consequences if they fired at us. We dropped off the precious cargo and made a hasty retreat. When we were back on the ground, a captain told us that there were enemy 51-caliber machine guns that kept the troops in that LZ pinned down all night. Thus, "Happiness was having two gunships flying cover for us."

On one mission, we landed in the smallest confined area that I had ever seen. It was one small hole in the midst of 100-foot-tall trees. The door gunners were instructed to warn us if our main rotor or tail rotor came too close to the trees. Beeping up the rotor RPM we carefully inched our way down to the bottom. Once the ship was unloaded, we carefully inched our way back to the top completing our day by "hauling log". On the last run of the day, the main generator warning light came on. However, we still had standby generator power. We wanted to complete the important resupply mission. We were carrying an important load of flack vests, "C" rations, water, ammunition, and medical supplies onboard. The cargo was desperately needed by the ground troops. We passed over a shell hole as we landed. The cargo was quickly retrieved by the ground troops and we returned to base for the repair on the main generator.

It made our crew feel good that the troops on the ground would not go hungry or be unprotected on our watch. Lately, there had been a good deal of VC activity at that LZ. Many VC were killed or captured. Many caches of VC weapons and supplies were found. Many of the VC hiding places were dug into rugged inaccessible remote places in the side of steep mountains. On the way back, we flew over the burnt wreckage of a UH-1D that had crashed over a year ago.

We pulled more RRF duty on Monday, 17 October 1966, at Hammond Field. We were called upon to extract troops from 1st the 7th Cavalry at LZ Mosley. Later, we flew log missions for Charging Bear. We were a replacement aircraft for one Slick that had crashed and was destroyed upon landing in the LZ. One troop on the ground was killed. Another Slick (809) went down due to an engine failure. I was assigned to aircraft 809 the day before. I noticed that the tail pipe temperature was running high. With that high operating temperature indication, I suspected that the power turbine in the engine was about to fail. Already two Slicks had been lost that day. I was lucky that the engine did not fail when I was flying 809 only one day before. Thank you, Lord. We logged 5.2 hours that day.

Early in the evening my back was hurting. I woke up thinking someone had massaged my back with a sledgehammer. About the same time, our perimeter radar detected movement to the west of us. We began preparing for a mortar attack, but nothing materialized. The activity was probably a friendly troop patrol.

On Tuesday morning, we flew back to LZ Lane for a scheduled day off. It was extremely hot and uncomfortable. We only logged 0.5 hours. I practiced more on my guitar and wrote a few letters. That evening many joined in my guitar playing as we conducted group singing.

The first mission of the day on Wednesday, 19 October 1966, was to haul log for Silent Panther of the 1st of the 7th Cavalry. The weather was terrible, but for the most part, I enjoyed the flight. We made two passes over a free fire zone. On both passes, both of our door guns jammed. I suspected the problem was a bad lot of ammunition. Such a condition with faulty ammunition could be dangerous when facing the enemy. We noticed that enemy rounds were fired at a Slick that was ahead of us on final approach into the LZ. Our gunship escort immediately tore up the side of the hill with rocket and machine gun fire. Death rained down at 550 rounds per minute. No more hostile ground fire was reported. We logged another 7.4 hours. A thought that

I had heard before ran through my mind: "A brave man lives in a place of honor even if his house is only a hut. A coward, no matter how rich he is, cannot buy honor." Some ancient writing stated: "Young men prize their strength and old men prize there wisdom. But all prize bravery." Many of the young men in Vietnam were truly brave even though some were foolish. To be strong, wise, and brave was the winning combination in my estimation.

Our unit moved north to LZ Crystal which was about halfway between Qui Nhon and Bong Son on Thursday, 20 October 1966. Personally, I anticipated yet another move further north. We flew another courier mission for the Signal Corps. We stopped at Hammond Field, Phu My, and Bong Son. On approach into Bong Son, we received ground fire but "Charlie" was not able to hit us. On the mission that afternoon, we airlifted two Red Cross Girls (round eyes) to Hammond Field. We flew low level to try and impress them. Between getting fired at and transporting the Red Cross girls, that was an interesting day. Back at Crystal, the area was fairly soggy. All my equipment and clothes were soaking wet. However, the jungle fatigues and boots were designed to dry out from body heat; that was life in the jungle. We were sharing the LZ with an artillery battery and a company of infantry for security. Things were quiet. We flew 5.3 hours.

There was more RRF duty on Friday. We were in a forward combat area. As we sat on the ground, we prepared some personal defenses. We placed sandbags around our tent. We dug fox holes on the outside of our improvised bunks. If we received fire, we could just roll out of bed and into the foxhole. We also built shelves out of ammunition boxes to help keep our gear off the ground and dry. It rained all day as we sat comfortably in our tent. When it rained, some of our troops stripped down and headed outside with a bar of soap to shower in the heavy rain which certainly did the trick. When else would you relish the rain for a shower under normal circumstances of freedom and peacefulness?

Only one mission was flown that afternoon. We performed one extraction and then returned to LZ Crystal. Our formation performed a 360-degree overhead break over LZ Crystal. The troops on the ground said that we looked good. We logged 1.4 hours. At that time, I could play and sing three songs on my guitar without rebellion from my friends. My red mustache continued to grow to the point that I could start to wax and twist the ends of it. Positioned near our tent, a large 8-inch, self-propelled gun was parked only a few feet away. The gun started firing after dark. Each time that heavy tracked artillery piece fired at night, it scared us to death. The inside of the tent was illuminated and the top and the sides of the tent flapped as the result of the flash and concussion caused by the muzzle blast. A mustache meant nothing even for a second when we were under attack. The small things in life are quickly forgotten.

We were experiencing heavy rain again on Saturday, 22 October 1966. The sandbags around our tent helped channel the rising water away. The outgoing artillery continually pounded away at suspected enemy positions. Our friendly artillery battery could fire projectiles to points many miles away. Some of those guns supported "fire missions" at targets that were called in by the outlying units trained artillery spotters.

Sunday, 23 October 1966, marked two full months since I had arrived in Vietnam. That day was the first time that it did not rain. I felt as though I was a seasoned combat troop and I was an integral part of the lift unit. We thought of each other almost as brothers. Between rainstorms we played softball and volleyball. I played my guitar and some of us sang together. There was more talk of a mortar attack as our perimeter anti-personnel radar detected movement outside of our perimeter. The artillery fired a concentrated barrage into the side of a nearby hill. We cautiously remained on constant standby alert.

Monday was another day of remaining on standby. The weather was ridiculously hot. We played softball and volleyball to take our minds off the possibility of death. I practiced more on my guitar until my fingertips were sore. As we went to bed, we always contemplated the possibility of a mortar attack. We kept our gear and weapons close at hand and didn't want to sleep with one eye open, but almost had to, constantly.

My Last Flight in a UH-1D Slick

We were back on RRF duty on Tuesday, 25 October 1966. Troops from "A" Alpha Company of the 5th of the 7th Cavalry were transported from LZ Savage to LZ Falcon. We were not able to land because of tall elephant grass and rocks. We hovered as low as we could and told the door gunners to "kick everyone out." The legs of three troops were broken during that airlift. We flew several more routine missions and then returned to LZ Crystal without getting swallowed like a rat. We logged 7.8 flying hours.

Our crew had an exciting experience on Wednesday, 26 October 1966. I was flying with our 1st Lieutenant, platoon leader, call sign OX or "Oscar X-ray". OX was at the controls. We were heavily loaded as we made a steep pinnacle approach into LZ Venus, which was perched on the top of a steep mountain. Without warning either the fuel control or the RPM governor temporarily failed. As OX applied power to come to a hover, the rotor RPM was rapidly declining and the low rotor RPM warning was blaring. The immediate focus for all of us was to save the aircraft.

The quick-thinking OX brilliantly made a pedal turn and pointed the nose of the aircraft down to the valley below. For a short time, we were dragging the landing skids through the tree tops. The entire crews' "pucker factor" was mounting as we feared crashing into the trees. The main rotor system began to unload as the aircraft's forward airspeed achieved translational lift. As a result, the rotor RPM began to climb back to the normal operating range. The aircraft staggered back into controlled flight. Hacksaw Six was observing as that incident was unfolding. Hacksaw Six keyed the radio and complimented OX on a great piece of flying. OX was a great leader and he was one of the best pilots in the unit. I was very fond of OX and hoped to learn more from him.

We circled back after the last helicopter had landed in the LZ and dropped off our frightened combat troops in the LZ. They may have been happy to get back safely on the ground. We completed a few more airlifts, uneventfully, and we returned to LZ Crystal. That venture was the first of many missions that I would fly into the dangerous Happy Valley. We flew 2.5 hours. As it turned out, that mission was my last flight in a UH-1D in Vietnam. Later that evening I received an official message that I was to return to the CH-47 Chinook 228th Assault Support Helicopter Battalion the next day.

I was experiencing mixed emotions about departing. However, the last exciting flight that day was the culmination of a dramatic end of my 60 harrowing days of flying Bell UH-1D Slicks in Vietnam. I was to receive a Distinguished Flying Cross and several Air Medals from that dangerous temporary duty. I was proud of the fact that I had not crashed an aircraft and my crew had not even incurred as much as a scratch. We were never hit by ground fire, I had made enduring friendships, and had gained the respect of the other pilots. I could depart the 229th AHB with my head held high. I was very thankful that no one in my crew or in my aircraft had been killed on my watch. I was even more proud of the lives that we had saved. Under my watch and God's grace, we never became rats swallowed whole by the VC pythons.

After two months of my TDY experience, I thought that going back to flying Chinooks was going to be "a piece of cake." Like a child getting off one exciting roller coaster ride in a theme park, I was wondering what the next ride and adventures would be like. Little did I know, at that time, that I still had to come to grips with a full range of feelings, circumstances, emotions, tragedies, and life changing experiences before I would depart Vietnam. Providence would still provide many new lessons for me to experience and to learn from each day. I had completed the required 60 days of my temporary duty assignment with "A" Alpha Company of the 229th Assault Helicopter Battalion on Thursday, 27 October 1966.

I rode back to An Khe on the UH-1D courier flight about 1400 hours. As I was flying back to An Khe as a passenger, I reflected back on the exciting missions and activities of the previous 60 days. Our 1st Cavalry Division Second Team Slick Unit had become a closely knit team that were bonded to each other like brothers. We respected each other. That made me feel good as I was departing.

The more skilled pilots mentored the weaker ones. We had flown in close formation together, fought together, had fun together, and had experienced a full range of dangerous combat activities together. We had lost a few aircraft but no one in our unit had been killed. Our *Second Team* unit was well respected and it was a valuable asset for the 1st Cavalry Division. I was very thankful and enormously proud of that. I thank God for all that happened to me and did not happen to me.

After we landed at An Khe, I reported to and saluted Major Jackson, Hacksaw Six, as part of the exit protocol. The commander thanked me for my service and for the good job that I had accomplished for him. As Hacksaw Six reached out and shook my hand, he said, "I wish I had more pilots like you." I had found acceptance with "A" Alpha Company of the 229th AHB and I wanted to stay longer but I knew that was not possible. As I departed the "A" Alpha Company area on the southern end of the "golf course" area, I noticed that Serpent 7 was coiled up and was sleeping in his pen. I looked at the python and thought about how he did not get me.

Not far from there, I saw that a new squad tent was placed over the cement foundation of the "Continental Palace" that I had helped construct when I first arrived. I was glad that I took photographs and that I recorded all the activities of the last 60 days in my journal. I gathered up all my gear and my guitar from the "Continental Palace" and was driven in a Jeep to the CH-47, 228th ASHB Battalion area, at the north end of the "golf course". I had arrived with much apprehension, but I was departing 60 days later as a valued member of the 229 Assault Helicopter Battalion. With pride and excitement my anticipation for flying the Chinook once again filled me with memories of my boyhood dreams.

Back to Flying CH-47 Chinooks

As I was on my way back to my Chinook unit on Thursday, 27 October 1966, I knew that I was taking back with me a vast amount of flying skills from Vietnam. What I had previously learned in the 1st Cavalry Division in Korea, as an instructor pilot at Fort Rucker, and in the previous 60-days as a combat UH-1D Slick pilot helped temper me for the next challenge as a heavy lift CH-47A Chinook pilot. Verses from Ecclesiastes flooded my mind as I sat embracing this new time ahead.

> *There is an appointed time for everything. And there is a time for every event under heaven— A time to give birth and a time to die; A time to plant and a time to uproot what is planted. A time to kill and a time to heal; A time to tear down and a time to build up. A time to weep and a time to laugh; A time to mourn and a time to dance. A time to throw stones and a time to gather stones; A time to embrace and a time to shun embracing. A time to search and a time to give up as lost; A time to keep and a time to throw away. A time to tear apart and a time to sew together; A time to be silent and a time to speak. A time to love and a time to hate; A time for war and a time for peace. What profit is there to the worker from that in which he toils? I have seen the task which God has given the sons of men with which to occupy themselves.*
>
> *--Ecclesiastes Chapter 3*

The door to Company "A" of the 229th AHB as a UH-1D Slick pilot had officially closed. It was a time to be grateful I had survived, a time of mourning for the brave soldiers who had been lost, a time of pride for becoming an accomplished combat pilot, and a time of joy for the love of flying.

As Providence would have it, another door opened as a Company "C" of the 228th ASHB Chinook pilot. Upon reflection, my experience flying "Slicks" was to become my biggest asset as a Chinook combat pilot in Vietnam. I prayed that this new experience would provide a time to mend a broken nation and war-torn world through the hope of peace.

Officially a Circle "C" Cowboy

When I reached our company area, I immediately reported to Major Fountain, the commander of "C" Company. Major Fountain was a tall slim career soldier who looked sharp and stately in his uniform. He spoke with a slight Southern accent yet had an authoritative presence about him. Everyone respected him. I was now officially one of the "Circle 'C' Cowboys". Major Fountain knew that I wanted to stay with the Company "A" of the 229th AHB, but he kindly said to me, "Jim, I can't let you go. I need Chinook pilots." He also told me about a possible infusion where another Chinook company might be established down south around Saigon. I immediately smiled at the thought of seeing my friend Captain Bob Bradley whom I believed to be stationed somewhere in that area.

In anticipation of returning to my Chinook unit, I had shaved off my red handlebar mustache the night before. The commander gave me a pat on my shoulder and said that he was glad to get me back. It felt good to be back among my Chinook friends. I was happy to reacquaint with several of our assigned Chinook pilots who were my classmates in the Chinook Transition Training Class at Fort Rucker, Alabama. My friends wanted to hear all about my exploits in flying combat assaults in Bell UH-1D Slicks. I proudly recounted those war stories, but never felt cocky. God was my guide, and He was entitled to my reverence and honor.

I began again to perceive the familiar sounds and smells of our Chinook company area. At night, there were the different sounds of the outgoing artillery fire, the steady hum of power generators, the sound of insects, and the distinct sound that was made by what American troops described as a "'FU' lizard." That species of lizard produced a distinct "FU" sound as it frequently called out to others. Our lizard lived in a tree that was adjacent to the south end of our shower bunker on the west end of our company area. I gladly welcomed an "FU" lizard over a Serpent 7. One would gobble you up; the other did not have the capacity to do so.

The 1st Cavalry Division CH-47 Chinooks at An Khe were parked on evenly spaced pierced steel planking (PSP) parking pads, on the row next to the 1,200-foot PSP runway on the "golf course." I noticed that many of the Chinooks had scab patch repairs installed that were the result of bullet holes and shrapnel damage. Some of the patches covered the damage received while flying, while other punctures were the result of earlier mortar attacks.

When I first returned to the Chinook Unit, I discovered that the food in our mess hall was considerably better due to the pilots who were higher ranking. Maybe the lower ranks should eat better? I noticed many more officers and Chief Warrant Officers with many years of flying experience. What I didn't know, at the time, was that the experience that I gained from flying Slicks would later prove to be invaluable to "*The Second Team*." I did not need a local area check out since I was thoroughly familiar with all the LZs. I had already flown into most of the LZs in the 1st Cavalry Division combat area from Qui Nhon to the area around Bong Son and I certainly had the direct experience of flying in combat assaults and facing the enemy eye to eye.

"Winged Warriors" plaque in the CH-47 Officer's Club at An Khe.

Back to Chinook Life

My flying with the 229th AHB was exclusively limited to the area between Qui Nhon and Happy Valley which was just northwest of Bong Son. The Chinook cargo missions ranged over a much larger area. During the reminder of my tour in Vietnam, I flew Chinook missions as far south as Saigon and as far north as Duc Pho, which was located several miles northeast of Bong Son near the seacoast.

Since I had recently finished my Chinook training and did not have much experience, I was paired up with other older seasoned CH-47 pilots until I gained more mission flight experience in the aircraft. I was pleasantly surprised when I ran into my old friend, Sergeant

Durham, from the church where we both attended in Ozark, Alabama, while at Fort Rucker. He had been assigned to the Chinook unit while I was away flying Slicks. It was good to catch up on the news of the folks in the congregation back home. It gave me some comfort and moral support to know that he was there.

Standing proudly with a "C" Company Chinook.

On Friday, 28 October 1966, I stowed my gear on a vacant steel cot in an available tent. I drew bedding supplies and a mosquito net from supply and began to set up my area. I located and plugged my refrigerator into a spare electrical outlet which was connected to one of the portable power generators. Later that afternoon, our commander held a meeting to discuss some of the upcoming missions. We enjoyed a hot meal in our semi-permanent wooden mess hall building that was built during one of our previous building projects. I went to bed early and slept well.

On Saturday morning, I began to intently review the pilot's operator's manual for the Ch-47A Chinook. It had been three months since I had finished my Chinook training at Fort Rucker, Alabama. The Chinook was a complex tandem rotor helicopter with two flight controls and a utility hydraulic system, five transmissions, a drive train of several segments between all the transmissions, and a rescue hoist. The Chinook had internal web seats that could accommodate thirty-three passengers. That meant we could airlift a U.S. Army platoon of soldiers. A thorough knowledge and understanding of the Chinook aircraft systems and the emergency procedures were essential survival skills. I would rest easier knowing that I would be able to handle any of the complex emergency procedures.

That afternoon, I flew 1.4 hours of Chinook flight training for the first time since 27 July 1966 when I had flown my last flight in CH-47 Class PTC # 66-8. Since it was a training flight, I was at the controls most of that time. The next flight was to hook up an external load consisting of a bulldozer's tracks and blade and sling load them to a Special Forces Camp in Happy Valley. I knew the exact location of the LZ since my last Slick flight was into Happy Valley. It felt good to be able to lift a heavy 8,000 pound load again.

That night, we ate supper and watched, *The Flight of the Phoenix*. One might find it horrifying to watch a movie about a plane crash while being a wartime pilot, but I found it mindless and entertaining and I needed that. In fact, we all needed that. Mostly, I was exceedingly happy that I did not have to wait many days to begin flying. Our company area was at the north end of a 1,200-foot pierced steel plank runway on the west side of the "golf course" at Camp Radcliffe where we heard C-130 aircraft periodically depart at the north end of the runway only a few hundred yards away across a dirt road and just beyond our outhouse (crapper).

We did not fly on Saturday except for a short flight to the "Green Line," where we dispersed our flyable aircraft for the night. The aircraft dispersal procedure made it harder for "Charlie" to destroy our aircraft during mortar attacks. We learned a costly lesson during the last mortar attack in September. At 1630 hours, I was asked to present a Chinook orientation briefing for some of the new ground troops and gladly got them up to speed and prepared for what was to come. I ended my day by helping with the construction of benches for our combination bunker and shower. Our shower was "high end" compared to others, the sides were constructed of thick steel reinforced concrete and was covered by a heavy gauge steel roof. We even had both hot and cold running water. Two large steel shipping containers were placed on the roof. One stored cold water, the other was modified to include an immersion heater which heated the water. Both containers were plumbed for hot and cold water faucets. That was a plush feature by Vietnam standards.

An Khe on Alpha Row of the "golf course".

Hook Up Crews

Monday was payday, but I did not get paid. My records were all messed up since my last move. Administration would have to sort that out. Yet, I was never worried about money more than my life. I flew 7 hours that day and ended up with over 90 flying hours for the month of October. We flew several CH-47 sorties. We hauled about 100 troops and ammunition. It was much faster to haul supplies in external cargo nets. The aircraft could hover over the drop zone and release the supplies without having to unload them from the cargo bay. That action drastically reduced the exposure time to enemy ground fire.

There was also a defined crew procedure for hooking up external loads. When approaching a load, the pilot that was flying and on the controls spoke the command, "Hook armed." The other pilot reached up to the overhead panel and placed the cargo hook switch to the armed position and verbally confirmed, "Hook armed." Any time the cargo hook switch was armed, either pilot could hit the cargo release switch (pickle button) on the cyclic stick and release the load. In flight, the cargo hook switch was normally placed in the "Safe" position. As the Chinook flew through the air, a huge charge of static electricity built up in the airframe. While hovering low over a load, the hook up man used a handheld aluminum hook up tool (wand) that was grounded by a cable to the earth. The first procedure was to touch the hook up wand to the aircraft cargo hook. Once the static electricity was discharged, the hookup man could safely attach the nylon cargo sling into the cargo hook by hand without getting shocked. When the static electricity was released, the crew chief, who was lying on the cargo floor and looking through the open cargo hook hatch, provided directions to the pilots to center the aircraft over the external load.

I always reminded the hook up crews, in case of an engine power loss, I would guide the aircraft to the left and the hook up man should go to the right to avoid being crushed. Once the load was hooked, the aircraft was slowly raised until tension was felt on the cargo hook. Next, power was slowly applied until the crew chief confirmed that the load had cleared the ground. The pilot ensured that the thrust power gauges were in the green range and the aircraft was not overloaded. "If you can hover, then you can fly."

Finally, we received clearance for takeoff. The next step was to slowly transition from a hover into forward flight. Once the aircraft progressed through translational lift, about 20 knots, less power was required to maintain forward flight. Once the aircraft cleared the populated areas and it reached about 70 knots the pilot at the controls gave the command, "Hook safe." Thus, the load could not be dropped until the cargo hook was rearmed.

That afternoon, our aircraft and two others were ordered to Pleiku to augment an "A" Alpha Company operation. Pleiku was west of An Khe on Highway 19 and I had never traveled there, so that mission was a new experience. Intelligence provided information that VC were heading to the Pleiku area en masse. Our staging area was called LZ Oasis. Pleiku was considered another dangerous place at the time. It was known for its red clay. In the dry season, grated landing areas produced a thick cloud of red dust when coming to a hover. Enroute to Pleiku, we observed one of the most beautiful and majestic sunsets I'd ever seen, yet I did not want to let my guard down and be vulnerable by any kind of beauty. We arrived after dark which made it difficult to find a suitable place to park the aircraft. As it turned out, we unwittingly landed in the middle of the ammunition storage area.

The cockpit of a CH-47A Chinook 1966.

First Flying Missions as a Chinook Pilot

Outgoing machine gun fire was heard during most of the night on Tuesday. I think that the ground troops were jumpy. That next morning, we flew two missions to Duc Co near the Cambodian border. The U.S. Army was not permitted to conduct combat operations in Cambodia. However, the VC supply route, known as the Ho Chi Minh Trail, often traveled through Cambodia. Our first sortie was an internal load of a Jeep and trailer. The second sortie was a standard piggyback load of a 105 Howitzer and 50 artillery rounds, code name, Scorpion.

One of the two indicators needles of our thrust gauge failed so we diverted to Camp Holloway in order to get fuel and to try and repair the problem. The gauge failure could not be repaired and we flew back to LZ Oasis. Later, we returned to An Khe and spent the night there.

We had flown only 1.3 hours. I was concerned thinking about mechanical issues and could only hope that listening to the aircraft, routine inspections and prayer would be enough to fend off the Grim Reaper in the future.

During the Vietnam War, "Charlie" was always listening to our radio transmissions. To maintain radio discipline, Cambodia was referred to as "Stormy Weather." If an aircraft drifted across the border the long-range radar controller would say, "You are entering Stormy Weather." This was another scenario very well could end with rotting cattle in the rice paddy fields.

On Wednesday, 2 November 1966, we returned and accomplished a variety of missions at Pleiku. We hauled several different kinds of loads; we slung fully loaded fuel bladders, or blivets, and backhauled the empty ones. We hooked up and delivered a 105 Howitzer and 50 rounds of Scorpion artillery shells to a field unit. Next, we underslung a load from a downed UH-1B from a field area. That was my first of many downed helicopter recoveries. We delivered several more internal loads and then we returned to An Khe. That was a good day's work and we had flown for 6 hours. It was exhilarating flying the big and powerful Chinook.

I practiced my guitar that night and enjoyed the relief from stress this pasttime provided as it helped me unwind and reminded me of home. Again, I reminisced of singing with my younger sister Marilyn, who was the artistic child in our family. She played "Liesl" in her high school production of *The Sound of Music*. I could almost play and sing "Somewhere My Love" from the soundtrack of *Doctor Zhivago*. It was a beautiful song and I imagined that Marilyn would be impressed. As my fellow pilots walked by when I was playing and singing, they would poke fun by saying things like, "Jim don't give up your day job." Yet, this was a significant improvement to my previous guitar playing skills; I wasn't bothered by it, it was a pleasant distraction from the war.

I noticed that the outside air was beginning to get cooler at night. The sunset was gorgeous. The cool weather was a welcomed change. My only flight on Thursday was 0.4 hours as we dispersed an aircraft to the Green Line. In the downtime, I helped construct one of our semi-permanent Bachelor Officer's Quarters buildings.

To my disappointment, the problem of my pay still was not resolved, yet I realized that this was not about money, in the least. Rotting cattle would not be able to earn a penny nor would a devoured rat or chicken.

Landing on a Navy Ship

I had the new and novel experience of landing on a Navy ship on Friday, 4 November 1966. Our mission was to take reparable parts to the USS Corpus Christi Bay, for repair. I flew with my good friend, Chief Warrant Officer Billy Joe Waymire, who had an easy-going character whom I really enjoyed being around as well as an outstanding Chinook pilot. The ship was anchored in Cam Rahn Bay. The only permanent U.S. Army Helicopter Depot was located at Corpus Christi, Texas, thus, that ship was a mobile extension of that operation. The scenery, while flying down the coast, was beautiful. The ocean was a beautiful green color that met the shoreline with the steepest of cliffs. Whenever possible, we flew over the water to avoid ground fire.

That large ship had a limited depot level maintenance capability that was operated by the U.S. Army. It was a floating machine shop. There was plenty of room on the landing pad and we had no difficulty landing and shutting down the aircraft. I took a few photos after we landed on the deck. The U.S. Army personnel onboard the ship enjoyed safe surroundings and good food. We were parked on the ship for less than one hour, and that was the only ship I ever landed on. On the flight back, our crew drank the orange juice that we scrounged. It was an unbelievably delicious treat and another reminder of times back home in Florida. On our return flight, we flew low level over the beautiful ocean. We flew 5.0 hours.

The landing pad of the U.S.S Corpus Christi Bay 1966.

Flying Golf Romeo Missions

Bright and early Saturday morning, 5 November 1966, we flew to Hammond Field in support of "B" Bravo Company on a combined mission duty. That amounted to flying various random support missions that came up. We dropped off some personnel at LZ Lane and at another site nearby logging 3.3 hours. On one sortie, we also picked up the body of a young soldier an E-3 enlisted man. There was a tag that provided the necessary identification details. He was killed in action (KIA). He was placed on a stretcher and was covered by a rubber poncho. For me, it was another sad and gruesome sight like the rotting cattle in the field, the horror was all too real and seemed senseless. His was one of many body bags that we carried out of Hammond Field and other field sites. I transported many body bags while flying Slicks. I was to learn the next step in the process of transporting deceased U.S. soldiers back home. The body bags were consolidated at Hammond Field and on the last mission of the day, all the body bags were lined up in the cargo bay of a Chinook and then transported to Qui Nhon. There was a grave registration (GR) also referred to as the "Golf Romeo" unit located at the airport in Qui Nhon and it troubled us all. It was such a traumatic and somber experience that many Vietnam Veterans may not even be able to speak of it to this day.

That unit sent the GR information to the receiving unit in the United States of America as they prepared the bodies for air shipment home. As a Chinook pilot, I was to perform many of those sad "Golf Romeo" missions. As I looked over my shoulder, from the pilot's seat, and saw the gray body bags lined up in the cargo bay, I felt the bitter realization of the ultimate cost of war. On each GR mission, I was always reminded that God, on many occasions, had placed His hand between me and the Grim Reaper. Death was a passenger in our cargo bay and reminded me that the death grip, like that of the serpent, from the daily risk of war, could strike at any time without warning.

We flew many more missions of both external sling loads and internal loads that day. We were told that one mission was to relocate a VC defector and his family to another remote area. The defector surrendered himself to a U.S. Special Forces unit and traded information concerning VC troop and supply locations for the safe passage of his family and their belongings. We were to airlift his family, his household belongings, a cow, and a pig. I thought that would be interesting, however, I was not unhappy that another aircraft was selected to fly that mission. We had more problems on our minds.

As that day proceeded, I experienced more and more sad reflections about the psychology of war. I noticed that our young door gunner had a peculiar malevolent characteristic that really disturbed me. He appeared to have a chip on his shoulder as I compared his actions to other valiant door gunners that I had recently flown with. By comparison, the best door gunner that I flew with when flying Slicks, always showed an innate concern for humanity and for protecting the lives of innocent women and children. Sadly, that disturbed Chinook door gunner rejected authority and back-talked when the pilots gave him direct orders. He bragged that he liked being a door gunner to kill people. He gave examples of when he served as a ground troop when he killed, beat, and subjected VC prisoners and villagers in a variety of tortures. In my opinion, he was a true "ugly American" and a disgrace as a U.S. soldier. When I was later assigned to another Chinook, I was happy to be away from him as he seemed to be friends with the Grim Reaper.

Our mission on Sunday, 6 November 1966, was in support the Special Forces, call sign "Colt Standby". The areas of concern were Pleiku and Duc Co near the Cambodian border. We remained on standby in order to airlift reinforcement troops in case any of the bases were being overrun by VC troops in the daytime. Like some of my previous Slick missions, at any time, a flight might turn into an experiment in terror for all concerned. Having to contend with the bad Pleiku weather made the missions even more dangerous. As the day ended, we returned to LZ Lane. We logged 3.0 hours.

After a supper of roast beef, which I loved, I watched *The Sound of*

Music and lightly strummed along on my guitar the cords to the songs I knew. Most of the other pilots' recreation of choice during their downtime was drinking and getting drunk. I'm sure for some it numbed the horrors and pain of war.

Next, we ended up flying 6.0 hours on Monday, 7 November 1966. The first in a variety of missions was a sad sortie to transport the body of a 21-year-old soldier "Golf Romeo" to Qui Nhon for processing before he was shipped back home. He had been shot through the head while on patrol in the jungle. That was another example of the tragedy of war as the Grim Reaper claimed one more victim as senseless as the rotting cattle that could be seen in the fields.

Other missions consisted of: sling loading artillery rounds (lobsters), transporting 35 troops, hauling a Jeep and trailer, sling loading rolls of defensive barbed wire, and an external load of white prosperous artillery nicknamed, "Willy Peter" shells. The final mission was to sling load another damaged Slick back to An Khe. One of the UH-1B rotor blades broke off on the way back. We had to reduce our air speed as that isometric sling load began to oscillate wildly. We were heading back to An Khe since our aft transmission started leaking oil from a main oil seal. Our flight engineer monitored the leak on the way back.

After we landed, I received a few letters from home which always made me happy. Letters were the only lifeline to my friends and family back home. Occasionally, I saw UH-1D Slicks flying on various missions. That reminded me of my previous assignment. However, it was good being back flying Chinooks. Circumstances were about to change again as I would be assigned to another short TDY mission further south in Phan Thiet.

November's Change of Pace

The previous months in Vietnam were like focused high-intensity consecutive roller coaster rides. On many days, we flew long hours and into extremely dangerous areas. By contrast, the days that I spent at Phan Thiet and Vung Tau were a much slower pace and somewhat more relaxed. Looking back, I wonder if my commander recognized that I needed to recharge my mental batteries before I burned out.

The Phan Thiet region was still a dangerous area, but for me, it was a time of reflection and renewal. In Vietnam, I was still on a mission to discover who I was. I found myself thinking about both tours in Korea and in Vietnam where I witnessed men at their absolute best and at their worst. Such was my perception of life at that time. I wondered how others perceived me as I was evolving as a pilot and as a man. I wanted my family to be proud of me, and mostly, I wanted to prove to myself that I was somebody of value.

Oh, would some Power give us the gift
To see ourselves as others see us!
It would from many a blunder free us.
-Robert Burns, 1786

I knew I still had much to learn and to endure, but the war in Vietnam was creating a different person inside me. Most of the religious people that I knew seemed to try to solve the "mysteries of life" on a personal level. Similarly, I pondered the questions; "Where did I come from?" and "What was my mission on this earth?" and "Where was I going?" Even now as an older man, I still ponder those same questions. While at Phan Thiet and Vung Tau, I was in closer contact with both the enemy forces and with the South Vietnamese people. Although I escaped previous missions unharmed, I still wondered what lay ahead as the missions would become even more dangerous. I prayed I would not succumb to the grips of the python nor become scattered as cattle.

More Changes

On Tuesday, 8 November 1966, for once in a long time, I was able to sleep past sunrise at An Khe. I was summoned to the "C" Company Commander's tent. After I saluted and reported to him, he informed me that I was to take over the vacating "C" Company Mess Officer's position. That really caught me by complete surprise. I said to Major Fountain, "Sir, I can't tell the difference between chicken crap and chicken salad." He laughed and said, "You will do fine." Next, I spent time that morning meeting the mess personnel and signing for the company's mess equipment. At that point, I became responsible for our "C" Company mess hall.

At that same meeting with the commander, I was also told that I would be sent as a replacement pilot for one of our small 1st Cavalry Division operations at Phan Thiet. So, I packed up my gear and after lunch I was driven to the airfield where I boarded the daily CV-2 Caribou courier flight to Phan Thiet. The flight to Phan Thiet lasted 1 hour and 30 minutes. It was an uneventful flight. The surrounding flat green costal valley reminded me of the flat lands of Texas in the springtime in contrast to the familiar highlands around An Khe. After landing, I was met at the airfield and driven with the mail sack to our camp.

Our camp was right on the coast of the South China Sea. The sea breeze brought in the fresh smell of salt water. I grew up on Tampa Bay and the fresh salty air reminded me once again of home. I was assigned a place to sleep in one of the tents and stowed my gear there. A beautiful sunset marked the end of the day. I seemed to be moving around frequently. I was looking forward to the activities of the next few days and I was also looking forward to visiting the port city of Vung Tao.

On Wednesday, 9 November 1966, it was a terribly slow day in a relaxed environment; there was not much to do. We only flew one scheduled 45-minute sortie to a nearby LZ each day. We only logged 0.3 hours on my first flight at Phan Thiet.

We drove into downtown Phan Thiet to look around. It appeared to be a typical Vietnamese town. There was, however, one major difference: Phan Thiet was the place where the smelly fish sauce (Nuoc Mam) was made. Nuoc Mam reminded me of the pungent Kimchi smell when I was in Korea. The stench permeated everything. Even when flying over Phan Thiet above the low clouds, the fish sauce smell could still be detected. After driving through the town, I did not see anything of any interest to me, and, as always, I carried my 38-caliber pistol and I always was on alert in case of a VC threat. After returning to our compound, I practiced my guitar as I pondered over what I would do once I had separated from the U.S. Army and left Vietnam. Because of my love for aviation I joined the Army for flight training and to serve my country. I believed that once I had accumulated enough flight experience that I would be qualified for many different civilian jobs. I knew that I wanted to marry a sweet girl and start a family. However, I still had several months ahead before anything might transpire.

Operation Byrd

Phan Thiet was a three ship Chinook mission in support of "Operation Byrd." Two Chinooks were from "C" Charlie 228th ASHB and one of them was from "A" Alpha Company. Slicks were from "C" Charlie Company from the 229th AHB, and a few gunships and ARA ships from "D" Delta Company were also supporting that operation.

Our flight operations were located inside a squad tent not far from where our Chinooks were parked. At the entrance to the tent was a modified 55-gallon drum that kept canned drinks cold. The drum had been split in half horizontally and hinges were installed on one side. There was a handle on the top to lift the top half. The lower drum half was buried in the ground up to about 2 inches from the top of the lower half. Ice was available at our camp so we could keep drinks cold inside the insulated drum. It got hot in Phan Thiet and the cold drinks were a pleasant relief from the heat.

The primary LZs in that wide valley were designated; Benny, Virginia, Anne, and Buffalo. Some of those LZs were triangular shaped fortresses. They were surrounded by moats and land mines. A great deal of rice was grown in that area of Vietnam. It seemed that part of the local government's defense strategy was to control the rice harvest and to keep it from falling into VC hands. A great deal of rice was previously captured by the VC. At that time of the year, Phan Thiet was very dry and dusty. We ate our meals in the nearby 15th Medical Detachment mess hall; the food in the mess hall was not as good as our mess hall at An Khe - I should know since I was officially a Mess Officer.

One of the best attributes of Phan Thiet was the prevailing cooling breeze from the ocean. That helped prevent the smell of Nuoc Mam, the Vietnamese fish sauce, from reaching our area. On the way back from a resupply mission, we flew over the sea for some target practice with our two door guns. We flew low and threw out some empty ammunition boxes into the sea. While in Korea, I had been an assistant armament officer where I learned how to tear down and reassemble M-60 machine guns in only a few minutes. However, I had never fired a machine gun before and always wondered what it was like shooting out of a moving target. At Phan Thiet, I was finally given the opportunity to fire one of the M-60 machine guns. I took a turn as a door gunner. I quickly learned that at a high airspeed, the aiming point was well behind the target. As I fired the M-60, I would make final adjustments by guiding the arching red tracer fire onto the target. I think I could have become proficient at that. However, I liked being a Chinook pilot much better.

I only flew 10 minutes on Thursday. Happily, I did receive several letters on the daily CV-2 courier flight. Later, a few of the officers and crew got together for a cookout. We cooked some pinto beans and steaks for supper. The steaks were scrounged from the 15th Medical mess hall. The beans were sent airmail to one of the officers who attended the cookout which turned out to be a feast. That night another enlisted man played my guitar for entertainment. He played significantly better than I and carried quite a melody. He had played in a band back in the U.S. so that explained his talent and high entertainment value. The pleasant evening was quite a comparison to the night before where there was a firefight outside our perimeter where two VC were killed and another one was wounded and captured. I enjoyed the one-man band a thousand times over the sound of incoming fire of the Grim Reaper.

On Friday, 11 November 1966, as we were going to lunch in the mess hall of the nearby 15th Medical Battalion, I witnessed another horrifying tragedy. While we were eating lunch, a UH-1D medical evacuation helicopter, Dustoff, with the distinctive large Red Cross insignia painted on its side and nose, hastily made an approach to the nearby emergency medical landing pad. Ground medical crew, who were bare from the waist, up ran out and recovered the wounded troop who was on a stretcher. The victim, a young soldier, had stepped on an anti-personnel mine out in the valley while he was part of a patrol. He was afflicted by many fragmentation cuts. He had blood-soaked stains in the pants of his jungle fatigues which were in shreds. His right foot was missing from the top of his boot downward. A medic in the field had tried to stop the bleeding and patch him up for the flight to the 15th Medical unit. A tree limb had been employed as an improvised splint that was secured by his belt and a bandoleer to immobilize his leg and to slow the bleeding. The soldier's other leg was intact but it was badly cut by fragments from the anti-personnel mine. I noticed that he was breathing heavily and that his chest was rising and falling rapidly. The aircrew had administered a plastic bag of plasma, during the flight back to the aid station, which was dripping into his arm. He had lost a lot of blood. I could tell that he was both in shock and in great pain. The expression on his face screamed silent agony. The amazing medical technicians were trying as hard as they could to keep life in his body while the Grim Reaper was wrestling for his life. All that I could think was, "Please God, help him."

As soon as the wounded soldier was carried inside the medical aid station, the medical technicians immediately started a flow of whole blood into his veins. All members of the U.S. Armed Forces were required to wear metal identification tags around their necks. The dog tags listed, the name, the religious affiliation, and the blood type of the wounded soldier. Thus, from the start of the medical evacuation by the Dustoff helicopter, the medical technicians knew what type of blood was needed for the blood transfusion as soon as they arrived. The information on the dog tags concerning the religious affiliation, was to alert the various chaplains of different "Faiths" to perform such things as last rights. After starting the blood flow, the medical technicians removed the improvised field dressings and began cleaning and dressing the wounds to stop the blood loss. All that could be done at that aid station was to stabilize his condition, administer medications for; shock, infection, and pain. Once stabilized the patient would be air evacuated to a field hospital for further advanced treatment. I often wondered what happened to him. My senses indicated that I was a witness to the saving of his life.

For me, it was sickening to realize the war devices we had to kill each other. I greatly admired the Dustoff pilots. Their task was to save people and not to kill them. I think that the Dustoff role, for many of the pilots, was a solution for their own inner struggle of not to having to kill other human beings. Of the many missions that I had flown thus far in Vietnam, the ones that helped rescue and preserve life were the most rewarding. All that I accomplished the rest of the day was playing my guitar, solemnly, in private. As I strummed my thoughts wandered to my truck crash in 1954. I knew what it felt like to endure pain and suffering. I was rescued and my life was preserved for a greater purpose. I knew that my part of my purpose was to help in rescuing others. One of the guys popped in my tent, so I put down my guitar and brushed aside my thoughts as we made a trip into Phan Thiet. I dropped off my laundry and bought a new set of guitar strings.

Not much happened the next day, Saturday. We ended up flying only 2.0 hours. Thoughts of curiosity occupied my mind as I considered what our next mission might be. I was also beginning to think about running the "C" Company mess hall at An Khe once I returned. I started to take notice of the other mess halls that I visited for ideas. I was off station ever since I was assigned the duty as mess officer.

We flew a 1-hour mission to LZ Virginia Sunday morning, 13 November 1966. We were forced to abort a second mission because the N-1 Governor on the number two engine failed. We could only achieve 72% power on the number two engine. We were grounded and awaited replacement parts. That afternoon we enjoyed another barbeque of steak and chili, always a favorite. I kept practicing on my guitar, wrote letters, and recorded the recent events in my journal. I missed the excitement of flying Slicks but relished being alive. I was ready to return to An Khe.

Monday passed without much flying activities. I was there for about a week and I had flown relatively little. I was, however, aware of a rumor circulating that Phan Thiet may be attacked soon. The bunkers were being reinforced and everyone kept their weapons close by.

Loss of Helicopters and Loss of Friends

Each day a confidential report came down from battalion headquarters. The report described the action of the past 24 hours and the information that was gained from the interrogation of VC prisoners. The colonel in command thought that the VC might try to overrun our compound so everyone was apprehensive and on high alert. I became more aware of the activities at Phan Thiet. On a typical day, "Air America" maintained a scheduled helicopter courier flight in and out of Phan Thiet. That day the wind blew the loose dry sand across our compound. In the distance, we heard the sound of artillery exploding out in the valley. We logged one hour on our one sortie to LZ Virginia.

The night before, the VC attacked with mortars, machine gun, and small arms fire. Several people were hit by small arms fire. However, we did not take any direct hits in our area. To keep from staying idle, we completed the installation of wooden floor in the operations tent. It felt good to accomplish something and helped pass the time. The food in the mess hall seemed to be getting worse so much so that even I could have made suggestions. By then I had been at Phan Thiet for about two weeks. When I wasn't flying on a mission, I was finding myself, bored. This pace was much too slow for me and felt as if a pause button had been permanently pressed.

The boredom was broken when I took a disturbing land line call on Saturday, 19 November 1966, at the Phan Thiet headquarters also called the "head shed" from our company headquarters at An Khe. As I recall, it was Captain Ken Sines on the other end. The purpose of the call was to inform the unit at Phan Thiet that one of our "C" Company Chinooks crashed on Friday, 18 November 1966. Aircraft 37910 had come apart in the air and fell to the ground from an altitude of four thousand feet. All in the Chinook crew were tragically lost. Both pilots CWO Billy Joe Waymire and CWO James Leach, who were good friends of mine were now gone. I was shocked and in disbelief that the Grim Reaper had claimed those two great patriots. That was our first Chinook loss and I was stunned, saddened, and overwhelmed for days and months ahead. I had flown with Billy Joe to the ship in Cam Rahn Bay. I went through Chinook training with Jim Leach. Jim was tall and thin and had a great smile. He was always happy and joking. I then had the solemn task of informing the others in our unit at Phan Thiet. That was another onerous duty for me to perform. The Grim Reaper had snatched away two of my close friends and that was hard to accept. It was very painful.

My mind wandered back as I thought of my first similar tragic experience of losing a friend while I was serving with the 1st Cavalry Division in Korea. LTC Rudolf F. Giglio, the commander of the 15th Aviation Battalion, crashed in an OH-13D Raven Helicopter in the village of Ma Dong on 9 February 1965. He was on his way back from visiting one of his companies at Inchon when the crash occurred. All of us were in shock as the result of his sudden death. He was a highly admired commander and I really liked him.

The accident investigation team quickly determined that the cause of the Korean crash was due to faulty maintenance. One of the bolts, on one of the flight control rod end bearings on the swash plate, had fallen out in flight. All the bolts on the OH-23D swash plate were secured by castellated nuts and cotter pins. During a previous maintenance action, that nut was reinstalled on the swash plate but without the critical locking cotter pin. As a result of vibration, the nut came loose and the bolt worked its way out of the swash plate. With the bolt missing the aircraft became uncontrollable and it plummeted into the village. LTC Giglio and a small child were killed because of that tragic crash. All these deaths seemed tragic and unnecessary. It reminded me of the phrase, "Sometimes the dragon wins."

Similarly, our "C" Company Chinook also fell prey to faulty aircraft maintenance. One of the bolts in one of the control actuators that connected the actuator to the aft swash plate also had fallen out. The bolts on the swash plate were also secured by castellated nuts and cotter pins. During a previous maintenance procedure, the maintenance personnel had again failed to install one of the locking cotter pins that kept the castellated nut securely in position just as in Korea. On this occasion with the bolt missing, the aft swash plate caused the aft blades to violently flex downward and strike the fuselage. The aircraft then immediately disintegrated in flight. Due to the resulting extreme gravitational g-forces, the crew was probably killed within only a few seconds. Three more of my good personal friends had been killed due to faulty aircraft maintenance procedures. After that Chinook crash, I insisted that more attention be given to our preflight inspections.

We flew few 3.4 hours that sad day. Resupply sorties were flown to LZ Virginia and LZ Buffalo. On the way back we made another firing pass over the ocean. Since Phan Thiet was located on the coast we often flew out over the South China Sea to periodically test fire our door guns. The crew lashed together a few wooden ammunition or rocket shipping containers together that we used as a floating target.

We scanned the area for fishing boats or other sea craft so no one was in danger of being hit by our machine gun fire. We descended the aircraft to about 500 feet above the sea and pushed the target off the rear ramp. The M-60 Machine guns fired flawlessly and did not jam. Ammunition was drawn from a container adjacent to the input feed of the gun. The disintegrating belts had tracers installed every fifth round. As the guns were fired laterally from the aircraft at different forward speeds, the tracers formed distinct arcs that were used to walk the stream of projectiles into a ground aiming point. An experienced door gunner was proficient at that technique. On different occasions, I took turns at firing the door guns. Back then, one never knew when that skill could become valuable. I was mentally prepared and had the skill to man the door gun if a crew member became incapacitated or if we were in a circumstance of trying to fend off the enemy after being forced down in a hostile area. It had been an emotionally exhausting day reflecting on losing LTC Giglio in Korea, notifying our unit that we lost Billy Joe Waymire and James Leach. I was determined to keep my crew safe through more thorough pre-flight inspections and the mental capability and skill to fend off "Charlie" if I had to take over as a gunner. Already I had lost too many friends and I certainly didn't want to lose anyone on my watch if I could keep them out of the coils of the python and the strike of the Two Step Viper.

Lessons Learned in Korea

While in Korea in 1964 and 1965, other than being the 1st Cavalry Divisions Commander's pilot, I was also given the assignment of Assistant Armament Officer. This additional duty included accounting for the live ammunition, small ordnance, and several M-60 Machine guns. As part of our unit battle plan, should an attack be launched from North Korea, the ammunition and machine guns would be issued to defend ourselves. As a pilot, I was partly responsible to provide instructions on installing the two M-60 Machine Guns on our fleet of OH-23 Ravens and bore sighting them. I took great pride in the fact that I had become proficient enough to tear down and reassemble the M-60 in less than two or three minutes.

We were scheduled for two missions on Sunday, 20 November 1966. One sortie was to resupply LZ Virginia and the other was to resupply LZ Buffalo. We logged 1.0 hour. Once again I found myself bored so I rode with the driver to the airstrip to pick up our mail from the Caribou courier flight when it landed. When the Caribou was on final approach, the pilot dropped the aircraft wing into the prevailing wind and aligned the aircraft with the runway for landing. We strained to see if the aircraft bore a 1st Cavalry patch on the tail. It was indeed the courier flight so we quickly located our mail sack and headed back to our area for mail call. Mail from wives or sweethearts were often referred to as "sugar reports." As with the accounts from every foreign conflict, a few times the mail included "Dear John" letters from sweethearts or wives whose shallow affections and passions could not endure the test of time or the long-distance love between them. All through my previous tour in Korea, I heard personal accounts from men whose wives and girlfriends formed other liaisons while they were away serving their country. I remembered one account of a sergeant who said that when he returned home early to surprise her, he found some other man living in his house with his wife. Of the men that I knew well in Korea, I had the most respect for the moral straight arrows who remained true to their wives. For amusement for the remainder of that day, I practiced more on my guitar and dreamed of finding a girlfriend who had the same convictions when I returned home.

On Monday, 21 November 1966, it was my father's and my brother's birthday. After returning from flying, I wrote a few letters and sent a money order home to buy Christmas presents for my family members. Soon after that, we were scheduled to fly to Vung Tao for a scheduled 100 Hours Intermediate Maintenance Inspection accomplished on our aircraft. At first, we thought that we would be in Vung Tau in about three days from then. However, our plans had be changed. Maintenance personnel cannibalized a few hydraulic lines from our aircraft to return another Chinook to flyable status. Our aircraft would probably be down for maintenance until the replacement lines arrived the next day on the courier flight.

Bad news travels fast and scuttlebutt indicated that another Chinook crashed at the Special Forces camp at LZ Oasis in Pleiku. There were all kinds of rumors, but we were not yet officially notified of the cause of the mishap. Later, we learned that tragically, the Chinook had broken up into pieces in flight and struck the ground and burned. The crew's bodies were dismembered and severely burned. No one had survived the crash. I never found out the cause of that crash and mourned the loss of yet another crew. I thought that it might have been the result of either a maintenance failure or a possible hit from friendly or unfriendly artillery fire. During my previous tour in Korea as the 1st Cavalry Division Commanding General's pilot, I learned many valuable lessons that I applied to my flying in Vietnam. I was cautioned by the more experienced pilots, soon after I arrived in Korea, of always being acutely aware of the danger of being hit by friendly artillery fire. Being hit by an artillery round could ruin your whole day.

Unit pilots in Korea on many occasions flew high ranking VIPs to live fire demonstrations on various artillery ranges near the DMZ. It was important to know both the location of the artillery batteries and the impact areas. I learned to navigate, either behind the guns or to fly low level with a ridge between my aircraft and the muzzle of the nearby gun, with prowess. As pilots in Vietnam, we monitored artillery nets that provided the locations of artillery batteries and active firing times. One hazard existed from the firings from unreported artillery batteries. On some missions, I was more concerned about being hit by friendly artillery fire than by ground fire from the enemy. My time in Korea gave me an advantage and experience that would prepare me for the future.

When I was not flying, I had plenty of time to ponder what I would do after I returned home. I played my guitar until my fingertips were sore, yet again, as I tried to relax and think about home through each simple strum.

Thanksgiving Week in Vung Tao

Each day, we continued to receive confidential reports concerning the activities of the previous day. The reports covered combat assaults, casualties, and the number of captured VC and supplies. The captured VC prisoners were interrogated to find VC locations and caches of hidden enemy supplies.

On Tuesday, 22 November 1966, we flew several flights into LZ Virginia. A new forward operations base was being set up at Sung Mao. That afternoon, we were scheduled to airlift heavy equipment to that site. On the first sortie, we slung loaded fuel bladders and ammunition. On the next sortie, our rotor downwash blew down a square corrugated metal building in a landing zone. The ground controller requested that the heavy external load be dropped near the building. I tried to explain to the ground controller that the rotor downwash would destroy the building like the strong forced winds of a tornado. However, they insisted that the load had to be dropped off there. I knew from previous experiences that it would not work. To prevent foreign object damage (FOD) to our aircraft, I pointed the nose of the Chinook toward the building.

Slowly approaching the drop off area I could see that the building was under a heavy wind load and it started to shudder. A second later, I saw the corrugated steel panels flying in the air and luckily being pushed away from the forward rotor disc by the strong forward rotor downwash. After the flying debris settled, I dropped the load onto the designated landing pad and wondered what the ground controller thought.

On the return flight, we saw three Skyraiders dropping napalm on a position in the jungle. They climbed to about 5,000 feet and then dove down to about 1,000 feet and dropped their bombs with great precision. At about 1600 hours, we loaded our gear in Chinook 143 and headed out for Vung Tau to start our scheduled intermediate maintenance inspection. That was my first flight to Vung Tao on 22 November 1966. It was a beautiful city and it was much cleaner than most Vietnamese cities. Notably, there was a French influence there which was evident in the food and the fresh baked French bread was mouthwatering. The people there seem to enjoy a better standard of living. Vung Tau was also considered an "in country" Rest and Recuperation (R&R) center for our troops. It was a common sight to see troops engaged in leisure activities and heading to the beach.

We stayed at the leased Hotel Pacific. It had nice comfortable bunks. The perimeter was guarded by American troops so we felt safe. We ate supper at their "O" Club and the shrimp and other seafood was fresh and cooked to perfection. As a pianist was playing a popular song on the piano we relaxed and enjoyed a pleasant evening. The other pilot in our crew liked to drink. He talked freely about his wife and family back home and how he missed them. That first night I had to guide him back to the hotel, which was a more frequent occurrence than not. Alcohol was a numbing force from all the stress and chaos that existed. I was not one to judge; I just chose to stay sober.

The following day, Wednesday, we drove out to the airfield to check on the status of our aircraft. Some unexpected major components needed to be changed out even the aft transmission on Chinook 143 had to be replaced altogether. An increasing high frequency vibration in flight was a symptom that the pinion gear was starting to fail. A replacement transmission would be flown in by a C-130 flight from An Khe. On the way back from the airstrip, we stopped at the PX to pick up a few things.

Thursday, 24 November 1966, was Thanksgiving Day. I had been in Vietnam for three months. Unfortunately, there were more expected delays in repairing our aircraft because one of the engines failed a power turbine inspection and it also needed to be replaced. With not much to do, we hailed a taxicab and headed into town to spend some time on Vung Tau beach. The beach at Vung Tau had beautiful white sand like the beaches I was familiar with in Florida. There were local people cooking and I certainly did not recognize the smells or the looks of the food. I was afraid to try anything for fear of dysentery. It was nice to put my toes in the sand and swim in the South China Sea with my mind floating back to memories of family and friends on the beaches of St. Petersburg, Florida. My mind also floated to a faraway place as I wrestled with the harshness and troubled times of my youth. I realized that God had given me everything I had hoped for in my boyhood dreams and that He in fact provided emotional freedom and great purpose. I knew I was changing. I knew I was forgiving those that had wronged me in my past, I accepted the accident of 1954, and realized they were all lessons I needed to fully appreciate all of God's Providential events, still to come, in my life. I was wrestling with the tragedy I had experienced in the war, images of rotting cattle, body bags and all. I did not have all the answers, but I was content knowing that God did, and that prayer and faith mattered. Overcome with complete peace and tranquility, I relished in the sun and enjoyed the majesty of nature that God had given to me as a gift that day.

When we arrived back at the hotel I was worn out from the sun and took advantage of my time with a long afternoon nap. Down the street from our billets, we discovered a French bakery. The French rolls were another tasty reminder of the inviting meals my sisters Margaret Anne and Harriett often made. It felt comforting to close my eyes and experience the tastes and smells of the good memories of home.

There were many bars lining the street that were frequented by our soldiers. While strolling down the street, we noticed a Vietnamese movie house. Following the theme of the French bakery, we bought tickets to see a French version of "The "*Count of Monte Cristo*" with Vietnamese sub-titles. It was an indescribable entertainment experience. Instead of popcorn, the locals ate fruit, nuts, sugar cane, and many other things. The children laughed and giggled most of the time. The oddest thing to me was watching previews of upcoming films. It seemed funny to me hearing American cowboys speaking French. I returned to the hotel and went to bed early. I slept well that night as war stayed distant from my dreams.

Friday, the next morning, from my room at the Hotel Pacific, I could stand on the balcony and look out over the harbor and see many Navy ships. We were still awaiting the repairs of our aircraft to be completed and were still killing time, so that afternoon we went to the local movie house again. This time we saw a film that was made in India. It was a poorly made *Tarzan* movie. My fear that day at the beach had come true as I not only developed another case of the runs, but also a sore throat on Sunday, 27 November 1966. Illness was not what one wanted in combat because feeling less than 100% was psychologically as well as physically damaging.

After checking with maintenance, our aft transmission and engine still had not arrived from An Khe. Being bored and restless after already having explored the local area, twice, I decided to go to the beach again even though I still had suffered the runs and a sore throat. After returning we went to the airfield so I could pick up more clean clothes and my guitar from inside the aircraft. While at Vung Tau, we had one particularly interesting encounter. We visited the Australian Aussie camp that was located near the airfield. The Aussies were remarkably fascinating and good people. In the evenings, the Aussies liked to gather together, to drink, and to sing. I sang along with them a few times. One interesting practice of the Aussies was to stencil a small red kangaroo on the side of every aircraft that parked nearby on the ramp at the Vung Tau airfield. On one trip to the airfield, I noticed that a signature red kangaroo was painted on our Chinook's crew entrance door. In that moment I understood how she got her Aussie mark of approval.

I went to the airfield again on Tuesday, 29 November 1966. Not much had changed. It appeared as though we would be there another week or two for parts and maintenance so we visited the Australian camp near the airfield again that day. The Aussies were easy going and I loved listening to their "British" accent. It was always a pleasant time visiting with them.

I was still on the mend from my dysentery and sore throat so I stayed back at the hotel and practiced playing my guitar and soothingly thinking of home. I had been restless and bored with all the down time and was anxious to get back to the business of flying missions. Even moreso, I was bored with being stuck down in Vung Tau. I felt somewhat better on Wednesday, 30 November 1966. As it turned out, that was another wasted day without flying, but a needed day for recuperation so I guess it was a blessing in disguise. We made another trip to the Vung Tau beach and strolled along by the ocean and viewed the ships in the harbor. I took in a deep breath of the salty air as the month of November 1966, in Phan Thiet, ended.

A Prelude to the Trauma

To put it lightly, intense personal traumatic events transpired during the month of December in 1966. The impact of the events on 18 December 1966 fostered another profound change in the direction of my life that would linger in my mind forever. I later would discover just how much I had in common with the numerous casualties of those in the poem by Alfred Lord Tennyson. This poem of 1854 was composed amidst great casualties, during the Battle of Balaclava when the United Kingdom was engaged in the Crimean War. The words of this poem seemed to sum up the feelings that consumed me as I look back at a host of soldiers, we lost that day.

The Charge of the Light Brigade

Was there a man dismy'd
Not tho' the soldier knew
Someone had blunder'd
Theirs not to make reply,
Theirs not to reason why,
Theirs but to do and die:
Into the valley of Death
Rode the six hundred.

- Alfred Lord Tennyson

Broke and Restless

My TDY to Phan Thiet that began on, 8 November 1966, and our maintenance down time at Vung Tao dragged on. We were running low on money and all our crew expected to be paid on Thursday, 1 December 1966. I guess that we were too far south at Vung Tao for the old man to travel there. My personal cash was nearly depleted. The bulk of my Vietnam military pay was in an envelope in the company safe at An Khe. We spent much of the day at the airfield eagerly hoping that our company commander would arrive. Mail from home was a lifeline for a Vietnam soldier and we were desperately waiting for the courier to deliver ours. Broke and restless, we were in great need of hope and encouragement.

I was restless and anxious to get back to flying missions. I loved being a helicopter pilot and I wanted to be flying instead of sitting on the ground. Our company commander finally did show up at 1830 hours and I finally got paid. Some of our crew, to whom I had lent money, also paid me back, which brought me even more financial relief. I had received a few letters and three packages from the folks at home. That day, life became a little easier as I read the letters and thought of my brother and sisters, extended family, church family, neighbors, and friends. Letters can heal a man, believe it or not, and ground them in something normal, something loving. I know that day, for me, it did.

We spent most of the day on Friday getting our aircraft (129) ready to fly. It took a good deal of time in reviewing the extensive maintenance records to ensure that every single maintenance task, for that complex periodic inspection, was properly documented in the aircraft forms. Ever since the mechanical failures and lost Chinook pilots took place, I personally and meticulously reviewed all the many pages of entries in the aircraft forms. We made sure that all the replaced components and the required inspections' tasks were fully documented, thoroughly inspected, and signed off as completed tasks. I was not comfortable leaving my life and the lives of my crew members solely in the trust of the maintenance crew.

Reflection of Fears and Dangers

The next day, Saturday, 3 December 1966, we waited around all morning for our aircraft to be test-flown by the maintenance officer and then released for flight. Once everything was completed, our crew rounded up all our belongings and headed for the airfield. After being grounded for 11 days, we departed Vung Tau in the late afternoon and arrived at Phan Thiet a little after sunset. It was good to be flying again and to be back with our operational detachment. As I thought about this time in Phan Thiet and Vung Tau, it was a time of reflection, anxiety, and a major milestone in my life.

The maintenance downtime and the boredom fostered a time for me to reconcile my past and to seek another direction in my future life. I began thinking about what I would pursue in my life after Vietnam. I had only six and a half months left before I would separate from the U.S. Army. My superiors constantly encouraged me to extend my tour of duty and to remain in the U.S. Army, but I struggled to determine, "How I would fulfill my true mission in life?" I knew that I wanted to make my living as a pilot, but I was not sure about staying married to the U.S. Army. I had proven to myself that I was an excellent Army pilot and was happy with the course I had set in aviation. What I really longed for was a wife and family of my own.

The fear and dangers that I faced in the previous missions in Vietnam were always on my mind. I could have perished many times over, yet I had remained unscathed. I knew any plans for my future must include a good relationship with God, my friends, a wife, the church, and my family. Pondering those heavy thoughts produced a good deal of extreme personal anxiety and apprehension concerning the remainder of my tour in Vietnam. I thought about my friends and fellow soldiers who had recently died and that added fuel to my anxiety. I wondered if one day my luck would also run out. I had no idea, at that time, how the combat pace would rapidly escalate and that I would face one of the greatest traumatic events of my life. It was the calm before the storm, rotting cattle in the field or the rat of my existence swallowed whole by a python.

The Calm before the Storm

There was not much happening the next day on Sunday, 4 December 1966. It felt good to be back in Phan Thiet and to be part of the mission there. I began feeling increasingly better as I was almost over my cold. Flying kept my mind in focus. I drew comfort as I recorded what I was thinking and what I was doing in my journal. I always hoped that one day I would have friends, a wife, and children to share it with at a comfortable home filled with love, free of the anxiousness that war gives a man each day.

I did not fly on Monday. There was not much action at Phan Thiet. Since I was thinking about my Uncle Vernon and Aunt Carrie, I took time to pen a letter, catch them up on my journey, and thank them for the kindness and compassion that they instilled in me. I knew that God had placed them in my life to fill me with the goodness of life. I practiced strumming another *Sound of Music* song on my guitar. That seemed to help keep my mind occupied and at ease. I cautiously rode downtown to check out what the local people were doing. I knew that

I must always remain on high alert in case there was an imbedded sniper. No matter how I tried to pass the time and keep busy, I couldn't take my mind off the need to get back to flying frequent missions again.

I heard that the weather at An Khe was bad and the courier flight delivering the mail would be delayed. I did some of my laundry by hand, using plenty of lemon scented soap so I would have some clean clothes to wear. I probably over-sudsed them so I made sure to make extra rinses while wringing them out. In combat, how my gear looked was not as important as how they smelled and I was determined to remove the stench of souring sweat. After I finished my laundry, my thoughts were refocused on our combat situation and the defense of our compound at Phan Thiet.

While we were away in Vung Tau, the perimeter security guards continued to kill a few VC intruders at Phan Thiet every now and then. Concertina barbed wire, trip flares, and Claymore mines around the perimeter were the first lines of defense that protected our compound. But for the most part, it was normally quiet.

The next morning, Tuesday, 6 December 1966, we flew out to LZ Virginia with a 7,500 pounds on our sling load. Chinooks were notorious for breaking down frequently and constant repairs were required. In this instance, the throttle beep or rotor speed control went out on the number one engine. We could only get eighty-nine percent compressor speed and only seven hundred pounds of torque on the engine. That was not enough power to maintain a hover with the heavy sling load. That resulted in landing the external load a little too hard but luckily neither the load nor the helicopter was damaged. Our planned landing technique was to flare at the last moment to avoid the high-power setting that was required to hover. As soon as the water bladders or sling load of blivets rested on the ground, and the gross weight of the aircraft was reduced, the descent stopped and we were able to maintain a hover. After dropping the load and reducing the gross weight, we did not have any problem returning to Phan Thiet. Maintenance personnel tried to fix the problem, but they could not. That afternoon, we flew the aircraft back to Vung Tau for field level maintenance to repair it. We again stayed at the Pacific Hotel. We saw another movie with Vietnamese subtitles and walked downtown and bought some of my favorite French bread still warm from the oven. I tore off a piece and it melted in my mouth as I inhaled the aroma of yeast that filled the air. It seemed that yeast rolls brought me as much joy as anything else while at war.

We drove to the airfield at 0900 hours on Wednesday. Maintenance personnel were still troubleshooting an electrical problem, so we stayed at the airfield until the aircraft was finally repaired. The Maintenance personnel finally isolated the problem to a loose connection in the number two engine control panel. After a successful repair, we flew our Chinook back to Phan Thiet. I was happy as a kid building a model airplane, as I was glad to be flying again.

My one-month TDY to Phan Thiet came to an end and I was informed that I would return to An Khe on the next day. I was anxious to return and to pick up the combat mission pace. Charlie Company would be moving to Lane Field which was a much better area than Pleiku. I had become remarkably familiar with that area when I flew the Slick helicopters with the 7th Cavalry. I thought that maybe I would see some of my UH-1D friends there. We were still having trouble with the beep or rotor speed control on aircraft 108 so we did not fly at all on Thursday. The beep problem lingered on until Friday.

That afternoon, we flew that aircraft from Phan Thiet back to An Khe, it was a very enjoyable flight of 3 hours and 15 minutes. We made one fuel stop on the way back and arrived at An Khe soon after sunset. It was good to be back at An Khe and to sleep in my own bed.

Operation Rat Hole

On Saturday morning, 10 December 1966, I reorganized my gear and prepared for another mission to Lane Field. I also went to finance and personnel to straighten out my pay. That afternoon, we flew aircraft 133 to Lane Field. Our company commander accompanied us. We made one stop at Hammond Field at Phu Cat. It was nice to be back at Lane Field. I spent a few weeks there while I was flying UH-1D's with "A" Alpha Company of the 229th Assault Helicopter Battalion of the 7th Cavalry.

I was familiar with Lane Field where there was a PX and an "O" Club. I was sleeping in a hexagon or "hex tent" with the other Warrant Officers. I had built a bunk and some shelves out of readily available building materials, empty rocket and ammo boxes to store my gear. At 2100 hours, I went to a briefing. The 1st Brigade was replacing the 3rd Brigade at Hammond Field. We would be relieving "B" Bravo Company of the 228th Assault Support Helicopter Battalion. We were told there would be a three or four additional Chinooks operating out of Hammond Field.

We were beginning to be involved in a new experimental tactic called, "Operation Rat Hole". The VC had become accustomed to our combat tactics. They were aware of how we flew and how we operated. When we air assaulted a new area, we sent out scouting patrols, and then we pulled back at night. "Charlie" simply moved farther away at night, and after we would leave the area, then the VC returned back again. To "Charlie," we had become predictable and this was more than dangerous. This would be our rotting cattle in a field of rice paddies if we did not figure something else out.

To solve the problem, some research theorists studied the behavior of rats within a maze or labyrinth. As a result of the study, several holes or routes were established by the rats in a normal routine. When seeking food and water, they followed a learned route in the maze. If the rats were agitated by an outside source and became frightened, their behavior would change. As the rats became afraid, they would retreat to the nearest hole for protection. Similarly, the VC were detected in following the same type of pattern. The VC troop locations and movement patterns were largely determined and plotted from routine OV-1 Mohawk infra-red and radar reconnaissance flights.

The VC established known hiding places, supply routes, and communication networks. "Operation Rat Hole" was designed to scare the enemy and break their established dispersal and resupply patterns. Instead of assaulting LZ's by day and then withdrawing at night, the new strategy was to leave some of our troops hidden within the area. Hopefully "Charlie" would think that we had withdrawn from the LZ and then the VC would sneak back in. Our troops would be well supplied and would be able to remain without further supplies for a few days at a time. The intent was to keep a low profile and then ambush the VC as they were returning at night.

With the new tactic in play, seventy-five percent of the fighting would be conducted at night. In my view, that could be dangerous and would subject our troops to friendly fire incidents. At night, gunships could not differentiate the friendly from the enemy troops. Tactical emergencies, such as urgent resupply missions or medical evacuations could only be approved by the brigade commander. I experienced that type of mission when I flew UH-1Ds with the 7th Cavalry. The airmobile concept was designed for daylight operations before night vision goggles came into practical use. Because of the lack of nighttime visibility, the lives of the crew and the aircraft were secondary to the needs of the mission. I was always fearful of night resupply missions. My anxiety increased as rumors began floating around that sometime the following month, I might be infused into a unit that would be supporting dangerous nighttime missions. I was anxious to find out where we would be going. I wanted to avoid this reckless type of warfare. In my view, it was inherently dangerous and a disgrace to consider soldiers and aircraft expendable, but it was a reality of war to shift strategies when needed.

There was some speculation that the new unit headquarters might be based at An Khe. The mission aircraft would be first deployed to Lane Field. Aircraft would have to meet a 30-minute response reaction time from Lane Field to Hammond Field at Phu Cat. If the aircraft could not meet the 30-minute reaction time, then the base camp would be relocated further north to Hammond Field which had fewer facilities and would be more dangerous for pilots at night due to enemy mortar and ground attacks.

In the meantime, I was trying to get a handle on my mess officer duties. We had to coordinate and draw mess supplies from different food distribution supply points. The mess sergeant, SGT. Berger, took care of most of the normal day to day mess responsibilities. The mess truck and trailer contained the mess tent, the gas cooking stoves and ovens, a refrigerator, folding tables, chairs, pots and pans, cooking utensils, and other equipment. The refrigeration of perishable food items was always a concern in that hot climate. Most of the meat products were received in frozen containers which helped preserve the shelf life. Many of the vegetables were issued in large gallon cans. Perishable items were force-issued on an almost daily basis. I remember one incident when we were at An Khe that the refrigeration unit on a C-141 had failed and we received many cases of steaks that were starting to thaw. We had grilled steak for a few meals in a row; however, no one complained. In true pilot fashion, I was still much more concerned about flying than worrying about my mess officer duties. The upside to the addition of mess officer duties was that they kept me busy when I wasn't flying and occupied my mind.

Another rumor had poured in that we would be evacuating friendly Vietnamese civilians, household goods, and livestock from the Crows Foot area near Bong Son. That area was declared a free fire zone due to imbedded VC troops and snipers. It was not unheard of to receive ground fire from that area and was always an interesting boondoggle when we air transported the local civilians.

The red web seats in the Chinook could accommodate thirty-three combat troops. However, when we transported Vietnamese villagers, we stowed the seats in the upright position and had the passengers sit on the floor. Most of the villagers were so afraid to fly that they experienced involuntary defecation and urination during the flight. After the villagers exited the helicopter, it was easier to clean up the mess from the floor than from the seats. A Chinook could airlift far more than thirty-three Vietnamese passengers and boy did we pack them in. In flight I asked the flight engineer, "How many do we have back there?" He responded, "One hundred and six." By that time, I learned to gauge the weight of the internal load by the engine torque that was required to hover. "If you can hover, then you can fly."

The heavy rains that time of year inundated the roads and all transport was by air. For some reason, the Slick availability was down and the Chinooks had to assume more of the flying burden which had increased our workload. I also heard that one of my former Fort Rucker students in the "Q" course, which was a fixed-wing qualification course at Shell Field, crashed a UH-1B Gun Ship. One of his gunners was killed and he was severely injured. The crash, again, was due to maintenance problems. I think that the drive shaft between the engine and the transmission fractured. I was happy to hear that my friend survived that crash and that he was not claimed by the Grim Reaper.

Occasionally, I encountered the Korean Tiger Division in the Qui Nhon and Phu Cat areas. One Korean division arrived in Vietnam on 22 September 1965. One of their missions was to protect supply routes and vital arteries such as Route 1 north and Route 19 west to An Khe and Pleiku, as well as rice-growing areas along those routes.

While I was in Vietnam, the Tiger Division provided ground security for the area from Qui Nhon to the location north and east of Phu Cat. On occasion, we airlifted some of them for different combat missions. There were many stories circulating about them. They were fierce warriors and the VC greatly feared them. The Tiger Division had been involved in many search and destroy missions in that area. They were excellent marksmen and were martial arts experts. Occasionally, while I was at Lane Field, I could hear their fierce cries as they executed different moves while they were practicing Karate in a mass formation. I certainly would not want to tangle with them. The Tiger Division later returned home to Korea on 11 March 1973.

From the Mess Hall to the Chili Pot

I began my mess officer duties on Sunday, 11 December 1966. I went with Sergeant Berger to ration breakdown at Quin Nhon to see for myself how the mess supply system operated. It took up most of the morning just to drive around Lane Field and Quin Nhon to the various food distribution storage centers. To make matters worse, thick red mud covered the roads. The adjacent rice fields were full of dark green growing rice. Compounds were surrounded by barbed wire that was stretched in all directions. While driving by their camp, the Republic of Korea Tiger troops were practicing Karate. Tin shacks lined the roadsides. Some of the locals set up improvised shops that displayed a variety of goods. The aim of the local merchants was to get the troops' money any way that they could. In another separate incident, our mess truck got stuck in the deep mud while hauling sandbags. A wrecker was dispatched and it also became stuck. A third wrecker was called and it pulled the other two vehicles out of the deep mud. A simple trip to town was not always all that simple. Overall, the duties and responsibilities of being the mess officer weren't that difficult. The hardest part was hearing many of our troops gripe all of the time about the food in the mess hall. I visited enough mess halls in Vietnam to know, by comparison, that the food in our mess hall was above average and they really didn't have much to complain about. It was said that GIs were like seagulls, "They eat, crap, and squawk all of the time." The standard meal that was served several times per week was roast beef, mashed potatoes and gravy, and green beans. That meal was acceptable to all "faiths."

Being the mess officer, I also enjoyed some small yet satisfying perks. I kept some cheddar cheese, hamburger, and other snacks in the refrigerator in my hex tent. Once when I was staying in a hexagon tent with my friends and Chinook classmate, CWO John Greene. John and I were often paired together for missions and John's wife regularly sent him the ingredients to make chili from scratch. As you know, chili cookouts were one of our favorite evening past-times. I kept the cheddar cheese and hamburger in my refrigerator always hoping for a spontaneous chili cookout. The process of making our chili was simple.

We began by browning the hamburger in a pot and then adding tomato paste, seasonings, dry pinto beans, and just enough water to achieve the right consistency. All the ingredients were brought to a boil and then simmered. John's chili was always on the spicier side which filled the air and made me salivate in anticipation. The pacing item in the process was waiting for the dried pinto beans to fully cook. That usually took at least one hour. Once the chili was done, thin slices of cheddar cheese were placed on top of the individual servings of hot chili served on paper plates. John's wife even sent yellow vacuum-packed cans of El Paso Tortillas which we too, devoured with the meal.

Most of the invited guests drank beer while the chili was lightly simmering on the small one-burner camping cook stove. Since John was a few years older than me he would say, as the chili was cooking, "Boy, go get me a beer." On one of those instances, I shook the beer can vigorously while I was out of sight on the errand. I returned and handed the can of beer over to John. The look on John's face was priceless as he pulled the beer can tab and the contents sprayed all over him. He did not think that was funny as we all laughed at his reaction. The flip side is, he never did tell me to go get him a beer again. Still, John and I had become close friends and we trusted each other.

When the chili was cooked down and ready to serve, I placed chili and cheddar cheese inside my tortilla and wrapped it tightly before sinking my teeth into it. To this day chili is still one of my favorite dishes and it always brings happy memories of down-time with my friend in Vietnam.

Learning from the Indochina War

About that time, I finished reading the book, *Doctor Zhivago*, and I then began to read a book on Vietnam history and the "Indochina

War." The book provided a history of the events leading up to the United States' participation in the Vietnam Conflict. I learned that the French were ambushed in June of 1954 and that the French suffered heavy casualties. Many French soldiers were buried in a cemetery near the site of the battle at the Mang Yang Pass. Years later in 2002, the movie, *We Were Soldiers*, intensely depicted that opening scene.

As my Army release date in June of 1967 approached, I spent time once again pondering what I would do when I got out. I thought that I would look for something related to aviation. As I often looked back during various stages in my life, I had no advanced perceptions of how my life and personal perspective of things were about to radically change in the next few days and months in Vietnam.

Monday, 12 December 1966, was a good flying day. We flew a total of 7 hours and 5 minutes. We flew several sorties of troops, four or five sorties of sling loads of 105 howitzers with an attached suspended container of 50 rounds (called a scorpion) of ammunition, a round portable rubber fuel (POL), and drinking water containers (blivets). Those heavy items were some of the major necessities in order to set up a forward artillery fire base. At the end of the day, we were exhausted but the flying was good as I enjoyed flying heavy sling loads.

We had a heavy projected flying schedule for the next day around Bong Son, so I retired early that night. I had already become familiar with the region around Bong Son when I was flying Slicks. Occasionally, I saw some of my Hacksaw Slick comrades. When I was with them, the bond was still strong and somehow a part of me still wished I could fly Slicks with them.

At times, my thoughts returned to my home, my family, and my friends. They were not perfect, and like me, we all had our own faults. However, they were my people because they made me who I am. They were part of me and I loved them dearly. I knew I could not continue to live far away from them and looked forward to returning to the United States. I hoped and prayed that God would help make us all better people that could be made more aware of each other's feelings. Those thoughts reminded me of a popular song of that era, "*No Man is an Island.*" No one lives to himself and no one dies to himself. I hoped that I could make them proud of me.

Tuesday was another big day for us. We flew aircraft 111 (triple 1) back to An Khe for scheduled maintenance. There, we picked up my fateful Chinook aircraft 637901 and set out for Hammond Field at Phu Cat. It was our unit's standard practice for the same aircrew to man the helicopter for 25 hours until the next intermediate inspection came due.

Back at Hammond Field, we flew several external loads of 155-millimeter ammunition lobsters and a follow-on sortie of water blivets to LZ Stewart for a unit call sign, Tail Boom. From there, we back-hauled thirty-six VCS (Viet Cong Suspects) to Hammond Field for interrogation and processing. Next, we airlifted Republic of Korea Tiger Team troops. We dropped them off at Phu Cat Mountain east of Hammond Field. We did not return until after dark.

Part of the ROK Army mission was to provide perimeter security for Hammond Field. The ROK Army also sent out hunter killer patrols in that area. That time of year, the weather was notoriously bad around Hammond Field. It rained much of the time. As the air cooled after sundown, heavy thick fog formed. As the night progressed, the fog became extremely thick and made it impossible to maintain ground visibility during a hover. I feared being caught in those dangerous conditions.

The other aircraft pilots complained continuously about having to fly so much. It rained so much that the red mud was ankle deep. That red mud clung to my jungle boots in huge globs. It was a little easier to walk when I took off my heavy chest protector. After tromping through the red mud the evening ended on a good note. Several letters had caught up with me that day which put a smile on my face and comfort in my heart as I read them and thought of home.

As my mind drifted back from those happy memories, I heard outside of our tent radio chatter, the sound of running generators and the sound of the heavy rain showers cluttering the quiet peacefulness of the night. Closer to me, I could occasionally hear the chirping of a cricket. Our hex tent was also plagued with frogs. Beds were hastily made of 105-millimeter ammo boxes, but they kept us relatively dry while we slept with one eye open. Air mattresses, ponchos, and mosquito nets were readily available. There was one socket and light bulb hanging from the center tent pole.

I reflected on the book that I was reading about Indochina. In a way, I felt sorry for the Vietnamese. They had been fighting for such a long time. They fought the French at Dien Bien Phu in 1954. That was the first Indochina War between the French Far East Expeditionary Force and the determined Viet Minh Communist-Nationalist Revolutionaries. The Viet Minh staged a clever ambush in June of 1954 and the French suffered heavy casualties. I took off my muddy jungle boots and went peacefully to sleep. There was no telling what would happen the next day.

The Fear of Broken Arrow

We were on standby on Wednesday, 14 December 1966. We did not accomplish any flying. Part of the combat "Ready Reaction Force" standby strategy was to not commit all the forces at one time. The RRF was a reserve force that could immediately respond in case of a tactical emergency. We all knew what to expect if a dangerous emergency condition, called, "Broken Arrow", arose and if we had to respond immediately on short notice. Pilots always feared such dangerous missions. I wrote a few letters and built some shelves out of ammunition boxes. I practiced on my guitar until my calloused fingers could no longer take it. It was good to be able to rest, but I would rather be flying.

We flew almost nine long and hard hours on Thursday. Other than quick shutdowns to check our aircraft we hot refueled from fuel blivets and continued flying. My poor rear end sure hurt from the prolonged sitting in the armored seat. The weather was so bad, at times, that we could not get into some of the landing zones. It was lethal to fly helicopters in those severe weather conditions.

Hot refueling point from fuel bladders.

A good portion of our mission, that day, was to move replacement troops to positions further north. We loaded all kinds of other articles tightly bound to a Jeep in the cargo bay.

There was always a danger of transporting shifting cargo that was not properly secured and tied down. If cargo shifted, it changed the aircraft's center of gravity and, if that happened, it might get wedged in and be difficult to unload or it could damage the aircraft structure.

We airlifted all kinds of essential supplies by sling loads. Everything that was essential for a unit's survival in the field was airlifted by helicopters. As a rule, we liked transporting cargo by sling loads. If we lost an engine or experienced a severe power loss, we could always pickle the load and keep flying. Seasoned pilots always checked the torque or power indicator when coming to a hover. Sometimes the weight of the load was miscalculated by the ground crew. As you know, my rule of thumb was, "If you can't hover, then you can't fly." On occasion, I rejected loads that were entirely too heavy to lift.

Another problem for the Chinook was that when at a hover, there was a down-wash of up to hurricane force winds. Sometimes, the ground troops would place tents and other loose objects near the designated landing helipad. Thus, tents and other loose objects were blown into the air like a tornado and they were scattered in every direction. If such objects hit the rotor blades, they could destroy the aircraft.

We frequently received obscene finger gestures as the loose gear of the infantry on the ground was violently blown in all directions. On one occasion, I arrived when the troops were eating in a mess tent that was positioned near the landing pad. Putting it nicely, they were not happy when their plates, cups, beer, and food were launched and scattered into the air. Eventually the infantry learned to stow their lighter supplies within heavy containers and to erect mess tents away from the marked landing pads.

In another instance, we were delivering round water blivets to a LZ on top of a steep hill. I cautioned the troops on the ground to make sure that they securely chocked the water blivets to prevent them from rolling downhill. However, something went wrong. As soon as I hit the pickle button and the load was released, the blivets began to roll down the steep hill. As we departed, I could see the blivets had rested at the bottom of the hill. In its path the blivets had rolled over tents and destroyed whatever else was in their path on the way down. However, the blivets were not ruptured and the cargo sling was still attached. We returned to the bottom of the hill and hooked up the load again. This time when we dropped off the load the troops properly chocked the water blivets.

There was always a scramble as the troops rushed to hold down their loose gear when the aircraft was on final approach to a landing pad. That day was frustrating because many things did not seem to go well. Our crew was on standby that night and there was always a chance that we might be tasked with a hairy mission.

I went to ration breakdown the morning of Friday, 16 December 1966, with my mess troops. Other than observing the requisition process, I didn't accomplish much. Most of the food supply decisions were made by the mess sergeant. However, as mess officer, most of the officer's and pilot's complaints were directed to me. I always tried to anticipate the serving times and late dinners for returning pilots who were off flying combat missions. I knew from my own flying experience how nice it was to have a hot meal ready when I was tired and had flown for many hours. I visited many mess halls on my flights around Vietnam. I might have been biased, but I thought that chow in our field mess set the bar high in comparison to the others. It was still my personal goal to make it even better.

I was told that the day before, a Bamboo Viper was killed in our area. That snake had a fluorescent green skin color and it looked as though it had been painted with green lacquer paint. The locals called it the Two Step Viper. It had long sharp fangs. If you were bitten by one, then within two steps most people became paralyzed and died.

The VC also made booby traps by hanging those vipers by their tails in their underground tunnels and in trees along paths where our troops were likely to pass. If our tunnel rats (troops who crawl into VC tunnels with a flashlight and pistol) were not careful, they could be bitten, which would result in immediate death.

Moreover, the Korean Tiger Troops who were positioned around us, were operating in the area near Phu Cat. The Tiger Troops were very tough and the seasoned troops and the VC were deathly afraid of them. Recently, I heard more stories about the Tiger Troops. It was said that if a Korean patrol took fire from a village and one of their troops were killed, then the Koreans would kill everyone in the village and their livestock. For sure, the Vietnamese villagers were terrified of them.

That afternoon, the sun came out and there was a break in the cloud cover for a short time. But soon after, the dark clouds and the heavy rains of the storm front moved back in. I had our unit patches sewn onto my newly issued jungle fatigues. After I rested, my mind drifted back to my home, my family, and my friends. It was a pleasant experience as I thought of riding around in my sporty powder blue Triumph TR-3 with a pretty girl at my side in the other seat. I also pondered again what I would do when I got back home.

Tensions Mounting

Saturday, 17 December 1966, was a long, hard hectic day of facing many problems and flying exceedingly difficult and dangerous missions. We flew 5.5 hours. I flew my very first resupply missions into the fateful LZ Bird that day. LZ Bird was an intensely hot area that was surrounded by hidden VC and North Vietnamese Army (NVA) troops. There was heavy fighting in the area between LZ Bragg and LZ Pony.

There were heavy casualties on both sides as the VC and NVA were determined to take and hold the ground around LZ Bird. Some of our ground troops in that area were already dead or wounded and they needed to be airlifted from the LZ. One Chinook was rigged with litters to make the task easier since less time would have to be spent on the ground. We did not have a working FM radio, so we were prohibited from taking that mission.

We did fly a sortie or two of transporting the walking wounded troops back to Hammond Field. Back at Hammond Field one of our newly arrived captains, Captain Wade, took over as my co-pilot. He was a well put together young man who recently had arrived in our unit. Captain Wade and I flew several more resupply sorties to LZ Galaxy and LZ Bird. We mainly ran sling loads of 155-millimeter Howitzer ammunition, lobsters. LZ Bird was stock piling artillery and canister rounds in preparation for a forecasted VC and NVA siege during the following night. A foreboding feeling was in the air and everyone was nervous. I felt the fear of a looming "Broken Arrow" condition at LZ Bird.

As the tension mounted, at 2100 hours, we were alerted for a Tactical Emergency Mission to extract a platoon size security force from an LZ southwest of the LZ Strip and to transport them to the Happy Valley Special Forces Camp. The ceiling was low and it was down to 800 feet above ground level (AGL) when we reached the river. As we continued the flight, the ceiling immediately dropped to 400 feet AGL. I became gravely concerned as we proceeded cautiously in those dangerous flying conditions as tension was building.

Those weather conditions had placed us in a very vulnerable and dangerous position of being exposed to enemy ground fire. The tension was building. At night, in such conditions, we turned off the exterior lights to make it more difficult for "Charlie" to see and to hit us. We flew a southerly heading until we entered a low-level scud cloud bank. We made an immediate 180 degree turn and descended to 400 feet AGL. We continued flying low level just above the river to maintain ground visibility. I keyed the intercom and warned our door gunners to be on high alert.

We contacted Camp Rustic Hobby and asked them to fire an illumination flare. As the flare illuminated, we had a strong visual reference to their location, and we were able to safely land. We quickly unloaded the troops and returned the same way that we came in. We traveled at an exceptionally low altitude over the river. After completing that very tense mission, we safely landed at Hammond Field and refueled. We breathed a sigh of relief and we hoped that we were finished for the night.

Soon after, however, the operation dispatcher informed us that we were ordered to fly one more urgent resupply mission into LZ Crystal. There was a temporary break in the clouds and Captain Wade had flown that mission without encountering any problems. We returned to Hammond Field refueled and then shut down for the night. That was one terrifying day. I had never seen the flying conditions that bad before. Surprisingly, my underwear did not speak of the terror I had just encountered. I was grateful to have dodged the Grim Reaper and thanked God that I was still alive. As I lay down that night, what I didn't know, was that the worst experience was yet to come.

The Trauma of December 18, 1966

After a long night of casualties, terrifying weather conditions and close calls I could feel the gravity that each succeeding emergency mission held. Each mission seemed more dangerous than the one prior and required more skill, vigilance, and courage. I was fearful that the next mission might exceed the capability of our aircraft and crew. I had a sense of foreboding and I could feel the tension rising. I was anxious about the future. Looking back to my military time, it reminds me of Job's trials in The Book of Job.

> *But reach out with Your hand now and touch all that he has; he will certainly curse You to Your face. Then the LORD said to Satan, behold, all that he has is in your power; only do not reach out and put your hand on him.*
>
> *-Job 1:11-12*

Emergency Tactical Resupply Mission

I was awakened at 0110 hours (1:10 am) on Sunday morning, 18 December 1966, by Captain Wade. He was sleeping in the operations tent. He said that we were still on standby and that we were ordered to take part in an emergency tactical resupply mission to LZ Bird. LZ Bird was thought to be under heavy attack by numerous NVA ground forces. Our troops at LZ Bird desperately needed medical supplies and more 155-millimeter Howitzer ammunition. Although it was pitch dark in the cool early morning and the weather conditions were horrible, the completion of the resupply mission was deemed more important than the safety of the aircraft and the crewmembers. It was a circumstance that I had most feared. The aviation community was to pay a horrible price in blood for the decisions that were made that night. I was very apprehensive and wondered if my "luck" would finally run out.

The weather forecast was reported as clear around the intended destination of LZ Bird. I was at the controls when we started up and I hovered to the sling load pickup staging area. At 0130 hours, I said, "Hook armed," and Captain Wade replied, "Hook armed." We hooked up to a sling load of 155-millimeter Howitzer ammunition and then proceeded on a compass heading of 360 degrees toward LZ Bird.

I could see the lights from LZ Crystal as we climbed to an altitude of 2,500 feet. We called LZ Crystal for an artillery advisory. It was standard operating procedures to contact fire bases to keep from getting hit by friendly artillery fire. Due to the extreme enemy action, the guns of LZ Crystal were constantly firing south into a hot area near LZ Pony. We secured a temporary artillery cease fire and we continued northward straight toward LZ Bird. As we continued flying north of LZ Crystal, I could see layers of heavy fog rapidly forming in the valley just north of the old artillery fire base at LZ Bragg. That was most certainly not a good sign and I was gravely concerned about the rapidly deteriorating weather conditions. The weather above the fog layer was still clear so I climbed to 3500 feet to clear the mountain tops. I had flown in that area many times before and I knew my current location while I recognized the landmarks on the tops of the mountains even in the dark of the early morning.

We called LZ Bird while heading there. As we flew over their position at LZ Bird they could hear the distinct sound of the Chinook aircraft and the rotor blades, but they were not able to make visible contact with us. Due to the cold temperatures, a very dense fog layer had just engulfed LZ Bird. We then made a 180 degree turn and headed east. At our request, LZ Bird fired two flares to mark their exact location. We could see the increasing white glow of the parachute flares as they emerged from the thick fog bank below. Those brilliant parachute flares then descended back down through the dense fog until the decreasing glow completely faded away and totally disappeared.

There were no visible breaks in the fogbank and nothing on the ground was visible. I could see that it would be impossible to safely land there. There was no way that we could safely drop off our sling load of ammunition. We radioed the Forward Air Controllers (black hats) at LZ Bird again and reported that the fog was too severe for us to try and land. They could not see us and they agreed with our decision and responded that it would be safer if we did not attempt to land.

Landing with an Airstrike in Progress

We then aborted the mission and headed south for Hammond Field. Shortly thereafter, either LZ Pony or LZ Bird transmitted a blanket radio call that an air strike was in progress near LZ Pony. I could see a few illuminating flare rounds that were being fired from LZ Pony. I headed eastward and then followed Highway 1 south to Hammond Field. As we proceeded down the highway, I could see the faint lights again from LZ Crystal and Hammond Field. The weather at Hammond Field was rapidly deteriorating as the heavy fog began to obscure the whole area on the ground. That was of increasingly great concern for me. One of the greatest fears for helicopter pilots was hovering in dense fog. I was trying to mentally prepare myself for that challenge. I was becoming very frightened at the prospect of losing control of the helicopter in the dense fog. All that I could think was, "Dear God, please help me."

Our unit operations dispatcher at Hammond Field then called and advised us to land and to remain at LZ Pony for the night. Even the dispatcher realized that it would be extremely dangerous for us to continue and attempt to land at Hammond Field in that rapidly deteriorating weather condition. We responded that LZ Pony was already completely obscured by fog Instrument Flight Rules (IFR) and that it would be impossible to land safely there. Our options for finding a safe place to land were rapidly diminishing. While all of that was going on, there was an increasing amount of frantic radio chatter as many of the LZ's and firebases were under simultaneous enemy attacks around the area. As we continued south, our unit dispatcher informed us that the weather was rapidly deteriorating and that more thick ground fog was forming. As we passed LZ Crystal and cleared the mountain tops, I began a descent from 3,500 feet into the flat Phu Cat Valley below.

Our unit dispatcher said that vehicle lights would illuminate the landing area where we would drop off the sling load and then land the aircraft. As we were on final approach, I recognized the lights and I had a general idea where we would come to a hover. The vehicles flashed their lights and we responded by flashing our landing lights. Everything seemed to be going well, but in the pit of my stomach I felt very apprehensive and frightened. My heart began to pound fiercely and my breathing became heavy and shallow. I clinched the controls in fear of the worst. I thought back to the many times before while I was flying Slicks and my experiences with many difficult and dangerous approaches into Hammond Field at night. However, the weather conditions and the thick fog at Hammond Field were the worst that I had ever encountered. I was at the controls and I knew that it would be the most dangerous landing that I had ever attempted.

I was intentionally cautious and hyper vigilant as we set up a 70-knot night textbook final approach into the landing area. On the short final approach, I attempted to maintain a slow ground speed just above the translation lift speed, about 20 knots, while at the same time maintain a slow rate of descent. It was imperative that we kept a visual contact with the ground. In that moment, I was fully cognizant of the many tragic helicopter crash accounts of experienced pilots who lost visible ground contact while at a hover. I gave the command: "Hook armed." Captain Wade responded, "Hook is armed." On that short final approach in those deceiving flying conditions, I realized that I was still a little too high. The actual ground clearance was obscured by the fog bank. I began to slow the aircraft and initiated a pedal turn to the left in order to try and maintain the visibility of the vehicles headlights. In the same instant I tried to avoid the populated tent areas and still possess the presence of mind not to fly into the nearby Little Hong Cong Mountain.

The Crash

Within seconds everything went from bad to worse and then to impossible. During the pedal turn, I entered a very dense patch of fog. I lost all ground references and the view of the vehicle headlights. Captain Wade could not see anything, either. I knew that we were in big trouble to say the least and I became terrified. At that time, it was well beyond my capability to hover on instruments, without any ground references. I feared the worst.

I looked at the attitude indicator to keep the aircraft level and I noticed the vertical speed indicator was indicating a descent of 500 feet per minute. I experienced spatial disorientation or vertigo and I lost control of the aircraft. The Chinook was obviously in an unusual descending altitude from which I did not have enough time to recover. As we descended, I felt the external sling load strike the ground. I frantically had fought for control of the aircraft right up until the time that I pulled pitch just seconds before the forward aircraft rotor blades impacted the ground.

Once the Chinook forward rotor blades struck the ground the aircraft began to rapidly break apart and beat itself to death. Once all motion stopped, the main part of the aircraft fuselage came to a final rest on its side. The cockpit area was broken apart but remained relatively upright. The aft rotor blades were stacked on top of each other as they struck the ground. It was fortunate for us that both engines flamed out after the violent ground impact. The cyclic control lever and the thrust lever had been ripped from my hands. Parts of the disintegrated cockpit was strewn all over the immediate area. I experienced the sensation of rolling over and being tossed through the crash wreckage.

That moment became petrifyingly dark and instantaneously quiet as the motion and sounds of the aircraft ceased and the electrical wiring was severed. It was the deafening sound of silence. I was severely dazed by that violent hard landing. I had taken a hard blow to my head from a piece of wreckage that had ripped off my flight helmet. For an instant, I thought that I might be dead having succumbed to the ultimate squeeze of the python and making my way into eternity. I thought that I had encountered my own Two Step Viper.

I could smell JP-4 jet fuel and hydraulic fluid permeating the early morning fog. The familiar vapor of jet fuel (that smells like kerosene) and hydraulic fluid (that smells like automobile automatic transmission fluid), penetrated the darkness and awakened my senses. After realizing that I was not dead, I was able to release my seat belt and shoulder harness. It registered with me that I was no longer inside the aircraft cockpit. My armored seat had been dislodged from the cockpit floor and thrown several feet away during the violent impact. Strapped in, I was laying on the back of the pilot's seat on the ground facing upward toward the obscured sky. The armored seat, my gloves, chest protector, boots, and flight helmet had shielded my body from much of the crash debris and the disintegrating wreckage when the aircraft was violently breaking up. Later on, I noticed a deep gouge in my chest protector and I knew that, without my helmet and chest protector, I surely would not have survived the final squeeze of the python. God made sure that I was protected.

Semi-Conscious and Seeing the Light

Captain Wade's flashlight, which was positioned on the center console between us, had miraculously turned on upon impact and it was lying illuminated not far from my right hand. Due to the trauma and the shock of the violent impact and a severe blow to my flight helmet, my mind was in a semi-conscious state. When I was able to stand up, I picked up the flashlight wondering if I was hallucinating. My helmet was ripped off and I didn't see it anywhere. I realized that I was alive and that I had just survived a tragic helicopter crash. I was outside of our perimeter, in the dead of night, with my crew. A major epiphany of my life began to unfold. At that point, I got goose bumps and the hair on the back of my neck stood up because I knew I was alive, and I knew that God had intervened, but my mind went straight to my crew. I prayed that they were out of the grips of the python, too.

With the flashlight in my hand, I began searching for the aircraft crew. The flight engineer, the gunner, and the crew chief had survived the crash and had found their way out of the broken cargo compartment. I thought that Captain Wade was probably still strapped in his seat somewhere in the crash debris. After intently searching for him, I finally saw some of the crash debris begin to move. I had found Captain Wade. I unbuckled his seat belt with my left hand and with my right hand, I grabbed him firmly under his left arm and began slowly moving him away from the crash site. I could tell that he was in shock and in great pain. His armored seat had also been thrown clear of the aircraft. With my grip under his arm and support, he was slowly limping away from the aircraft wreckage. As we began making our way from the aircraft wreckage, the Chinook caught fire and started to burn. I could see that the fire originated under the left fuel tank filler cap. The fire began slowly, at first, and then progressed rapidly into a blazing inferno. The main part of the fuselage appeared mainly intact, but it began to burn more furiously. Again, the Grim Reaper, the python, rotting cattle, and the Two Step Viper were all taunting us in unison. The finality of our lives flashed through my mind.

Rescued after the Explosion

In a commanding and frantic tone, I shouted to my nearby gunner for assistance. I was afraid that the aircraft would immediately explode before we could reach a safe enough distance away. Without hesitation, he helped me pull Captain Wade even further away from the flaming wreckage. I held onto Captain Wade's left arm and the gunner held onto his right arm. With adrenalin pumping through our bodies, we hustled as rapidly as our injured bodies could move trying desperately to evade what I thought would be an impending explosion.

In the distance, I noticed a mound in the area, about forty yards from the burning crash site, and my gut reaction was to make it to that point for protection. Time was running out and that mound was our only hope if we were to dodge the shrapnel and flying debris from the brewing explosion. We all clustered behind the mound hoping to be shielded from the imminent inferno. As God would have it, all of my crewmembers were sheltered safely behind the mound while the aircraft was completely engulfed in flames. Soon thereafter, the fuel tanks exploded into large orange fire balls, one followed by the other. Even from the distance, we could feel the heat of the flames. Some of the nearby 155-millimeter powder canisters ignited and soon exploded like a firework display on the fourth of July. Small arms ammunition also began to erupt from the intense heat and the new sounds accented the deep droning sound of flames with rapidly piercing pops. A few minutes later the ammunition stopped exploding, but the flames continued to feed on the JP-4 in the fuel tanks.

The crash site of CH-47A Chinook 63-7901 at Phu Cat.

As our Providential good fortune continued after the crash, the intense heat from the aircraft fire burned away the fog in the immediate area. Later, our operations personnel told me that when the sound of the hovering Chinook engines and rotor blades ceased, they feared the worst. The aircraft fire provided a flaming beacon to the nearby personnel at Hammond Field. A nearby medical evacuation Medevac UH-1D was quickly dispatched to our crash site. I would be rescued in a Slick like I had done for so many others. So many feelings seared through me but I set them aside to focus on the rescue of my crew. We had made it that far and I wasn't going to let anyone die on my watch if I could help it.

I signaled our location, behind the mound, with the flashlight and the chopper picked us up and hovered back to the medical tent to administer first aid. By the grace of God, they were able to rescue us all. Captain Wade had suffered the worst injury and incurred a broken leg. The flight engineer obtained several deep bruises. The crew chief experienced deep cuts on his forehead and in his hands. He also experienced a wrenched neck. The gunner received deep cuts that required many stitches. I suffered a badly sprained ankle and I received large bumps and bruises on my head since my flight helmet came off upon ground impact. My neck muscles were sore, and I had a bad scrape on my right leg. The right pant leg of my jungle fatigues had been caught on something and it was ripped completely off even though, my right boot remained in place.

Once we were safely back to camp and being tended to, we were able to give an account for the evening and ponder the events. I shared with the crew that my intent was to try to ascend out of the fog, drop the load, and fly to another safe location for landing. On that occasion my luck ran out and my efforts to save the aircraft proved futile. I remembered the flight jargon phrase: "I ran out of pitch, power, and ideas all at the same time."

The next day, we were told that the mound that shielded us that night was an abandoned giant termite hill. The analysis of the accident investigation team later reported that I was in a nose down attitude when the forward rotor blades had first contacted the ground. We were injured, but God had not allowed anyone to perish in that helicopter on my watch as aircraft commander. Once again, God had placed His hand between our crew and the Grim Reaper, and the python was forced to release its grasp.

After the brief helicopter rescue mission, I entered the medical tent where I noticed an enlisted man lying on a stretcher. The medical assistant said that he was the lone survivor from another helicopter crash that occurred on a mission that same night. I was informed that a few other helicopters had crashed that same night while they were attempting emergency resupply missions into the LZs that were under heavy attack. The crew members of the other aircraft that crashed were not as fortunate as my crew. They had all been killed. Again, I felt very blessed and morose both at the same time. Momentarily, I looked down and I noticed that my 38-caliber side arm and my survival knife were missing. That did not matter to me because we were all immensely overjoyed to still be alive. By God's Providence, that dreadful night, all my crew members were spared. I thanked God that none of my crewmembers were trapped inside the Chinook or were left to burn to death. That would have haunted me forever as my own emotional Two Step Viper attack on my mind.

The Accident Investigation

Later that day, a group of several colonels interviewed the crew as part of the preliminary accident investigation inquiry. They told me that due to the weather conditions, the crash was probably inevitable and the aircraft would be declared a combat loss. They thanked me for having the presence of mind to help rescue Captain Wade. I am forever thankful that I remained conscious enough after impact, though still in a daze, to complete the rescue.

I answered many of their probing questions. After answering their questions, I worked on my personal accident report statement. The tragic events of that early morning had touched the lives and families of many brave men, both friends and enemies. Many people had died and each soldier who perished left grieving family members. It was a catastrophic day as some of our other aircraft also had crashed that night leaving no survivors. Although I was responsible for the aircraft loss, gratefully, all of my crewmembers had safely made it out alive.

Learning to Endure the Pain

After daybreak, I returned with some others to the nearby crash site. After viewing the charred aircraft wreckage, I was amazed that we all had made it out alive. Later that same day, the accident team was sifting through the wreckage, but they did not find my pistol or my survival knife. Not long after that, I was issued another flight helmet, a chest protector, a pistol, and a survival knife.

On the way back from the crash site, I visited the aid station to get my ankle x-rayed and wrapped with an elastic bandage. My whole body, and especially my ankle, was increasing in pain and my leg was throbbing. I walked with a pronounced painful limp. I realized that pain was an integral part of our life experience. I was very thankful to still be alive after that tragic crash and that pain meant that I was alive.

My thoughts drifted back to my teen years in Florida and the lessons I had learned in understanding pain. I learned many lessons in life and how to endure pain from a sweet 85-year-old lady, Mrs. P. L. Harper. We first met her when I was a young teenager. She lived with her son only a few blocks from our house. She was in her 80's at the time when one Sunday morning, my mother spotted her walking in the direction of the church building. Mother stopped and she gladly accepted a ride since Mrs. Harper still had several blocks to go.

From that time on, we began stopping by her home on the way to church to give her a ride each Sunday. I noticed that when she was sitting ahead of us in church that her head twitched. Mother told me that she had a mild case of Bell's Palsy. My mother liked looking out for her and continued to drive her to church every Sunday. I came to love her like a grandmother. She had the old-time ability as a storyteller, like my grandmother Mama Hall, had. Mrs. Harper told such wonderful stories of the old days when she was a little girl in Tennessee before the turn of the century. I could hardly wait to hear her stories every Sunday on the ride to church. She always had the place of honor and sat in the front seat on the passenger side of our 1956 Chevy.

One Sunday morning, while getting into our car, she slammed the front passenger car door on the fingers of her right hand. After that incident, I noticed that more than one of her fingers were bleeding and I knew that it hurt her. Mother wanted to stop and tend to her injury. Mrs. Harper just took an ornate lace fringed handkerchief from her purse and wrapped it around her bleeding fingers and said, "When you get old, you learn to endure all kinds of pain." For me, that was one powerful lesson in pain management. We continued to church, without any more stories that day, and when we got there she washed and bandaged her fingers. The powerful example of her kind manner and unwavering strength within her, influenced my entire life. I learned a good deal from her example that influenced my faith and positive perspective during times of trial. Even today as a man nearing her age, I frequently look back to my early teen years and realize how much that kind old Mrs. Harper loved and believed in me.

Mrs. Harper died a few years after I was released from the Army in 1967. She was in her 90's when she passed on. She died not long after my wife and I married in November of 1967. Shortly before her death, my wife and I came home for a visit from Alabama and dropped by to see Mrs. Harper. As it turned out, on that visit, I saw her for the last time. She was bedridden and very thin. Her frail, thin body was just worn out. She was immensely proud of me and happy that I had found a good wife.

I sat there after my crash and as memories of Mrs. Harper consumed me, because of her example, I did not complain about the pain from my own injuries. Compared to Mrs. Harper, I was still young and I had plenty of time to heal. I was very thankful that God had spared all our lives. I was more than happy to endure the pain as Mrs. Harper had once taught me.

Over the years, I have recounted the life-changing events of that tragic night of 18 December 1966. A strange phenomenon occurred, at the precise time that I crashed in Vietnam. My mother, who was living in Florida, sensed the trauma that I had experienced during the crash. Later as I would find out my mother felt that something had happened to me and even my sisters at home sensed it after watching the evening news that a Chinook had crashed in Vietnam; and, then, my Mother said aloud, "that's Sonny". Later in the afternoon, I caught a flight back to my unit at Lane Field. I was tired, weary, still extremely traumatized and; yet, humbled and very thankful to be alive.

When my next letter reached home, those feelings of my mother and sisters were confirmed. I was mainly happy that I had not been killed so that my family did not have to endure receiving a telegram of my death stating that I was killed in action. That notification would have been followed by a delivered casket just before Christmas in 1966; and, I certainly didn't want them to have to face a tragedy of sadness.

Hindsight

On Monday, 19 December 1966, the news of my accident had preceded me when I arrived back at Lane Field. When everyone asked, “How are you,” I jokingly said, “It’s so nice to be here!” My whole body was still very sore. I sat around and finished filling out my personal accident report statement. Repeatedly, I had to recount the tragic events that resulted in the crash of the helicopter, to the other pilots.

My good friend, CWO John Greene, had been genuinely concerned about the circumstances of that tragic accident. We had flown many missions and logged many hours together. While looking me straight in the eye, he laid his hand on my shoulder and said, “If I had been with you that never would have happened.” I realized in that somber moment that he was probably right. Part of the problem was not having a well experienced copilot to help control the aircraft in that difficult situation.

It was officially confirmed that the aircraft would be declared a combat loss. It was the judgment of the crash investigation panel that I would not be held responsible for the crash of the aircraft under those difficult combat flying conditions. I continued to rest and to heal.

I was commended by the panel for the rescue of Captain Wade from the aircraft. If he had been left abandoned in the aircraft, he surely would have burned to death in that inferno. They shared with me some of the crash photos. The clock in the instrument panel had stopped at 0232 hours when the fire had charred it and caused it to freeze in time.

As part of the follow-on accident investigation procedures, I was given a post-accident flight physical by a flight surgeon. It was the flight surgeon's responsibility to determine if I was fit enough to continue flying combat missions. During my flight physical, the flight surgeon asked me, "Are you afraid to fly?" I confidently looked at him and said, "No sir. I know what happened and I will never make that mistake again." My superficial injuries were beginning to heal. Doc said that from a medical standpoint, I could return to flying status.

A big contributing factor to that tragic incident was my lack of instrument training. I was not instrument-rated and thus I was not prepared to cope with the demanding circumstances that I faced. From the time that I lost any ground references to the time that the aircraft's forward rotors struck the ground was at most 15 - 20 seconds.

We had not experienced any problems landing at Hammond Field on the two previous earlier flights on that same fateful night. We had not experienced any difficulties with that final flight up until the time that the visual references to the ground were lost.

In looking back with 20/20 hindsight, I thought about many other ways that I might have prevented the crash. At that time, I was overwhelmed by the circumstances that were happening too quickly and the ground came up to smite me. It was overwhelming. That night I did not have the luxury of being paired with one of the seasoned and more experienced Chief Warrant Officers.

My mind was still racing when I finally went to bed about 0400 hours. I tried to rest but I could not sleep with my mind racing, as it would for days to come.

Spared for a Greater Purpose

It is interesting how the mind reacts during traumatic events. For a short time in my dazed condition, I felt as though time had stopped just like the clock on the instrument panel. In that altered state, my mind was blending the events of a violent childhood truck accident in June of 1954, with that Chinook crash in December 1966. In both events, I passionately believed that God had spared my life for a greater purpose. I still believe that to this day, even as an older man. The sheer fact that I survived that horrible crash was a spiritual experience for me.

Amidst all the explosions and chaos, the Divine message that consumed my mind immediately after the Chinook crash was, "Son remember the covenant that you made with Me when you were eleven years old. I have preserved your life so you can teach others." Both of those tragic events were very profound life-changing experiences. I looked up toward the sky and said, "Thank You Lord." I knew God was with me and that He was actively piloting my life.

It was many years later as my wife, my children, and I were visiting Israel that I felt a similar experience. As I entered the Garden Tomb in Jerusalem, I had the same feeling of goose bumps and the hair on the back of my neck standing up in the same way that it had when I first saw the flashlight shining in the darkness at the Chinook crash site. It was the same spiritual circumstance now for the third time in my life. In the Garden Tomb, as my thoughts began to clear, my mind was drifting back to the reality of the Chinook crash situation. Each time God had shown me my path in life and every time I wanted to take full advantage of the moment to maintain my initial boyhood covenant. My understanding of the importance of life had been radically altered, again, forever, after my Chinook crash. That event was a wakeup call for me. The Grim Reaper wanted to destroy us that fateful night, but

God would not allow him to put his hand on us. I felt determined to be more cautious, to get more instrument training, and to become more attuned to the power of the spiritual realm. Suddenly, life had taken on more meaning for me. I felt closer to God, but I always regretted the fact that I had crashed a Chinook and lost so many friends in Vietnam.

The Late December Carnage at LZ Bird

It would be five days until Christmas on Tuesday. I was so thankful that all our crew had survived to see another Christmas. Flying combat missions in Vietnam was not a typical way to celebrate festivities leading up to a joyous holiday, but we were relieved to be alive and breathing. Even though we had been afforded the gift of life that dark perilous morning, we had suffered defeat to the fog. As I replayed the moments leading up to the crash over and over in my mind, the words of Sun Tzu came to mind.

> *"If you know the enemy and know yourself, you need not fear the result of a hundred battles. If you know yourself but not the enemy, for every victory gained you will also suffer a defeat. If you know neither the enemy nor yourself, you will succumb in every battle."*
>
> *- Sun Tzu, The Art of War*

For many nights to follow I went to bed reliving the crash always awaking in a same semi-conscious state just moments after the crash. Once fully awake my mind focused on those last few seconds before the aircraft struck the ground. I think my mind was fixated on how it transpired so fast because it was still a mystery that bothered me. I repeatedly asked myself why I had failed, and why I had succumbed to losing that Chinook. Even though I could not solve the mystery of that night, I knew that I never wanted a scenario like that to every play out on my watch, ever again. I had learned from other pilots before me that had already lost their lives due to faulty maintenance. To protect my crew in the future I started conducting my own additional inspections. I was troubled trying to figure out what I needed to learn to master similar situations in the future.

The Full Report

I still did not fully understand, with certainty, what the aircraft attitude was when the Chinook first contacted the ground. Feelings could be deceiving. The accident investigation team examined all the evidence and published their findings. The official accident report established the most likely sequence of events after I lost visibility of all ground references.

The report indicated that the aircraft was in a nose low attitude while drifting to the right upon impacting the ground. Upon impact the cockpit had broken up and had separated from the main fuselage at the pilot's compartment bulkhead. The main fuselage continued to roll away to the left from the demolished cockpit area. Large sections of crash debris came to rest and were littered all over the immediate area.

Part of the floor, with the flight controls still intact, had been located not far off and the complete instrument panel and the center console was also strewn nearby. The two pilot's seats were found relatively close in proximity to each other. The aircraft had plowed up the soft damp mud during the impact sequence before coming to rest. It was estimated that the damp mud cushioned the impact and helped reduced the chance of a sudden impact fire.

During the accident investigation the following morning, I

recalled how obvious it was, from the footprints at the crash site, that some of the village scavengers had already begun to carrying away what valuable debris they could salvage. The M-60 door machine guns, ammunition, and the crew's personally issued weapons were missing. Some of the unburned powder canisters and the 155-millimeter shell casings had also been carried away by the villagers.

Consequently, a detail of ground troops and a Vietnamese interpreter arrived at the crash scene early in the morning to provide security. A villager was discovered at the crash scene who was then captured and beaten by the troops until he confessed that the weapons, the ammunition, and the artillery shell casings were concealed in a nearby rice paddy.

Some of the other metal wreckage was also carried away and hidden. My 38-caliber pistol was located within the buried cache of weapons although it was severely burned in the aircraft fire and the live cartridges in the cylinder had exploded from the intense heat. My damaged flight helmet and my survival knife were also recovered. I had suspected that my flight helmet had perished in the ensuing aircraft fire. It was soberingly surreal to hold my half-beaten flight helmet in my hands, knowing that in the process, it helped save my life. That helmet was God's hand between me and the Grim Reaper. Sadly, we were not the only crash that dreadful night. A total of six helicopters went down that foggy dark morning, ours happened to be the only one with all survivors. It was sobering to consider that of the six flights that night, not only did my entire crew survive, but it was also the only flight that had escaped the coiling squeeze of the python. Chills came over me as I held that flight helmet deeply understanding the spiritual magnitude of Providence.

On that same day, our company commander had also experienced another tragedy. He had performed a heroic act at Pleiku that afternoon by helping wounded soldiers climb up the ladder into a hovering Chinook. After getting all the troops on board, the python squeezed its coils even tighter until the aircraft suddenly burst into flames and crashed violently onto the ground. Another senseless and gruesome act scattering heroes across the rice paddies. The commander watched in horror as the aircraft, the crew, and the passengers were all incinerated, instantaneously. I never did hear what caused that Chinook to crash. My best guess was that the aircraft was hit by an enemy artillery round. Pleiku was a dreadfully dangerous place and other Chinooks had similarly crashed due to enemy artillery fire. Two Step Vipers were at every turn.

When our company commander heard the news that we, too, had crashed he expected to hear the news of more charred bodies. Upon his return, our company commander visited the field hospital where several of the crew members, including myself, were recovering. He saw that we were injured but was relieved that we were still very much alive. Major Fountain was overcome with comfort and solace that we had escaped the doom of that dreadful night. Captain Wade told the captain that we were sorry that we had lost one of his assigned aircraft. Captain Wade went on to tell the Major that when we hit the ground, he said to himself, "Goodbye cruel world." Captain Wade thought, "We had bought the farm."

I expressed to Major Fountain that I was at the controls and the accident was my fault and that I did the best I could under the circumstances. He did not blame me, and he was relieved that the entire crew had survived the crash. The commander assured me that the urgency and priority of that combat resupply mission into LZ Bird that night had far outweighed the cost of the aircraft and the safety and the lives of the aircrew. That, in and of itself, was comforting to know.

I became keenly aware of the gravity of the situation that had taken place at LZ Bird. A battalion of our troops at LZ Bird had been under periodic heavy enemy attack and it had been feared that they would be overrun. He said that under normal circumstances that I would never have been ordered to attempt such a dangerous mission nor in such bad weather conditions. That made me feel a little better about the events that transpired on my watch, but I still hated losing the aircraft. I carried that guilt for a long time. After the accident, I returned often to the field hospital to see Captain Wade and our crew chief. The captain would be evacuated to Japan for further treatment, and I would miss him, but I was glad to know that he would eventually make a full recovery. The crew chief would remain in Vietnam in the field hospital until his cuts healed.

Moving Forward

I remained in bed until 1100 hours on Wednesday, 21 December 1966. When I lay completely still, my body did not hurt nearly as much. I was not on any pain medication, and I did not have anything to do or any place to go. I remained quiet in the stillness of my mind and thoughts, allowing my body time to heal. Day by day the pain slowly subsided, and I thought of the story of a "bronc rider" who had been thrown. I had been thrown off the horse, but I wanted to get back in the saddle as soon as I could. I spent some time reading and playing my guitar because those activities were simple and soothing to me. It took my mind off the movie reel that had been looping in my head that awful night. I focused my mind on fully healing and spiritually growing. My limp began to lessen somewhat but my ankle was still very weak and achingly sore. I intentionally wore my jungle boots most of the time to provide some support for my aching ankle, but it still needed more time to heal, so I lay motionless for most of the afternoon.

Later in the evening, I had the good fortune of flying for about an hour with my good friend CWO-3 Webster C. (Web) Manuel who was several years older than me. We had been staying in the same tent at our home base at An Khe, and I genuinely enjoyed his company. In a short amount of time, we became good friends. He was a true American Cajun by descent, and he spoke French fluently having been raised in Louisiana. Web was one of the most interesting U.S. Army pilots that I had ever known. He had flown helicopters for many years and had earned an instrument rating. Prior to his Vietnam tour he had been an instrument instructor pilot. It was said that Web was one of the best instrument instructors at Fort Rucker, Alabama. Web was a master Chinook pilot and I really respected him as I always walked away learning more than I had expected.

During the Korean War, Web was an enlisted man and he had served as an interpreter with a French unit in Korea. Later elements of that same French Unit deployed to Indochina in Vietnam. Web told me that he had visited the French cemetery at the Mang Yang Pass where there was a memorial for the fallen French soldiers. Web said that he recognized the names of many of the French soldiers that had been killed in an ambush there in September of 1954.

After my Chinook accident, CWO Web Manual, CWO Jack King, CWO Harold Marquardt, and others of the more experienced Chief Warrant Officer pilots, wanted to ensure that I received some field instrument training. I greatly respected all of them and was grateful to take on this new skillset, and honored that they wanted to take me under their wings, as a student. They desired to provide me with enough tactical instrument instruction for me to get out of trouble if I again, inadvertently, went IFR in the clouds or in thick fog at night. I deeply appreciated their concern for me and valued the investment they were willing to make to further my aptitude as a pilot.

Those seasoned Chief Warrant Officers were some of the best helicopter pilots in the world. When flying with them I realized how good they really were and the skills that I had been lacking. I gleaned skills and lessons from each one of them. Web and all the other CWOs became my personal instrument flying mentors.

Our unit was informed of the harrowing missions that I had flown as a Slick pilot. And some of our pilots had already flown with me on dangerous missions in Chinooks. I was always well known to be sober and always ready to respond to emergency calls for help when so often others were not in a coherent state to respond. Many times, I was one of the only pilots in the "O" Club who had not been drinking when someone came in with an urgent request to fly, thus, my combat flying time accrued more rapidly than others. The unit knew that through my many combat missions that I had become accustomed to being shot at and with a sharpness of mind keenly outmaneuvered the enemy to bring the crew home safely.

From that time on, our unit Chinook pilots called me "Tiger" or "Tig" for short. Although sometimes, admittedly, they would jokingly refer to me as "Crash." My survival of the recent crash marked a turning point in my Vietnam tour. I became more acutely aware of my situational awareness; I was focused on my instrument training, and I felt more confident in general. God had been kind to me, and I felt that I had just as much purpose in life as that 11-year-old-boy many years ago. I focused on missions to come and was determined to become an even better combat Chinook pilot.

My Second Flight Back in the Saddle

Web and I began my second flight after my crash a few days earlier. After being bucked off my horse I was eager to climb back in the saddle to prove my resolve and passion to fly in combat, again. My body was still aching, and I certainly did not want to be thrown off anymore but I was more than ready to fly above the clouds to experience the serenity and love I had of flying. Web had always called me "Tig." As we put on our helmets and ear protection Web put his hand on my shoulder and looked me in the eye and said, "Tig, you got this. I'm proud of you." I knew I was in good hands and looked forward to my first instrument training session.

That second flight since the crash included my first sessions "under the hood" which meant that a device clipped onto our helmets that limited our view to only the instrument panel. Under the hood, I experienced vertigo easily just as I had that early December morning. The sensation my body was delivering made it a struggle for me to believe what I saw on the instrument panel. The physical sensation was deceptive because of the false sensory inputs that my body was feeling. I quickly trained myself to trust the flight instruments as sight and not feelings which had previously been my primary input for making decisions. Bravely, I assumed the controls for that entire flight. As we were flying, a request was received to take one load of 155-millimeter ammunition (lobsters) to the fateful LZ Bird and then to return to Lane Field. Thankfully, the weather was clear, and I easily dropped off the external load safely at LZ Bird. It felt good to have recovered so quickly from such a tragic experience not so many nights before. I was relieved.

From that flight on, I continued to gain more mastery over the complex Chinook helicopter. I frequently and intently studied the pilot's flight manual and continued to gain a good working knowledge of the aircraft systems and the emergency procedures. The skills and knowledge that I had learned from flying the Slicks into hot LZs, aided me in performing my duties as a Chinook pilot. I was becoming more skillful and comfortable in maneuvering the Chinook in similar combat conditions while trusting my instruments. Fortunately, I had outstanding depth perception and was well suited at carrying external sling loads.

On final approach into Lane Field, I observed tracer fire coming from the nearby hills. The fire quickly ceased so we continued the flight and landed. I was still a little apprehensive about getting caught again in IFR weather conditions, however, I was determined to improve my skills on the next instrument training flight.

We had flown several more sorties into the hot areas of LZ Bird and LZ Pony. There was constant heavy outgoing artillery fire from both of the LZs. Back and forth we flew into LZ Bird and LZ Pony to replenish the supply of artillery ammunition.

The reported VC activity and the subsequent artillery fire was steadily increasing. The artillery battery incessantly fired in all directions at reported VC and NVA locations. We radioed on "Fox Mike", to the Black Hat Pathfinders (forward area controllers who directed aircraft landings into the LZ Bird), but they were not able get the artillery fire lifted for us to land.

In addition to the artillery fire, the weather started to turn bad as moisture saturated scud clouds that were forming near the ground under the higher broken layer of clouds. My favorite expression was that we had been experiencing a “Chinese fire drill.” The Black Hats were frantically trying to stay in contact with both the artillery battery and the approaching aircraft.

Finally, the artillery fire was lifted long enough for us to land and drop off the artillery ammunition. We dropped the sling load and then we hooked up to a damaged 105 Howitzer as a back haul. The Howitzer had exploded during a previous fire mission at LZ Bird killing two artillery troops. The barrel of the cannon had been split and broken into pieces. We dropped off the load at Hammond Field and headed back to Lane Field. I was dog tired and in pain after that long day. Remembering the example set by Mrs. Harper, I did not complain because I was still alive. I planned to eat supper and go straight to bed because my whole body was hurting.

At the end of Thursday, 22 December 1966, we logged over eight long flight hours. I was more exhausted than usual, and my leg and ankle were in constant pain from sitting in the pilot's seat for such a long duration of time. The bruises on my head and body were beginning to fade. The scabs from my abrasions were beginning to loosen up and flaked off as I unconsciously picked at them. It had crossed my mind again that enduring pain was part of the life experience. The important thing was to heal and to keep moving forward in a positive direction.

In the process of that day's missions Web Manuel provided some flight instructions on performing a few ground controlled approaches (GCAs) on our return flights into Hammond Field. When we arrived back, I discovered that a new tactical radar set had recently been installed at Hammond Field. As I headed back to camp I thought about how helicopter instrument flying was truly a challenge for me.

I was thankful that Web Manual and the other CWOs were investing so much time into my flight training because I viewed mastering instrument training as a necessary survival skill that I was determined to master.

Christmas Eve Missions

It heavily rained all day on Friday, 23 December 1966. We sat at Lane Field for most of the day. Aircraft (133) was down for maintenance at LZ Lane. The auxiliary power unit (APU) was hard to start, and it needed to be changed out. After the APU repair was complete we delivered a few parts to LZ Lane near Qui Nhon and then returned. As we waited, I read and played my guitar to relax my mind and disconnect from the intensity that was demanded of the Vietnam War. I had bravely gotten back in the saddle, but psychologically, it was emotionally draining to stay ahead of the fear.

At about 1700 hours there was a break in the weather and we were scheduled for a few urgent missions. The water levels in the rivers and lakes were rising up north due to the torrential rains. We internally transported small boats inside our cargo bay to an area in the north. I supposed that the boats were to be used to rescue stranded people. We completed four missions and two of which were flown after dark. I practiced more instrument flying and accomplished two instrument take-offs (ITO). I was developing my skill at flying on instruments and gaining confidence.

Saturday was Christmas Eve Day and there were heavy rain showers, low clouds, and poor visibility at Lane Field. I slept until 0800 hours while it still was raining. We sat around waiting for the weather to break so we could fly aircraft (070) back to An Khe for structural repairs. While hauling boats internally the night before one of the boats was caught by a wind current and stuck the station #360 stringer in the rear of the aircraft. The stringer was significantly damaged and needed repairs.

At about 1300 hours we flew back to An Khe or "Alpha Kilo". We flew at a low level to Happy Valley and then slipped in under the clouds at the north pass. We continued "nap-of-the-earth" or flying very low in order to avoid enemy ground fire, for the remainder of the short flight from the north pass to the "golf course." As the natives would say we made it, "no sweat GI." A Jeep met us when we landed on the "golf course" and drove us back to the company area. I had received several Christmas cards and letters from the folks at home which brought back the happiest of family memories and made me smile.

Even though the weather was cool, and the rains continued, it just did not feel much like Christmas. Christmas carols were played on the radio from the Armed Forces Vietnam Network in Saigon. Homemade Christmas decorations were placed on our tents, in operations, and in the "O" Club. I felt as though I was a million miles from home, it was very lonely. I was still sore from the injuries that I received in the crash, and I was emotionally and mentally trying to heal.

Christmas Eve Cowboys

While I was flying on Christmas Eve Day, a hydraulic brake line ruptured and sprayed hydraulic fluid all over the cockpit area triggering a smell to memory response. The distinct smell of the hydraulic fluid sent my mind immediately to the crash that had occurred just a few days earlier. My body tensed up as if I were experiencing it all over again. When I inhaled the odor of spilled JP-4 and hydraulic fluid, like a broken record, my mind replayed how lucky I was to survive that crash. I was dazed and in a half-conscious state of mind after the crash. I can still vividly recall the smell of JP-4 jet fuel, the hydraulic fluid, the torn metal, the fresh plowed dirt, the gun powder, and my own blood. The smell, triggered by a simple ruptured hydraulic brake line, sent a simultaneous message to my brain reminding me that my life was spared that night for a higher purpose.

I decided to head over to the "O" Club to check out what others were doing to celebrate Christmas Day. Soon after, a discussion arose in the "O" Club while various pilots were drinking. With animation they were telling stories of their building material gathering exploits at Phan Thiet. Our company always tried to scrounge building material to construct our semi-permanent quarters and were always on the lookout for more. We noticed during our prior operation that there was an abundance of building materials at Phan Thiet. There had been a supply of plywood that was stacked up nearby where we typically parked our aircraft. No one seemed to have claimed the plywood and building supplies, so we conspired a secret mission to make a special Christmas Eve delivery to An Khe.

Our company commander and one of his subordinate captains decided to fly a Chinook from An Khe to Phan Thiet to stealthily abscond with the pile of lumber and other loose building materials that they located in that storage area. On Christmas Eve night, they commandeered a forklift and transported the materials to the aircraft. The secret Christmas Eve mission became known to several as the "moonlight requisition." Our commander instructed the forklift driver that, "He had not seen a thing." The tools and the building materials were easily traded for a couple of bottles of booze. The lumber and building materials were quickly loaded into the Chinook and the cargo ramp and door were closed to conceal the evidence. A portable gas cement mixer and some other hand tools were absconded and loaded aboard the aircraft at the same time. The aircraft was fully loaded with contraband building materials and tools. Our company commander was standing by the aircraft and had expected that at any time, the Criminal Investigation Detachment (CID) would show up. By chance, a full bird colonel drove up to the Chinook in a Jeep. He was a "ground pounder", or infantry commander, and he had never been inside a Chinook. Our commander, who always looked sharp in appearance, smartly saluted the colonel and said, "May I help you, Sir"?

The colonel asked if he could have a casual look inside the aircraft. Our commander responded, "I'm sorry Sir but this aircraft has been loaded with a new top secret radar array that is to be installed at An Khe. Unless you have a real need to know I would rather not reveal the contents." The colonel replied, "Maybe some other time" and he drove off as our commander stood there sweating bullets. The commander and crew started up the Chinook and immediately headed back to An Khe. As far as I know to this day, nothing more was ever said about the missing building materials. I think our commander would have had a difficult time convincing the colonel that the stolen cement mixer was a top-secret radar array. We all enjoyed a good laugh about that story late in the night at the "O" Club.

It ended up that the "moonlight requisition" mission, contributed significantly to our building program. Due to our escapades, we earned the title of the "Circle 'C' Cowboys." As the Circle 'C' Cowboys, we continued to pillage and scrounge while on missions. We were able to retrieve all kinds of useful building materials and even furniture. We obtained desks and chairs, power generators, air compressors, and more building materials to continue our pending projects. Every time a Chinook landed with contraband, the company commander asked, "How far behind you is the CID tailing you"? The commander kept saying, "You are going to get me a long prison sentence in Leavenworth."

Christmas Day

I slept until 0800 hours on Christmas Day, Monday. I got up and

I opened my Christmas presents from my mother, and my brother and sisters. I received several cards and letters from people back home that included Christmas family photos and a recap of 1966. It made me feel connected with a sense of belonging that several had taken the time to send mail over the holiday. I headed over to "B" Bravo Company mess hall to eat a full breakfast that Christmas morning. I thought about past Christmas mornings with my brother and sisters and remembered the feeling of joyful surprise and the smell of mother's cooking. Those smells triggered such positive feelings that I took a few deep breaths just to re-experience the positive emotions of back home. After breakfast I wrote a few letters home in reply to the stack I had opened and shared happy memories of my childhood or updated them on how I was doing. I missed seeing so many neighbors, family and friends, but I was happy for them all, that I was alive. Their love was a deep abiding and enduring kind of love. I knew that it would grieve so many of them deeply, had I been killed that night. However, only my ankle was still hurting something fierce, and I planned to see the flight surgeon on the next day.

Early Christmas afternoon we flew aircraft (143) to Hammond Field. The aircraft had a lateral vibration and an additional high frequency vibration from one of the engine nose gearboxes. We remained on standby at Hammond Field and we read magazines, mostly they were about stock car racing, Road and Track, sports, American Rifleman, and even Mad Magazine. We departed for An Khe about 1845 hours receiving a radar vector into An Khe and landed without experiencing any problems. Flying helped the time pass and it kept my mind focused. I was accumulating a decent amount of both instrument flying time and combat experiences. That night I reread some of my previous journal entries and daily jotted down the days' happenings even if the day was uneventful. I wanted to be able to share a full detailed account with my loved ones someday, which was one reason that I was so persistent with my journal entries. The realistically mortal side of me always wondered if my journal would abruptly end one day before my tour of duty was completed. It gave me peace of mind knowing that it would be sent home with my personal effects to my survivors if, in combat, God willed to call me home. I quickly dismissed that final thought as I remembered the verse from Ecclesiastes, "Where there is life there is hope. A live dog is better than a dead lion." The act of writing in my journal gave me peace and hope.

That timeframe after the crash was a reflective time for me. My mind continued to wrestle with the reality of war and death, even though consciously, I did not want to allow myself to succumb to a constant fear of dying. Since I arrived in Vietnam some of the missions and experiences were terrifying and intense, so I kept on telling myself, "Learn from the past and keep moving in a positive direction into the future." This kept me grounded and forwardly focused on success.

It was frequently said in Vietnam, and especially by Major Jackson, "No guts, no glory." I thought that every young man wanted to find his place in the eternal order of things. Sometimes God, Himself, puts us in critical learning circumstances. Thus, the conflict of the "flesh" and the "Spirit" continue to struggle within each of us, even today. I believed that my life was spared for a purpose and that I must continue to move forward to, one day, fulfill that purpose.

Entertainment from Afar

Since I continued to experience severe pain in my right leg for over a week after the injury, I went to see the flight surgeon concerning my injured ankle on Monday, 26 December 1966. Most of my cuts and bruises were almost healed but my ankle continued to be very sore and painful. When I saw the flight surgeon, he must have thought that my appointment was concerning, "a request to be removed, from flying" status. He asked me again, "Are you afraid to fly"? With a puzzled look on my face I said, "No sir, I am here about my sore ankle."

His question seemed odd to me since I already had been flying for the last few days. I had accumulated over 12 hours of combat flying time and had been under direct enemy fire at least one of those occasions. The flight surgeon explained to me that no bones were broken. He further told me to keep my ankle tightly wrapped with an elastic bandage and to stay off my feet as much as possible. While handing me another elastic bandage, I stood up and said "Thank you sir" and I departed the medical tent. Maybe part of the soreness was the result of the extra weight of wearing my heavy chest protector. I would wrap my ankle daily, endure the pain like Mrs. Harper, and continue flying.

At that very time, the Bob Hope show at An Khe was scheduled to begin. The weather was bad with zero visibility due to the overnight lingering thick fog, so I thought about going to the show to see all the pretty girls and enjoy listening to the music. By the time I arrived, the place was so crowded that I could not get in even if I wanted. I just sat down on a bench outside and listened to the music from a distance.

Anita Bryant, Joey Heatherton, Vic Damone, Miss World from India, Les Brown and his band, comedian Phillis Diller with her signature hairdo, and others were there to perform, but I did not get to see any of them. I remembered hearing Bob Hope ask Phillis Diller, "What do they called your hairdo." She responded, "A direct hit" and everyone burst out in a roar of belly laughs. When Joey Heatherton finished her provocative dance routine, Bob Hope said, "Go to my room and rest." Again, a much-needed distraction and release of tension as everyone continued to roar with laughter.

After listening to the show from afar I limped back to our company area on the "golf course." On the way back, just in walking, I twisted my weak ankle and it began hurting even more. When I returned to my tent, I looked through my handwritten statement that I would be submitting to the crash investigation team the next day. I wanted to make sure I had not left out any pertinent details. In throbbing pain, I fell asleep for the next couple of hours.

The following morning, I submitted the statement of my account of the crash, of CH-47A serial number 63-7901, so that it could be typed and become part of the official accident investigation report. It was interesting that the numbers were almost the same as Chinook tail number 63-7910 (only the last two digits were transposed) that had come apart in the air and took the lives of my friends while I was in Phan Thiet the prior month, in November. I walked away wondering what would ultimately come of my official accident investigation report.

The movie projector was inoperative so there was no movie that night. Instead, I walked over to our "O" Club even though that was a rare occasion for me. Typically, I only went over on special occasions, but there was nothing else to do that night and I did not want to be alone. A group of old Chief Warrant Officers were sitting around and drinking. In their charismatic and boisterous tone, they were trying to "out do" each other with their war stories and were "badmouthing" each other. When I had heard enough tales, I returned to my tent and went to bed and slept well.

When I awakened early in the morning of Tuesday, 27 December 1966, it was noticeably cooler and rainy as a cold front had drifted into the An Khe region. I read and organized my gear for a trip back to Hammond Field and for upcoming combat support missions. A little while later I received two letters from my mother where she related how she experienced intense feeling on the exact day when the crashed occurred. Call it ESP or mother's intuition, but she knew when it happened, she felt it all the way around the world as if we were on the same transmission frequency. She said that she had cried for a long time, but she was glad to receive my letter and hear that I was still alive. Her intuition knew something was wrong and had feared the worst. I hated to put her through that level of worry and traumatic experiences. My mother just seemed to perceive everything about her children. I looked forward to the day that I could hug her again and comfort her for the trauma and sadness that she went through on my account. War extends far beyond soldiers witnessing a field of rotting cattle to impact friends, families, the earth, mankind and generations that follow. I yearned for comfort and to comfort in such a senseless war of carnage.

North Vietnamese Attack

About that time, we heard the rapidly circulating stories that there was trouble the night before at LZ Bird. In the typical enemy fashion, the NVA violated a Christmas ceasefire truce and attacked LZ Bird and other nearby fire bases with a large force. The 1st of the Twelfth Cavalry were almost completely overrun by invading VC and NVA troops. Elements of two VC and NVA Battalions had stealthily infiltrated past the LZ's early warning listening posts. The NVA were not detected until they blew up a 155 Howitzer with a satchel charge. In that first attack about twenty-five American troops were killed and forty-five more were wounded. That was one of the worst conflicts for the 1st Cavalry Division in Vietnam since the previous assault on LZ

Xray in the Ia Drang valley in November 1965.

What had kept LZ Bird from being completely wiped out was a U.S. ground patrol that was returning to LZ Bird. The alert radio operator in that ground patrol alerted the friendly forces and frantically radioed aerial rocket artillery for emergency air support. ARA consisted of a UH-1B that was modified with twenty-four, 2.75-inch rockets mounted on each side of the aircraft. A brave standby ready reaction force from Hammond Field immediately prepared to respond to the emergency call for help. This was a "Broken Arrow" situation. The RRF rapidly boarded the Slick aircraft and expeditiously headed straight for the conflict area at LZ Bird. ARA and escort gunships were part of the RRF force. This time it was earlier in the night and the weather was much more cooperative.

Prior to the friendly RRF forces landing in the adjacent rice paddies, illumination flares lit up the whole area to identify the positions of the enemy attack forces. The plan was for the ARA and gunships to simultaneously arrive, to identify the enemy combatants, and to engage the enemy in a narrowly defined "kill zone" just beyond the perimeter of LZ Bird. The LZ Bird forward air controllers would help identify the intruders and coordinate the close air support attack.

Once the first ARA and the other gunships reached LZ Bird, illumination flares were fired high overhead from other nearby artillery firebases, and it began to appear in very bright clusters over LZ Bird. Some of the friendly ground troops also began to launch a series of handheld flares and popped colored smoke grenades, to distinguish the boundaries between the friendly and the enemy combatants.

The artillery flares began to "light up" the area almost as bright as daylight. Each ARA helicopter, each gunship armed with 48 2.75-inch rockets and deadly accurate quad machine guns, began to pour heavy fire into the startled enemy troop concentrations around LZ Bird. With the sudden flare illumination, the concealed enemy troops had their night vision impaired and became "sitting ducks." The gunships and ARA helicopters began a carnage in retribution for the attack during a declared, Christmas truce.

Following the violently executed rocket and machine gun attack, many of the enemy lay dead or wounded in the rice paddies with the ground soaking up their blood. Another soon-to-be scene of rotting cattle. After that initial gunship attack many of the enemy began to retreat in terror. Not much longer after that, the gunships fire was halted around the intended landing zone for the RRF Cavalry troops to land. The friendly brave RRF troop formations of Slicks began landing in formation in the rice paddies around LZ Bird and the troops rapidly dismounted. The assault force formation was escorted by more helicopter gunships that continued to orbit the area picking off enemy troops, with precision quad machine gun fire, as they fled.

Thankfully, the weather cooperated that night. As the flares continued to illuminate the whole area the landing force rapidly took cover and began engaging the enemy in a fierce fire fight. That was a night of heavy fighting and profuse bloodletting on both sides. By daylight, all the surviving enemy troops had fled the area. At dawn, once the LZ was finally secure, the Dustoff medical evacuation helicopters were busily transporting the seriously wounded troops to field hospitals. The troops that had been killed were lined up in body bags for transport to Qui Nhon for final processing.

On that same next morning following the attack on LZ Bird, we flew aircraft (108), which had just completed a routine 25-hour inspection from An Khe to Hammond Field. On our first assigned mission of the day, we sling-loaded a bulldozer to LZ Bird. The bulldozer was needed to aid in cleanup operations, and to repair the defensive positions that were battle damaged only a few hours earlier during the enemy attack. Upon arrival at LZ Bird, we noticed the sobering sight of many dead VC and NVA troops still lying in the rice paddies slaughtered like cattle. Our troops already had retrieved the enemy weapons that were not carried away after the battle. Many AK-47 and other weapons were retrieved from that field of somber decay.

After having dropped off the bulldozer, as a backhaul, we hooked up and sling-loaded a downed Slick, which was shot down the night before. We took the UH-1D back to Hammond Field and dropped it off. On the next assigned sortie to LZ Bird, we transported some NVA and VC KIA bodies to a village near LZ Pony. There were two NVA at LZ Bird who were gravely wounded, but they died as we were landing at Hammond Field. Their dead bodies had not been covered and it was a very eerie experience viewing their glazed eyes, staring out of blood-soaked faces, while lying in our cargo bay. I had hoped that they would have survived the trip.

Somehow in that carnage near a small nearby village, two young girls were found dead, probably from artillery fire. A weeping and distraught mother with her daughter came down from the nearby village of Phu My to identify and claim the bodies. It made me incredibly despondent to see the innocent children slaughtered as cattle and strewn out across the rice paddy. They had been bitten by their own Two Step Vipers. Sorrowful despair engulfed me for what I had just experienced. I looked at the mother and her daughter, but what could be said? They were simple and typical Vietnamese people who had unjustly become casualties of war. They wore dark clothes and even from afar I could see they had pierced ears with gold rings still in them. War really was hell. With a mournful countenance I choked back emotions as I said to my gunner, who also witnessed the carnage, "This makes a lot of sense doesn't it? People going around killing each other?" The close-up view of the dead killed in battle, was an image that never leaves one's mind. The killing of the innocent, as slaughtered cattle in a field, was the part of this war that I despised the most.

Protecting Defensive Positions from Enemy Attack

On one occasion, I saw our two-star Division Commander "Snortin" Norton personally assessing what had just transpired during the battle at LZ Bird. You could not miss him with those gleaming two stars that lit up on his approach. I wondered what he was thinking. I thought that he could have provided strategic leadership to keep his troops better protected and more alert. From history, everyone knew that "Charlie" had the custom of surprise attacks on or near holidays. We almost suffered a complete enemy overrun of LZ Bird because of the lack of foresight and vigilance.

This induced my recollection of the time that I was the 1st Cavalry Division Commander's pilot on Freedom's Frontier in Korea. After having spent months flying Major General Hugh Exton to the various division's defensive positions, I had learned from him the important strategies in protecting our defensive positions from enemy attacks. General Exton would have been appalled at what had just transpired at LZ Bird. General Exton always stressed the importance of vigilance and always being aware of your enemy's movements. General Exton always demanded strategic secure fields of fire in order protect the artillery and to keep the position from being overrun by the enemy. In my estimation adequate defensive preparation had not been made, and most of all, the enemy had been trusted to honor the ceasefire truce. The Grim Reaper was cunningly pleased that night, as many lives were snatched away into the realm of the dead.

The following year, on 20 February 1967, I would learn more information concerning the combat assault on LZ Bird. While chatting with my old Serpent 7 friends from "A" Alpha Company of the 229th AHB Company at Hammond Field they explained to me that they airlifted the RRF into LZ Bird on the tragic night of 27 December 1966 while it was under heavy attack during the Christmas ceasefire truce. One of the young pilots, who I knew well, was at the controls. His Slick was riddled with bullet holes and was forced down as they approached the rice paddy at LZ Bird. Luckily, no occupant in the downed aircraft was hit. As the ground troops exited the aircraft, the crew of the downed Slick were successfully rescued by his fellow pilots soon after the troops departed the aircraft and were on the ground. During that conversation, it dawned on me that it was that very same Slick that our Chinook crew had recovered later after daylight. To me, that incident appeared to be a profound coincidence. I felt a strong bond with that unit and had become a part of an even larger team that could still count on each other like brothers. It made me feel good to recover the very same Slick that I had flown only a few months prior.

I was sure that we would be more careful in tracking the enemy, and we would surely conduct more combat assault attacks to prevent the enemy from massing other large-scale attacks on any of our defensive positions. That type of tragedy, I knew, must never happen again.

Force Buildup

We experienced more aircraft maintenance problems on Wednesday, 28 December 1966. It took two hours to install a fuel pump in the right fuel tank. After dinner CWO-3 Hugh Barlow and I started up and headed back to Hammond Field. We flew for 1.50 hours when the number one engine low oil light came on. We headed to Lane Field to have field maintenance replace the sensor. Later that night a movie was shown in the mess hall, and it felt good to wind down.

We accomplished several sorties to various locations around the area completing missions to LZ Bird, LZ Pony, LZ English, LZ Govern, and LZ Uplift with most of the external loads being artillery ammunition. On a short final approach into LZ Bird, I saw a VC body lying on his side. His body was bloated and decomposing in a rice paddy about 50 meters southeast of the helipad. It was a gruesome sight that was forever etched in my collection of horrifying memories. At the time it was all I could do to breathe deep enough to remain calm as my stomach heaved trying to throw up from my gut reaction. I forced my mind to continue flying rather than allowing my emotions to hijack that flight. We accomplished many missions on Thursday and logged 9.25 hours which was a long day to spend in a hard seat with a heavy armored chest protector. My backend was so sore at the end of the day that I thought about putting a write up in the Dash 12 Maintenance Fault Form, "Pilot's rear end excessively worn." The crew chief did not think that was very funny.

Due to the increased VC activity and the losses suffered at LZ Bird the prevailing battle plan theme, seemed to include a "force buildup." Another reinforcement brigade would be arriving at Hammond Field from division headquarters at An Khe. Another Chinook company "A" Alpha Company also relocated to Hammond Field and would provide airlift support for the newly arriving brigade. As we airlifted more troops and more artillery pieces we experienced an increasing workload. The Vietnam War for the 1st Cavalry Division was escalating, significantly.

C-130 Hercules aircraft dropped off many incoming troops at Hammond Field and the Chinooks transported them to the various LZs. The artillery kept pounding the already scarred hillsides. As a precaution, bulldozers cleared away brush at various LZ's to provide advanced warning of VC incursions and better fields of fire. I supposed that the order had come down from headquarters. It was about time they took direct action to defend the fire bases.

Grueling Endurance

The low clouds persisted and it rained most of the time. The mud was thickening more with time as it stuck to our jungle boots when we walked on the ground. You could hear a sloppy suction sound with each adhering step. The rivers were filling up and some of them were even overflowing their banks. Occasionally farmers with water buffalo could be seen plowing their fields even amidst the adverse weather conditions. The brutal war dragged on and on.

Each evening mission status reports were radioed in and missions were scheduled for the next day unless there was another emergency. The sling loads for the next day's missions were consolidated and placed in large cargo nets and rigged with nylon slings for quick hookups. Captain Ken Sines coordinated that effort. Aircraft tail numbers with the pilots' names were kept posted on the operations boards for the designated standby alert crews. Most of the pilots sat around in the evening drinking and discussing the close calls of the day. Some read books or watched a movie or sat around talking and drinking beer. Beer appeared to be the favorite pastime activity and biggest distractions from the serpent-squeezing cattle-rotting war.

The ground crews continued working long after dark to get the aircraft ready for the next day's flights. There were daily inspections for bullet holes and other battle damage that might have been inflicted on the airframe. Bullet hole tears were stop-drilled to prevent the propagation of cracks until permanent repairs could be installed. It always seemed as though some component was always failing in one of the Chinook's complex operating systems. Common failures included fuel boost pumps, fuel control units, engine N1 and N2 speed sensors. The lord mounts in the drive train did not last long and we were always plagued with many hydraulic leaks.

There was a noticeable buildup of troops forming at Hammond Field. Pilots flew in close proximity missions to friendly artillery fire bases and were in constant danger of being hit. As I gained more combat experience and became familiar with our operational area, I was able to determine in what direction the artillery was most likely firing at the "bad guys." The air traffic corridor between Hammond Field and north to the Bong Son area was normally free of artillery fire during daylight hours.

Part of our two-pilot aircrew standard duties was for one pilot to fly the aircraft while the other monitored the aircraft systems status instruments and the various fire base radio nets as we passed by. During emergency combat conditions, it was tediously stressful to try and avoid being hit by artillery fire. In some instances, I was unknowingly directed near combat areas in which our flight path crossed low flying fighter jets that were actively bombing enemy targets. I can recall flying at an altitude of about 1500 feet and observing a F-105 Thunderchief in my chin bubble under my feet. The F-105 streaked under us from behind and was proceeding at a much faster airspeed on the same heading. That fly-under got our full attention and I had only hoped that my underwear would keep it a secret.

Looking back, I was more fearful of being hit from friendly

artillery activities or experiencing a mid-air collision, than from being hit by the enemy from ground fire. To avoid the known artillery fire, we either changed directions or requested that the fire be temporarily lifted as we were crossing the gun target line. Even more anxiety built up when two or more artillery positions were firing at the same time as it demanded strict full attention to our situational awareness.

As experience would have it, I learned from my previous tour in Korea how to avoid artillery fire while flying with the 1st Cavalry Division Commander, Major General Hugh M. Exton, to the various artillery firing ranges. As a failsafe rule of thumb, "If you knew where the artillery pieces were located then you went low level 'nap of the earth' and positioned a hill or mountain between your aircraft flight path and the tubes of the artillery battery." That technique was always successful unless we entered an impact area. If the artillery fire base disappeared from view as our aircraft dropped below a hilltop or mountain peak, then we were normally safe. "If you can't see the firebase then they can't hit you." That procedure worked every time. If a firebase could not be contacted, we often proceeded low level and fired artillery shells would safely travel in an arc high above us. That theory appeared to work well since our aircraft was never hit.

On one of our missions that day we noticed jet aircraft, ARA gunships and our own CH-47 Guns-A-Go-Go engaged in a ground attack. That combined airstrike was tearing up the countryside of a suspected VC location between LZ Bird and LZ Pony. I suspected that location was a staging area and was probably where the previous massive attack on LZ Bird was initiated. After enduring that grueling and long day we returned after dark. I was tired and my ankle was still very sore. I ate supper and went to be bed early believing that the next day would be filled with more dangerous missions.

We flew for five or six hours on Friday encountering more maintenance problems with aircraft (108). One engine torque meter had failed and the needle had begun to drift. The parking brake was inoperative (INOP), and the aft speed trim actuator had also stopped functioning. We flew one long haul sortie into LZ English and two more sorties into Bong Son or Two Bits.

The jets and artillery continued to pound the areas north of us. Normally it was the Republic F-105 Thunderchiefs that flew the ground attack missions. To me, those attacks were an indication of increased enemy activity north of us. With our increasing troop buildup, I expected that we would soon be assaulting those areas. We were fighting against an incredibly determined foe. Each day I felt stronger with less pain and hoped that I would soon be fully recovered from the physical effects of my injuries that were incurred just 13 days prior.

Saturday, 31 December 1966, was the last day of December, the last day of the year, and my mother's 50thbirthday. Before falling asleep I remembered her birthday celebration just one year earlier and hoped that she was enjoying another pleasant celebration, worry free. I was so exhausted that I slept until 0930 hours. Aircraft (108) was still down with a faulty torque meter and I suspected that repair might take a while. It was nice to get a slight reprieve from flying because most of us had also flown many hours and endured grueling circumstances that month due to the increased combat activities.

After lunch I retired once again, still exhausted, until 1745 hours. I ate a supper of fried chicken in the mess hall and went to the "O" Club to watch the 1966 western movie "*Waco*" thinking, "It always comes down to a gunfight, doesn't it?" I remained at the "O" Club for a while drinking a soda and waiting for the arrival of the New Year.

Compared to the other pilots, my lack of carousing and drinking must have appeared very dull to them. Enjoying my last drink of the year, I sat in the "O" Club grateful that the tragic days of December of the year of 1966 had finally come to an end. I was so wound up from the events of the month, that I felt as though I had been thrust into a higher plane in an upward cycle, spiraling through the mysteries of life. I realized that life spirals in cycles and I was ready to cycle through a calm peace and resolve to the ending of a wasteful war. I was ready to open a new chapter in life of family, stable predictability, and prosperity as a hard-working American citizen. I was very thankful to still be alive to ring in a new year, as a combat pilot, on a mission.

Treading on Desperate Ground

For me, the last half of 1966 was one of the most challenging periods of my life filled with traumatic life-threatening experiences and conflicting powerful emotions. After my crash on 18 December 1966, I was vividly reminded of the events of the truck crash when I was eleven years old. As a young boy my life was first drastically changed by Providence, as I experienced my first real terrifying fear of my own mortality. I had gone full circle in another cycle in the mysterious upward spiral of life, thirteen years later. It appeared to me that my life unfolded in cycles that lead me to a higher awareness in my ability to recognize each cycle. Compared to my mindset at age eleven, as a twenty-four old, I was more mature and more aware of my increasing knowledge and thirst for spiritual things. With God's protection I had survived two tragic events that shaped my life forever. I saw myself as very blessed to still be alive.

As I still recall, my life had reached a dramatic peak during the month of December 1966. I had survived a tragic crash and the 1st Cavalry Division had suffered a savage surprise attack on LZ Bird during a Christmas ceasefire truce. As the somber New Year began, I was hoping that 1967 would no longer be filled with more personal traumatic events and tragedy. God had my full attention.

On Sunday, 1 January 1967, I managed to stay awake to bring in the New Year at midnight. I went to bed about 0100 hours and I awakened at 0800. The traumatic events of December had profoundly affected my New Year's resolutions. The urge to find employment opportunities after I was to separate from the U.S. Army was growing increasingly stronger in my mind. The crash of 18 December 1966 and the rapidly escalating intense combat activities in the area around LZ Bird had precipitated a profound turning point in my life. The Grim Reaper had acted cunningly and was on the prowl during that timeframe as many souls had been snatched away on both sides by the hanging, Two Step Vipers. God's protective hands had miraculously spared some of us from certain death.

The Vietnam War had reached another critical peak for the 1st Cavalry Division at the end of December 1966. We had learned another powerful lesson about our enemy and the type of ground that we had been treading on. My thoughts were engulfed with the words of Sun Tzŭ and the "nine" varieties of war that he recognized.

> *The Nine Situations*
> 1. *Dispersive ground*
> 2. *Facile ground*
> 3. *Contentious ground*
> 4. *Open ground*
> 5. *Ground of Intersecting highways*
> 6. *Serious ground*
> 7. *Difficult ground*
> 8. *Hemmed-in ground*
> 9. *Desperate ground.*
>
> *- Sun Tzŭ, The Art of War, Chapter XI*

I reflected on our own combat missions and tactical measures. We had advanced to a stage where we were desperately fighting to save ourselves, simply, from destruction. We were flying an increasing amount of combat missions routinely treading on desperate ground.

New Year's Resolutions

For the most part throughout my life's journey, I always tried to remain two steps ahead. I was logistically minded and differed greatly from the majority of my peers who were only "living in the moment." By the time I arrived in Vietnam, I did not have any current bills to pay since I faithfully had saved most of my income each month. While in Vietnam, I was drawing combat pay in addition to my base and flight pay which was a helpful added perk. Compared to the frugal circumstances of my upbringing, I felt like I was getting rich. And even more liberating, I was feeling free to make my own decisions as a successful and honorable man.

My New Year's resolutions included safely completing my combat tour, being a good Christian, finding a good job, finding a good mate, marriage, and "living happily ever after." However, after my recent close encounter with the Grim Reaper my primary goals in life were to stay alive, hope for the best, and to move forward in a positive direction. I was resolved to be more cautious in my flying, to get more instrument training, to be more aware of the needs of others, and to focus my mind on a higher plane of understanding. I did not fly that day; the most exciting thing that I did was to reflect my thoughts in my journal and watch the 1965 movie, "*Viva Maria*".

As the winter of the New Year continued, I was fearful, I was tired, my body still ached, and I was weary from seeing the horrors of war. Unbeknown to myself at that point in my life, I had begun a metamorphosis to a higher level of spiritual awakening. My values and my perception of the meaning of life were rapidly evolving. I was deeply grateful to be alive after so many had already perished in the Vietnam War. I was deeply thankful that God had given me another chance at life. As a lowly worm transforms into a butterfly, I was experiencing intense conflicting emotions in my spiritual transformation that would ultimately define who I would become. My stark reality was that I could have perished young in life on many different occasions. I was humbled by the fact that it was God's intervention and grace (even from the young age of eleven) and not my own merits that preserved my life. I was extremely thankful to have another chance at life as the New Year might also bring the hope of new beginnings.

I was reminded of the story of the footprints in the sand. As the story goes; "Two sets of footprints appeared in the sand as two friends walked along together. At some point only one set of footprints remained in the sand. The one who had been walking with his friend asked, 'Lord why did you leave me'? He replied, 'I did not abandon you that was when I began carrying you'."

I was hoping that the year 1967 would be less intense and would transition into a better life for me. Pleasant thoughts crossed my mind in anticipating the relief of returning home and separating from the U.S. Army. I had about six months remaining in my tour in Vietnam. I looked forward to not being in combat situations any longer nor personally having to witness the carnage rotting in the fields that I had seen in the previous five months. The first few months of my tour in Vietnam were extremely intense, and I was rapidly accumulating greatly prized flying time.

Slaying Dragons and Giants

While growing up I developed a flair for the dramatic and heroic characters in books and movie scenes. I secretly dreamed about accomplishing monumental feats and slaying dragons. The character of "*Cyrano de Bergerac*", the swashbuckling sword fighting French soldier with the oversized nose in Edmond Rostand's play came to mind. I studied that play in college my freshman year in English and easily identified with Cyrano's personality. It was my favorite play and, still hidden deep inside my own mind, I desired to be like Cyrano and reflect his magnanimous personality with statements like, "Bring me giants" and to accomplish great feats. On the other hand, I was also somewhat of an introvert at the time and remembered another less boastful famous and contrasting line from the play, "I wear my adornments on my soul." In reality, even Cyrano de Bergerac would have grown weary of "slaying of dragons and giants" after a long-sustained period of five straight months in combat.

The true reality of war was tempering my thinking of what I now perceived as what is most important in life. I personally witnessed the wounding and violent deaths of our brave U.S. soldiers as we transported many of them in our cargo bays. I saw the aftermaths of the savage attacks on villages and the resultant deaths of innocent men, women, and children. Those experiences were hard to get out of my mind - like watching the coils of Serpent 7 crushing the bones of that chicken; and, as the thought of pursuing slaying dragons and giants, ceased being fun when the feeling of desperation for survival set in. The primary focus of my life after December 1966, was, staying alive.

Headquarter Briefing on LZ Bird

Monday was another slow day. Aircraft (108) was still grounded and awaiting parts. The "old man", our company commander, Major Fountain, arrived back in the company area and provided us with a headquarters briefing on what had transpired at LZ Bird on 27 December 1966. He recounted how LZ Bird had been attacked by between 700 to 800 VC and NVA troops from the ridge line running from LZ Bird to LZ Lee. Detailed maps were retrieved from the bodies of the enemy soldiers that remained on the battlefield. The maps clearly illustrated all the artillery and bunker positions of LZ Bird down to the smallest detail. The VC and the NVA had executed a very well-planned attack on LZ Bird. During a declared Christmas ceasefire truce, the enemy troops had slipped right up to the perimeter of the compound before anyone was aware of it. The VC then fired mortar rounds into LZ Bird, and knocked out the Commo Bunker known to hold the vital communications radios. The enemy battle plan strategy was to prevent LZ Bird from being able to radio for help, to overrun the fire base, to kill all the Americans, and to take away as many weapons and supplies that they could carry. As it turned out, it happened just like in the old western movies we had just watched and the cavalry arrived just in the nick time to save the day. A friendly long-range patrol arrived in the immediate area, and they witnessed the unfolding attack on LZ Bird.

The alert unit leader of the patrol called in artillery fire from the nearby fire bases and requested additional UH-1B ARA ships for close air support. The perimeter around LZ Bird had been lit up by a barrage of brilliant night artillery illumination flares, the enemy was surprised as the perimeter flares revealed their troop locations. The enemy troops were then made visible all around the perimeter. The VC troops had already blown up one 155-Millimeter Howitzer and two 105-millimeter Howitzers. The exploding enemy satchel charges also killed and wounded some of the members of LZ Bird's own gun crews.

Major Fountain included in his account the story of a LZ Bird's sergeant who was occupying a bunker with eight other troops. The VC were swarming by and threw grenades into the bunker. It was an enemy tactic to throw grenades into a bunker and then to shoot every living or dead soldier. As the first grenade exploded the concussion of the blast forced the sergeant into a corner of the bunker. As more waves of VC and NVA troops stormed past the bunker each group of the enemy threw in additional grenades and machine gunned the occupants.

The sergeant had been gravely wounded, but he miraculously was the only survivor that remained alive in the bunker. Due to the quick action of the long-range patrol, which immediately called in friendly artillery fire from LZ Pony, the course of the battle began to turn in our favor. The patrol broadcasted emergency messages to command-and-control (Charlie -Charlie) that were located at Hammond Field. They immediately launched in a UH-1D command-and-control aircraft. While in flight, orders were issued to launch ARA, escort gunships armed with four flex-mounted M-60 machine guns and 2.75 inch rockets, as well as the RRF. Aerial rocket artillery and gunships quickly departed within minutes and arrived first on the scene to provide up-close air support for our friendly ground forces. Fortunately, that night the weather was clear of fog and the air operations were not hampered.

The flex machine guns on the escort gunships were hydraulically driven and could be swiveled in all directions within the guns' prescribed stop limits. The guns were controlled from the cockpit by a pull-down pistol grip that was stowed out of view above the windshield. Integrated within the pistol grip, was a see-through, a small transparent glass plate on which the aiming recital sight was electronically projected. Once properly bore-sighted, that weapon was dead-on accurate, especially, at close range when individual enemy soldiers had been clearly visible.

Our classmates had a short period of gunnery instruction with that system when we were in flight training at Fort Rucker. I remembered asking one of our gunship escort pilots, "How accurate are the flex guns?" He replied, "I was about four hundred yards away from a suspected VC who was located within a declared free fire zone. I was escorting a Slick command and control aircraft when I was given orders to fire at that person. I aimed the dot on the recital at him and fired a short burst. I noticed that his body went limp and he fell to the ground. I really felt bad about that." A year later in 1968, I saw that same gunship pilot in the cast of the movie "*The Green Berets*" with John Wayne.

Thus, that timely intervention by the long-range patrol had set in motion the fortunate chain of events that spared LZ Bird from complete annihilation. After Major Fountain left, I reviewed and recorded my own journal entry of what had happened on the morning of 27 December 1966 shortly before I first arrived at LZ Bird. Many brave men, on both sides, had perished that night as the python squeezed out their last breaths. In my opinion, that had been the most significant single battle that occurred for "*The Second Team*" during my tour in Vietnam.

After the briefing by Major Fountain, we continued in the business of finding and destroying the VC and NVA. At the time we all thought that the enemy had moved further north. B-52 "Arc Light" strikes, aircraft strikes from the F-105 Thuds, artillery, combat assaults, and other forces would seek out and destroy the enemy. A concentration of fire power would rain down wrath and fury upon the enemy that had violated the Christmas truce. I was periodically taking photos and recorded each event, faithfully, in detail, in my journal.

Reviewing the Accident Report

The weather was unbelievably bad on Tuesday, 3 January 1967. The rain was dense and pounding hard as the wind blew so furiously that I thought the wind might blow down our hex tent. About 1100 hours CWO-3 Barlow and I flew aircraft (108) from our base at An Khe to Hammond Field. Upon arrival at Hammond Field, we picked up the battalion commander, a maintenance officer, and others for a personnel courier flight back to An Khe.

On that flight we experienced the worst turbulence that I had ever encountered in Vietnam. The turbulence bounced us around all over the sky. The clouds were low lying and blanketing the ground level and we were barely able to sneak in under the clouds at the An Khe Pass. But we made it without having to go IFR or by being struck by ground fire. After we arrived at An Khe things were very dull. There were only a few people at An Khe since most of the aircraft and troops had been deployed to the field in hot pursuit of the fleeing enemy.

The foul weather was the result of a severe cold front that had passed by, plummeting the temperature to a point that it began to feel quite cold. It almost felt like winter at home in Florida. Although it was a welcome change, it was hard to stay warm in our thin jungle fatigues. I went to the PX and bought a small radio so that I could listen to music from the Armed Forces Network while I was at An Khe. Unless we had gotten mortared that night it would be a quiet evening. I read and caught up on my letter writing and my journal entries. I had finished reading the book, "*Who is Afraid of Virginia Woolf*", even though it did not make a lot of sense to me.

There was not much going on the following day, Wednesday, 4 January 1967, so I remained in bed until 0830 hours. I had nearly frozen to death the night before after the cold front had swept in. The temperature only dropped to 55 degrees Fahrenheit but it felt considerably colder than that. I went over to Battalion S-3, which was part of the Administrative Duties and Training, to sign more papers concerning the crash on 18 December 1966. S-3 had the accident report typed up inclusive of photos.

The accident report stated that the aircraft struck the ground in a nose low attitude while sliding to the right front. The nose of the aircraft dug a hole three feet deep in the soft mud before it broke apart. Our crew was counted as lucky for surviving the crash. The loss of the aircraft was set at $1,100,000 dollars. I was given a set of the photos and the pilot's clock from the instrument panel that had stopped at 0232 hours on 18 December 1966. Thankfully, none of our lives had stopped that night, as the clock did. I still have that instrument panel clock today and every time I hold that charred clock in my hands, I am eternally thankful that all of my crew made it out alive. I will always hate the fact that I lost that CH-47A Chinook helicopter, but I will forever be grateful that it stayed together long enough for the crew to escape before it ignited into a fiery inferno and explosion.

The 1st Cavalry Division's Winter Campaign

During the Winter Campaign, our ground troops were involved in some skirmishes about seven miles southwest of Bong Son. The 1st of the 8th Cavalry had air assaulted into that area. They ran into a company of VC. Several of the bad guys were either killed or captured. The assault force had been dropped right into the lap of the VC unit while assault aircraft were taking heavy fire as they landed in the rice paddies. Our troops had to low crawl across the rice paddy to engage the enemy.

Slick door gunners helped pin down the VC until ARA aircraft and more reinforcement troops could arrive to drive the enemy into a retreat. That turned out to be quite a hot spot. The enemy tried to set up a crossfire but the aerial rocket artillery aircraft engaged and killed many of them with their rockets. That was an exciting day for the assault units.

I had not received much mail lately and I was ready to get back to flying.

I slept late again on Wednesday and tried to find ways to amuse myself. I played solitaire for hours before moving on to a book. After wasting most of the day, we finally were assigned aircraft (129). The aircraft had just completed a 700-hour periodic inspection (PE). After we took off, it was only 30 minutes before the aircraft went down for maintenance. A rod end bearing in the aft slider assembly of the thrust lever, was excessively worn and the ball was gouging into the metal of the race of the control tube. The control action of the thrust control lever felt very rough. I was surprised that this condition was not discovered during the periodic inspection and the maintenance test flight. We left aircraft (129) down for maintenance at Hammond Field and caught a ride back to Lane Field.

While I back at Lane Field I was able to watch a recording of the "*Bob Hope Show*" on TV in the "O" Club that was located there. The show was actually pretty amusing and I enjoyed watching it, since I had missed the first show due to the large crowds and my sore ankle. We relaxed for a while and discussed what was going on in the field.

Up north around LZ Pistol, our units were still in contact with the VC. As the clashes continued, I expected that we would soon leave Lane Field and move our base further north either to Hammond Field or maybe to LZ English.

The weather began to clear up somewhat on Friday, 6 January

1967. The cloud ceiling was higher but the sun was unable to penetrate the blanket of clouds to peek through and shine. After having been caught by surprise at LZ Bird, the pace of battle planning and troop movements was steadily increasing. We were all feeling more cautious yet determined to pursue and to engage with our enemy. "Charlie" had broken the Christmas truce and had to suffer the consequences.

As the war escalated, there was an increasing forecast for combined support sortie requirements. We caught a ride back to Hammond Field, but field level maintenance had not even begun to repair aircraft (129). We waited around for awhile and then caught a ride back to Lane Field. On some days nothing seemed to go right. I still had not received any mail for a few days. My mind wondered about our family affairs back home but sometimes no news is good news. Some of the reasons that I left home were to avoid the stress of family conflicts, to become my own man, and to find my own place in the sun. I felt more purpose in life since I joined the U.S. Army. I loved everything about aviation and flying and was proud to fly dangerous combat missions. Even so, the prolonged flying missions in Vietnam were increasingly taking their toll on my nerves as too many missions had recently become terrifying, frightful, and deadly.

Early Saturday morning, 7 January1967, we hopped a ride back to Hammond Field and waited for maintenance to sign off all off on the "write ups" for aircraft (129) to become flyable. Finally, after lunch, our crew took control of the aircraft. We ended up flying 3.3 hours that day. The aircraft seemed to perform well, and it certainly felt good to be among the clouds again. Upon our return from flying that afternoon I was pleased to discover that I had received a letter from home which made me feel connected to life back home and comforted to know that things were ok.

Navigation Beacon

We departed on Sunday morning for Hammond Field but were forced to land because of a severe hydraulic leak. An "O" ring had ruptured on a primary flight control hydraulic hose. I could see from the fluctuation of the hydraulic gauge that the fluid pressure in one of the two primary flight control systems was rapidly decreasing. We made an emergency landing at an ARVN strip to replace the O-ring. The crew worked about two hours, but could not repair the leak, so we started up and carefully limped back to Lane Field. En route to Lane Field, we encountered even more maintenance problems: the engine N1 and N2 compressor speed indicators stopped functioning, which added more maintenance squawks to repair. I seemed to have the reversed version of the "Midas touch" with every aircraft that I flew since I crashed aircraft 37901 at Phu Cat. As the day continued, the aircraft was repaired and we were back in the saddle again. Aircraft (129) operated well for the rest of that day. We flew a total of about 5 hours.

We completed several sorties into LZ Sooner and LZ Abbey. On the final flight, we sling loaded a downed OH-13S "Snoopy" from Bong Son back to Hammond Field. When I arrived back at Lane Field, I received another letter from home and discovered that there appeared to be more marital problems in the family that were escalating. It was still good to hear what was going on back home, I was physically feeling improvement from my injuries and more than anything I was glad to be back in "the saddle." I put clean sheets on my bed that evening and slept well that night.

I was informed that "C" Charlie Company was in the process of erecting a makeshift control tower in the forward support element (FSE) at Hammond Field. It was painted bright yellow. It was set up by

Captain Ken Sines, who oversaw the task of scheduling the Chinook sling loads. Captain Ken Sines and our company commander Major Fountain could normally be found in the FSE area. I remarked that the yellow tower was a good benchmark for aiming enemy mortar fire.

Hammond Field was becoming more congested with aircraft traffic, troops, and supplies. So, I was pleasantly surprised to hear that better tactical navigation aids had recently been installed. Many aircraft, including mine, had crashed when trying to find their way back in the fog. A new radar unit was installed on the top of Little Hong Cong hill to facilitate ground control approaches (GCA), and a navigation beacon had also been installed so pilots could more easily find their way back in bad weather conditions or at night. Artillery batteries were emerging everywhere in that area. Artillery pieces were recently positioned at Hammond Field and many other nearby fire bases. I knew that there would be more ground activities in that area very soon.

Artillery Fire

At night when my sleep was interrupted by the sound of artillery fire and it became more evident that even more caution was required of us to avoid friendly fire. Artillery batteries were set up at LZ Pony, LZ Orange, LZ Abby, LZ Sooner, and several others. We always contacted "Lion Cage" which was a code name for the 3rd Brigade Unit that tracked and reported to pilots known coordinates and locations of artillery fire missions in order for the aircraft to avoid being hit by friendly fire.

Whenever we were flying and fire bases could not be contacted, we flew low-level knowing that the artillery shells would arc high over the flight path of the aircraft. All types of aircraft, both U.S. Army and

U.S. Air Force, had been flying in every direction and at all speeds and altitudes, so contact with "Lion Cage" was most important. On another occasion, we had been flying at 500 feet AGL when I saw another flash of an F-105 Thud in my lower chin bubble flying past us at a high rate of speed. Normally they did not fly that low. Flying conditions were getting more congested and more hectic. I could sense the increasing intensity of the war rising. In that season of the year, you could count on the weather being bad most of the time. The weather, the artillery fire, and a potential midair collision with another aircraft was more of a threat than the enemy ground fire. Occasionally, "Charlie" popped off a few rounds at us. Thankfully, most of the times, "Charlie" was not proficient in leading the aircraft by aiming at a flying aircraft. Most of the time the rounds passed harmlessly under or behind us.

By the time we completed all assigned sorties on that long day of flying my butt felt like lead. I was constantly stressed over the multiple hazards that we continued to face every day. I noticed that most of the other pilots had started drinking more heavily, especially in the evening. My usual routine was to eat supper and then make my rounds as the mess officer. I remember one incident where one of our captains was raised in a Jewish home. But when he joined the U.S. Army he learned to love pork chops. I was standing behind the serving line at one meal, including pork chops, when he looked at me and said, "Give me some of that fish." We grinned knowing that he sure wanted those pork chops.

I wrote letters, went to bed early, and mentally tried to clear my mind for the next day's demanding flight activities. My ears were still ringing from the piercing high pitch noise of the forward transmission. I went to bed hoping that I would not be jolted awake by the sound and muzzle blast of a nearby heavy artillery piece. The sound of artillery fire would be tolerable if it wasn't enemy incoming artillery fire.

Another peculiarity of our missions was the procedure for dropping off our loads in various landing zones. Loads consisting of beer, ammunition, and medical supplies were always in high demand. On final approach into the general tactical coordinates of an unfamiliar new LZ, we requested that the ground controllers "pop smoke." The smoke grenade pinpointed the exact drop off location for the incoming sling load. When other LZ's were in close proximity, often, we saw smoke that popped in one or two other LZ's. We keyed the microphone and said, "Identify the color of your smoke." That was how we would know if we were delivering the goods to the right unit.

When the flying day was completed and we had returned back to camp, I had received a set of 8 X 10 inch black and white photos of my crash scene. I still wondered how we survived that tragedy. I ran my fingers over the smooth edges of the shiny black and white photos dumbfounded that anyone could walk away from that pile of wreckage. I was sure the photos would make for a good conversation piece once I returned home. Undoubtedly, I had earned the nickname "Crash" that some of my friends there still called me from time to time. I continued to ponder what the next five months might bring. Under the circumstances of a rapidly escalating war, I remained cautious and alert.

World's Largest Hedge Trimmer

Monday, 9 January 1967, was a good day for flying. All was progressing well until one of our forward rotor blades clipped the top branch of a tree as we were parking at LZ Pony. I set the parking brake since we were on a slight muddy incline that sloped down to the tree line. However, the locked wheels did not prevent us from sliding toward that tree on the slippery wet mud. I quickly raised the nose of the Chinook to avoid striking the small top limbs. Unfortunately, it was too late and the damage was already done. I repositioned the aircraft to a more level spot and we chocked one of the landing gears and shut down the engine to investigate the damage. That incident had caused a small, indented tear in the tip cap on one of the forward rotor blades. The hole in the tip cap caused a distinct loud whistling sound from the forward rotor system. We laughed that our ship became the "world's largest hedge trimmer." The tip cap on the rotor blade would have to be replaced, but it did not pose an immediate risk for flight, it was just a whistling reminder of our small mishap. Later after the tip cap was replaced the maintenance officer presented it to me in a mock ceremony that amused everyone. I still have that damaged yellow CH-47A rotor tip cap among my Vietnam War mementos and it makes me laugh every time I tell the story.

At the end of the day we received a radar vector back to An Khe, and we executed a practice ground controlled approach. The approach worked well and as we broke out of the clouds and were lined up with the runway. I was steadily gaining more confidence with instrument flying.

We lingered around waiting for the weather to improve on Tuesday morning. The weather remained raunchy, and the heavy rain created low scud clouds that inhibited visibility. Since I had a "been there done that" experience, I was even more cautious of that situation. After lunch we obtained a radar vector and headed IFR to Hammond Field. Upon arrival we executed another GCA and landed safely. I was gaining even more instrument flying experience while among the clouds. We accomplished several sorties on Tuesday including one mission where we even entered a hot area to recover a downed OH-13S "Snoopy."

Flying in the Highlands

We were on a "weather hold", off and on, all day, on Wednesday, 11 January 1967. Despite the inclement weather, we managed to fly 5 hours that day. We hauled loads into LZ Sooner, LZ Minh, LZ Pony, and LZ Uplift. When returning at the end of the day we entered actual instruments (AI) conditions. I was grateful to feel so confident using my flight instruments during such adverse conditions. We climbed to a safe ground clearance altitude, received a radar vector from Phu Cat in Hammond Field, and shot a ground-controlled approach into Qui Nhon.

The events of that last evening flight was eerily like the conditions that led up to my Chinook crash on 18 December 1966. If I had previously received instrument training or if I had been paired with a more experienced pilot, I would not have crashed at Phu Cat. Thus, with 20/20 hindsight, I felt more confident that we could survive the difficult weather situations ahead. I still thanked God every day that I was still alive after so many good pilots and close friends had perished.

Each Chinook could only accumulate twenty-five hours of flying time between intermediate inspections, which was mandatory. The unit policy was for a flight crew to fly a Chinook until the next twenty-five hour inspection came due. Once the twenty-five hour inspection came due the aircraft would be returned to An Khe for the accomplishment of the next intermediate inspection. We completed the remainder of the scheduled twenty-five hours on aircraft (129) on Thursday. Due to the demanding combat situation, the maintenance officer obtained clearance to extend the aircraft inspection for another five hours. The five hours' flight extension approval was entered into the aircraft forms and we were cleared to fly an additional five hours.

That day we had a new first experience with a new air rescue device. Our crew was chosen to fly a mission to test a "Jungle Penetrator" which was a recovery device that was designed to lift ground troops through the trees of the dense jungle into the Chinook. Every Chinook had a built-in winch with a long steel cable that could be configured to act as a rescue hoist. We were often called upon to rescue wounded troops from areas on the ground where there was not enough space to land. The "Jungle Penetrator" worked well on that mission because two troops could be lifted at a time. That was an encouraging experience that made our job easier and would prove helpful in future rescue missions.

When we completed our last sortie into LZ Pony on the return flight back, we took a detour east out over the South China Sea to test fire our M-60 7.62-millimeter door guns. Out of my pilot's window I could view the red tracers arching into the green water below. At that same time, I heard the familiar rapid reports of the muzzle blasts and felt the vibration in the airframe as the guns were firing. The M-60s operated as if they were factory-new and free from jamming. After landing from the mission, we picked up our gear from base camp and took off bound for home at An Khe. I flew "under the hood" for more instrument training on the way back to An Khe. I operated the flight controls for a time with the stability augmentation system (SAS) turned off. I performed better than I anticipated and was determined to improve my Chinook flying skills. Being frequently paired with greatly skilled mentors with many years of experience was something to capitalize on. Those great pilots willingly provided me with sound advice and instruction with no other motive than to help me advance my aviation skills. I had a profound respect for those seasoned Chinook pilots and learned everything I possibly could take in.

Since my Chinook crash I was resolved to master any combination of aircraft systems failures or any difficult adverse weather conditions that we might encounter. I pushed myself taking full responsibility to obtain additional training and to always focus acutely on my situational awareness. I was gaining more confidence with every mission each day. Since I had flown Slicks for a sixty days' TDY, I had gained a more detailed understanding of the tactics of the battlefield and the firsthand experience of flying combat assaults. After we arrived at An Khe, I hoped to be assigned with another crew to return on Friday or Saturday. I always volunteered for additional missions and that was part of the reason that I was referred to as "Tiger" or "Tig".

It was cool again that night like the winters back home. We enjoyed a good steak supper with a baked potato. It was comfort food and hit the spot. There were still rumors of creating the 213th Aviation Company and infusing some of our pilots into it. The substance of the rumors was that the infusion would take place in February. The rumors that circulated had gone from infusion, to diffusion, to confusion. I personally did not believe that it was ever going to happen.

At that time I was satisfied with my current assignment and I had made many good and well-respected friends. I had a great fondness for the 1st Cavalry Division since my first assignment in Korea. I wanted to complete my tour with the 1st Cavalry Division in Vietnam. If, in fact, that other "infusion alternative" was adopted, then I could be transferred to the Phu Loi area of Vietnam. Since I had flown in Phan Thiet and Vung Tau, I had no desire of being assigned to the southern part of Vietnam. I liked the highlands much better.

Instrument Regulations and Procedures

I had continued to recognize a noticeable buildup of troops and the increased enemy activities in the 1st Cavalry Division area. I would not have been surprised if An Khe soon suffered another mortar attack. Artillery fire and airstrikes kept pounding the area toward the Pleiku Pass. In addition, our reconnaissance aircraft and our friendly long-range patrols were discovering enemy troop movements and weapons buildups northwest of Bong Son. I expected that the area northwest of Bong Son would be selected to attack next. We had not yet operated in that dangerous area. That area consisted of very rugged terrain.

Back at An Khe, outgoing artillery fired all night long and periodic streams of tracers filled the sky. There was always some kind of defensive tactic occurring during the night at An Khe.

While at An Khe, I went to the dentist on Friday, 13 January 1967, because two of my molars had started aching. The dentist kindly filled two cavities and the aching subsided. During some downtime that day I intently studied more of the instrument flying procedures. My previous terror had been burned into my memory forever and I considered the mastery of instrument flying to be a vital survival skill.

Time seemed to be flying by as I continued to study more instrument procedures on Saturday. That night I had supper at the "O" Club and enjoyed another savory steak dinner. It was cold again that night and I was not looking forward to sleeping in frigid conditions. I kept my mind busy pondering what flying opportunities that I might have when I returned home. Later I watched another movie "*Lt. Robinson Crusoe, U.S.N.*" with Dick Van Dyke before retiring early. I had to endure yet another cold night.

I had 5 months left of my tour until I got out of the U.S. Army. It was a normal occurrence toward the end of a foreign tour, to start counting down the remaining days. I studied more instrument regulations and had discussions with the older well-experienced warrant officers on Sunday. Web Manual was especially helpful.

I checked with operations and I was assigned to another aircraft and crew on the next day. Our crew was up early on Monday, 16 January 1967, and pre-flighted another Chinook. I noticed that it was my parent's wedding anniversary and shifted my thoughts to the good times as a child. Somehow flying had brought out the good times and the trauma from my childhood was no longer such a prevailing presence. We went through our pilot's startup checklist, received clearance to take off, and we headed for Hammond Field. En route, the sun was beginning to come up and we viewed a most glorious sunrise.

A Not So Happy Valley

After we arrived at Hammond Field we received a mission over the FM radio for one sortie into LZ Snake in Happy Valley. There was nothing "Happy" about that valley. In fact, it had a history of being an extremely dangerous area. There were not many sorties scheduled for that day. Due to the lack of scheduled missions, we were directed to disperse the aircraft to Lane Field and to await further orders. That procedure helped reduce the increased traffic congestion at Hammond Field. In addition, the dispersed aircraft were protected from enemy mortar fire at Lane Field. We were then faced with another change of plans. A unit at Lane Field was putting up buildings in our designated parking area so we had to move to another parking area.

About 1730 hours we received an urgent call that a CH-47 aircraft (070) had been shot down in the An Lao Valley. The downed aircraft location was northwest of English Field up the north fork of the Bong Son River. The aircraft was on an artillery sling load mission when the aircraft was struck by enemy ground fire rounds through the combining transmission as well as the forward transmission oil cooler.

For a Chinook, that was like taking a round through the heart. The oil level in the combining transmission was rapidly depleting and the oil was draining into the cargo bay. Thankfully, the aircraft stayed together long enough for them to land immediately. They were incredibly lucky.

The entire "Happy Valley" area was an enemy stronghold, and it was crawling with VC and NVA troops. As anticipated, we were in the first stages of assaulting that area. A standby ready reaction force with gunship escorts was alerted and they were rushed to the scene of the downed Chinook. A protective perimeter was rapidly established by two companies of our RRF ground troops for security. Two or three gunships orbited over head to fly cover for the Chinook rescue operation. Our mission was to deliver a maintenance crew and the rigging equipment to configure the aircraft for being airlifted out of the area by a CH-54 Skycrane. The early CH-47A & B Chinooks did not have enough power to lift that much weight. Our landing was uneventful and the maintenance team disembarked and expeditiously began removing the six Chinook main rotor blades. Some of the concealed enemy snipers were firing at the troops in the area. When the positions of the snipers were detected the orbiting gunships immediately dispatched them with machine gun and rocket fire.

We departed that area and headed to LZ Pony to "lump up" or hot refuel. On the way back to An Khe we began to experience a severe vibration. We thought that maybe we had been hit by hostile gunfire. As a precaution we returned to LZ Pony to remain overnight (RON). We cautiously made the decision to remain at LZ Pony until field maintenance personnel could arrive and inspect the aircraft. LZ Pony was a forward battle area so for supper we choked down heated up "C" rations. The "C" rations were placed in a drum of hot water that was heated by an immersion heater. That was another long and cold night. The artillery batteries at LZ Pony fired all that night, Tuesday, 17 January 1967. I was startled a few times by the sound and muzzle blasts of the heavy guns that were positioned near our assigned tent. In the morning we located a field mess hall and ate breakfast and drank some coffee.

The maintenance team arrived and inspected our aircraft isolating the problem to air trapped in the hydraulic lines that controlled the main rotor actuators. They theorized that the trapped air had caused the severe vibration. The team did not find any evidence of being hit by ground fire. The team bled the hydraulic lines and released the aircraft back to us. After we departed LZ Pony we experienced a fire warning light on the number two engine. I began to wonder if I had jinxed another aircraft or if a gremlin had taken up residence in the helicopter. Our crew chief and flight engineer looked out of the rear window and viewed the engine located on the right side of the aircraft. There was no evidence of a fire and all the number two engine instruments remained within the normal operating range. Thus, we flew the aircraft back to Lane Field for repair.

The Mess Hall

After landing I was informed that that my new mess sergeant was to arrive soon. I was getting complaints about the food at the mess hall while I was away flying missions. One of the main customer complaints was being served roast beef, mashed potatoes, and green beans several times a week. There was nothing that I could do about the field rations that were force issued to our mess hall from the food distributions points. That did not seem to matter to the customers as they still complained about the frequency of eating the same dish multiple times per week.

In an attempt to improve things in the mess hall, I extended the serving hours and had food available for air crews that returned late from missions. I brought the complaints to the attention of the mess sergeant to seek more improvements. I made up a story and joked about a fictitious colonel who had eaten in my mess hall. After inspecting the premises, he remarked, "Chief, this is a real mess." I replied, "Thank you sir." It was a play on the word "mess" as "messed up" instead of an excellent field mess. I chuckled at my own joke and moved on.

Door Gunners Buying Enough Time

I was informed later that day of the cause of the engine warning light. As we were operating in to the An Lao Valley a wire shorted causing the errant fire warning light on the number two engine. Not long after that, we heard that another Chinook (107) was shot down in the same area. There was a report that a UH-1D command and control aircraft was also hit by ground fire. Those reports caused increasing fear and concern for all air crews that were to fly into that dangerous area.

There were more reports of friendly casualties and more body bags. As for our lucky crew we had not received a single hit from ground fire. However, we still were experiencing maintenance problems. While conducting a preflight inspection on the aircraft, a slider assembly on the forward rotor head was discovered to be excessively worn. After maintenance personnel evaluated the problem we were ordered to return the ship back to An Khe for repair.

On the flight back to An Khe, our left door gunner spotted a stream of machine gun tracer fire coming up at us from a hilltop in the jungle about a mile southwest of the An Khe Pass. The gunner immediately opened up with our own machine gun fire. It was my standard procedure to always give a briefing to the enlisted crew members before their first flight in a different aircraft. The flight engineer, the crew chief, and a door gunner were normally permanently assigned to the same aircraft.

During the initial mission briefing I faithfully instructed the door gunners that it was critical for them to immediately return fire on the enemy as soon as it was detected. I further explained to the crew that a rapid response of suppressive fire from our aircraft would take the fight to the enemy. The enemy would immediately realize that our ship was armed with defensive weapons. Our rapidly executed return fire would cause the enemy to seek cover and it might "buy us enough time" to safely fly out of range. That was another of my survival strategies embedded in me during my time flying Slicks. After our return fire from the aircraft was initiated, the entire air crew would then be informed that our aircraft was receiving ground fire. Our standard rules of engagement indicated that the aircraft could return enemy fire anywhere that it was encountered. Otherwise, an aircraft was not authorized to fire at targets on the ground unless that area was declared a Free Fire Zone (FFZ).

It made me feel good that the alert gunner heeded my instructions. I heard the noise of the outgoing muzzle blasts from the left M-60 gun port. A second or two later I heard over the intercom, "Tracers at ten o'clock." As previously instructed, the left door gunner was raining down suppressive M-60 fire into the hostile area. The bursts of the rising enemy tracer fire passed safely behind our aircraft. That enemy position did not fire at us again. I praised the gunner for his quick action over the intercom for all to hear. That incident really frightened the other pilot. I suppose that because I had flown more combat missions and had become accustomed to taking ground fire, it didn't rattle me the way it did him. Frightening combat missions filled with near-death encounters was the pilot's life in Vietnam and I had seen pythons coiled and ready to consume rats on all too many occasions. There was a common saying there in Vietnam, "If the golden bullet has your name written on it then there is nothing that you can do about that. However, you should always worry about the bullets that are addressed 'to whom it may concern'."

At that time, it appeared to me that the occurrences of the enemy firing at our aircraft were steadily increasing. The determined enemy was also engaging more of our troops in the ground war. That meant more casualties and more body bags; a gruesome rice paddy scene that I did not want to face. I felt certain that there were more concentrations of VC and NVA troops in the area northwest of Bong Son. That was proving to be a dangerous area.

Snoopy, Sling Loads and Sorties

Wednesday was a good day. I received a box of "goodies" in a care package from home. I felt relief that our crew had responded well the day prior during the ground fire incident. I continued studying more of the instrument flight procedures during downtimes. It was good to gain experience and more training. I had more confidence in flying combat missions in bad weather and relying on my instruments. I continued to ponder and daydream about what I would do when I returned home. One thing was for sure, I wanted to finish college. The memory of my crash was constantly on my mind and I was thankful every day that I was still alive, but I also wanted it to be over. So many of our brave soldiers were continually perishing in battle every day.

About that time, some of our ACH-47A "Guns-A-Go-Go"

gunships were taking enemy fire from a village near Bong Son. I talked with some of the "Go-Go" pilots in the "O" Club that night. The pilots were explaining to me that their mission the next day was to "shoot up" a village near Bong Son that had VC sympathizers. It made me sad to think that many innocent men, women, and children might unexpectedly die in that village the next day due to the hostile coercion by the VC. The Vietnam War was such a deadly game and people on both sides would die like the cattle slaughtered in the field. Many times, I saw up close the horror in the faces of villagers. Most of them just wanted to be left alone and to peacefully live lives as simple farmers.

On Thursday, 19 January 1967, I studied Federal Air Regulations and Air Traffic Control (ATC) procedures. Not much happened that day. I was patiently waiting for my turn to fly again. I played some ping pong at the "O" Club (which I had gotten rather good at). I played a good deal when I worked as a draftsman at an engineering firm just before I joined the U.S. Army and ping pong was my game of choice when I served in Korea.

The month of January seemed to be flying by. I read "*The Diary of Anne Frank*" most of the day on Friday which was another sad story. Anne, like many of the Jews in World War II just wanted to survive. It was tragic that Hitler thought that he had the power to define what was good and evil. I supposed that people in high places, define for us, what was deemed good and evil, even in Vietnam.

After reading the book it was time to decide what to do the rest of the afternoon. I knew that I was starting to look like a "hippie" and was desperately in need of a haircut. Unfortunately, I was not able to find a place to get a haircut that day so instead I played more ping pong until later that evening when I headed to the "O" Club to see the movie, "*The Agony and the Ecstasy.*" I thought it was very inspiring about

Michelangelo painting the ceiling of the Sistine Chapel. Before heading back to my tent I checked in with operations and saw that I was assigned to another aircraft for the next day.

I was up bright and early on Saturday, 21 January 1967, ready to fly to Lane Field. After experiencing some maintenance issues with the aircraft we took off about 1230 hours. The oil pressure on the forward transmission was indicating too high, as a result the oil pressure transducer was changed to fix the problem. We finally made it to Lane Field and had lunch. I had to reorganize my sleeping area since we had moved further north at Lane Field. The weather was somewhat warmer that day and it was much more pleasant. I spent some time engaged in my mess officer duties for our field mess at Lane Field.

Too Afraid to Fly

Once I was paired with an older pilot who seemed afraid of everything. I think he had a dreadful fear that he would be killed in the Vietnam War. He was always jumpy especially with any artillery fire and he went way out of his way to find any excuse to keep from flying. I did not like his attitude and had concern that he was at a grave disadvantage with his open disposition of fear. As Major Jackson would say "No guts no glory." We were all afraid when we flew, we just didn't openly show it like this pilot.

I remember being on standby together when we received an urgent mission to help recover an aircraft that was shot down in an extremely dangerous area. He was the senior pilot and refused to accept the mission. He grounded the aircraft for no apparent reason and failed to carry out his duty. I always thought his fear would turn into his own demise. To my surprise, a few years later I heard that he made it through the war and later was killed in a Chinook crash at Fort Rucker.

Sometimes fate creates an interesting twist, and the Grim Reaper can find you anywhere at any time, even where you least expect it.

Flying with the Major

Sunday, 22 January 1967 was a workday for our crew. Major Max McHaney and I departed in Chinook (917) in the early morning for Hammond Field. The major was well aware of my previous combat activities since we occupied the same tent at An Khe. He liked for me to tell him all about my combat exploits when I was flying Slicks. He also knew that I kept an incredibly detailed tactical map and was keenly familiar with all of the LZs in that region. He personally selected me to accompany him on that combat mission for the next twenty-five flying hours and I felt honored. We had become friends and I liked him very much. I gained an extensive amount of knowledge about aircraft maintenance from Major McHaney and was proud to join him. It was another miserable weather day and the ceiling was low with heavy rain showers. Low forming scud clouds reduced visibility and created dangerous flying conditions. While at Hammond Field we experienced more maintenance problems. The forward rotor head swash plate pivoting actuator had blown a high-pressure hydraulic oil seal and the actuator had to be replaced. That incident resulted in red hydraulic fluid leaking all over the cockpit area. It took all morning to change out the actuator and to clean up the hydraulic fluid. After the incident we had flown only two sorties before we returned to Lane Field. I enjoyed my time flying with Major McHaney.

No mail came for me that day. I normally shaved in the evening and prepared my flight gear for an early departure the next day, that way I didn't have to wake everyone up in the tent in the early morning. I read for a while and then went to bed. I liked to be fully rested with a clear mind when I started to fly any new mission.

On Monday, 23 January 1967, Major McHaney and I logged 5.5 hours of flight time. The only thing that went wrong was the failure of the forward speed trim actuator. We were partial mission capable (PMC), as long as we restricted the forward air speed to less than 100 knots. That day we sling-loaded twenty-six tons of cargo into the forward base of LZ Pony. The ceiling was low with reduced visibility. At the end of the day's missions, we returned to LZ Lane. That evening after chow I went to a movie, I do not remember what film we saw but I remember it being a mindless distraction from war. That night while brushing my teeth a filling in my upper third molar fell out. That would result in another trip to the dentist at An Khe when I had the chance. The tooth started to ache, but I ignored it thinking of the sweet Mrs. Harper.

The combat operations around Bong Son were steadily increasing. Aircraft were flying everywhere. Our ground troops were finding enemy bunkers and tunnel complexes in the area west of LZ Govern. About forty NVA were killed in that location a day or two earlier. It seemed as though the valley just north of the Phu Cat Mountains was another VC hot spot. We had launched a successful operation near there about two month earlier.

The Republic of Korea Tiger Division was pushing north through the Phu Cat Mountains. The Army of the Republic of Vietnam were positioned east of the road that paralleled Hammond Field. They were deployed in an eastern blocking position around Hammond Field. The U.S. Troops had taken blocking positions in the hills parallel with the Hammond Field airstrip and Highway 1. The defensive strategy was to protect the critical high volume of aviation traffic and the high value aviation assets at Hammond Field. In the Airmobile concept the troop movements and the resupply operations depended almost exclusively on the Slick and Chinook helicopters.

The VC were forced to abandon their position as they encountered the savage Republic of Korea (ROK) Tiger Division. The VC began fleeing to a lake that was located there. The VC hoped to flee across the lake from the Koreans. As some of the VC tried to cross the lake in boats, our helicopter gunships experienced a "Duck Shoot." Many of the enemy's dead were gathered up after that engagement. Concentrations of VC bodies were discovered in cleverly concealed camps northwest of the lake. Based on intelligence INTEL from ground patrols and from OV-1 Mohawk infrared surveillance, our artillery and airstrikes had zeroed in on their position a few days earlier. That was probably the artillery and air strikes that we had witnessed. Many of the VC soldiers had been slaughtered like cattle.

Major McHaney and I flew 8 hours on Tuesday, 24 January1967. We mainly accomplished "Ash and Trash" which was a resupply mission of normal food, beer, water, ammunition, fuel, and medical supplies into LZ Pony, LZ Abbey, and LZ Sooner. We backhauled, as needed, the wounded troops and the body bags of our soldiers that had been killed. That was an incredibly sad duty. The Grim Reaper had been terribly busy. We also accomplished a sling load recovery of a downed Slick from Bong Son. It was a good day and I hoped to fly at least fifty hours that month. As long as the aircraft did not go down for maintenance we could accrue more flight time the next day. We returned to Lane Field at the end of a long, arduous, emotionally exhausting day. I wondered if the python would ever cease killing its prey. I received a good deal of mail that evening and I relished in all the news and happenings back home.

There were reports of more enemy activity in the valley around LZ

Pony. An OH-13S Scout or "Snoopy" was flying over the trees at low level and spotted some armed VC troops. Nearby gunships were given the coordinates of the enemy location and quickly arrived and rained down fire on the enemy troops. Artillery fire was called in from LZ Pony followed by a combat assault of four or five Slicks into that same area. Later that day we passed over that same area and noticed bomb and shell craters as well as splintered palm trees, leveled grass huts, and the dead bodies of both people and animals: a graphic scene of carnage I most hated. That was a constant reminder for me of the need of always being aware of where artillery was both firing from and where it would be impacting.

The major and I logged another 8 hours on Wednesday and considered it a successful day. Most of our time related to heavy lifting supplies into LZ Pony. After returning again to Lane Field at the end of the day, I headed to supper and I watched another movie at the "O" Club disconnecting from the reality of war. After the movie I retired early to prepare for the next day's missions.

The major and I only flew 4 hours on Thursday since that was all that remained of the twenty-five hours allotment and the intermediate inspection was coming due; we had ferried aircraft (917) back to An Khe. My tooth was continually aching and I planned go to the dentist the next day, then I hoped to be assigned to another Chinook and to get back in the field. I set a personal goal to accrue another thirty hours before the end of January. After supper I saw the flick, "*The Lost Command*" *with Anthony Quinn.*" It was about a French Army colonel who came up through the ranks to fight in an important foreign battle. It kept my attention enough to distract me from my aching tooth. I received another care package from my sister, Margaret Anne, and in her note, she described trying to hook me up with a computer dating service. I indeed wanted a soul mate someday and I trusted that God would provide, at the perfect time, on His watch.

Early on Friday, 27 January 1967, I went in and had my tooth fixed; finally, no more pain. I returned and wrote a few letters and prepared my field gear for the next flight.

Major McHaney wanted to continue flying combat missions for awhile. The major and I departed in aircraft (902) for Hammond Field that next morning. Upon arrival we were given an expedited mission to recover another downed OH-13S Scout "Snoopy" helicopter which was down north of the Criminal Investigation and Detection Group (CIDG) camp in Happy Valley. The aircraft had been shot down by enemy ground fire in a remote area way out in the "boon docks." After the aircraft recovery mission, we accomplished more routine sorties. We ended up flying 5 hours that day. It was a long day. I planned to eat supper and go to bed early that night. I expected a good deal of flying the next day.

Saturday, 28 January 1967 turned out to be remarkably interesting. To start with, we were down because of the weather and we had taken off late. It was clear and cold the night before and in the early morning a thick fog bank engulfed our area. We received a report that the weather at Hammond Field was clear. At about 1000 hours we executed an instrument takeoff from Lane Field and headed straight for Hammond Field. We quickly broke out of the local fog bank and all was clear. I was able to identify the familiar mountain tops enroute to Hammond Field. The visibility was crystal clear and the countryside was green and beautiful.

Major McHaney and I flew two quick sorties into an area southwest of LZ Govern, which was located between Hammond Field and Happy Valley. It continued to be an extremely dangerous area where we were taking heavy losses. We sling loaded a large amount of C4 high explosives. Many caves and tunnels were discovered in that area and I imagined the C4 was to be used to blow them up. The LZ turned out to be "hairy" to land in since there were tall trees all around and there was not much rotor clearance. All I knew was that I did not want to become the world's largest hedge trimmer, again. Cautiously, we made it. We flew another sling load into LZ Pony. While at LZ Pony we anticipated hot refueling, shutting down to inspect the aircraft, and having a quick lunch. Flying with the Major had been routine, but things would quickly escalate in intensity

A Rescue Mission of Mercy

Immediately after we hot refueled and shut down the aircraft on Saturday, 28 January 1967, a group of medical personnel troops came running over to our aircraft. As fate would have it, we had, unknowingly, arrived in a dangerous forward area at the time that an urgent life-saving medical evacuation (MEDEVAC) rescue mission was desperately needed. We were then briefed that a patrol of American ground troops had been ambushed and had suffered fragmentation wounds at a site near Happy Valley. It was reported that there was one KIA and seven wounded in action (WIA) at that location. There was no area at that location large enough for a rescue helicopter to land. Only the Chinooks in our division had rescue hoists installed. Therefore, only our CH-47 aircraft was available at the scene with the necessary rescue hoist equipment. The brave Major McHaney willingly accepted the mission. The major said to me, "Well 'Tig' we have a hot one." He knew that he could count on me, in the most dangerous circumstances, especially under pressure. I respected and trusted him enough to follow him into the deepest valley.

"Treat your men as you would your own beloved sons. And they will follow you into the deepest valley."
-Sun Tzu, The Art of War

A Mission of Mercy

I carefully plotted the coordinates of the rescue location on my tactical map. In a readiness response to this new mission, our crew began to quickly reconfigure the aircraft for a hoist rescue operation. The cargo hook and beam were removed to facilitate hoisting the injured soldiers up through the cargo door compartment. The long winch cable was routed through a pulley that was secured to a hard point at the top of the cargo bay directly over the center of the cargo hook compartment.

At that same time 15th Medical Detachment personnel began to arrive with the necessary medical equipment. Stretchers, medical kits, plasma, and other supplies were strategically placed in our cargo bay. In essence, our cargo bay was to become a flying medical triage area. In addition, a third M-60 machine gun position was placed on our rear cargo ramp. The additional rear gunner, an infantry troop, donned a crew harness that was tethered to a cargo tie down ring. About a week or so prior a Chinook had been engaged in a similar combat rescue mission. One of the door gunners fired at a NVA sniper that was perched in a tree about 200 meters from the rear of the hovering aircraft. Since that incident, rescue missions required the addition of a rear gunner for added protection. With all the medical supplies and crew on board we took a deep breath and expeditiously launched out on our mission of mercy.

Hanging Between Heaven and Earth

With Major McHaney at the controls, I handled the radios, plotting the course, and performing all the other pilot duties in that frantic combat situation. After takeoff, the rear cargo ramp was lowered to a position level with the floor in the cargo bay for the rear gunner to have a clear field of fire.

Our radio contact on the ground was call sign "Steel Helmet 10." I followed the route to the LZ coordinates (BR730608) with my finger on my tactical map as I directed Major McHaney to that location. Those coordinates had placed us right on the top of a heavily wooded 2,400 foot hill. To complicate the rescue operation, en route our FM radio transmitter failed. A helicopter gunship call sign "Spark Gap 27" escorted us on that mission. In order not to abort the rescue mission, I called our escort "Spark Gap 27" on the UHF emergency (guard 243.0) channel and requested that he relay messages to "Steel Helmet 10." We were able hear "Steel Helmet 10", but we were not able to transmit.

As we approached the area I quickly pointed out the location of the LZ to Major McHaney and requested through the gunship pilot that "Steel Helmet 10" pop smoke for confirmation of that location. Smoke was popped and the color of the smoke was confirmed. As we approached the rescue location a 20-foot hole in the dense jungle with tall trees became visible.

The clearing had been hastily cut by chainsaws to facilitate the rescue effort. The tree trunks were facing away from the center of the LZ. My heart began to pound as I realized the gravity of that situation. The brave Major McHaney brought the Chinook into a stable hover just over the treetops at the center of that small opening in the dense jungle. I could see several bloody troops in the clearing below with bandages all over them. The situation became frightening as the Grim Reaper was again lurking on that hilltop.

We were precariously hanging between heaven and earth. While hovering above the LZ, one of the wounded troops on the ground was near death and the unit medics were fighting to save his life. That critically wounded soldier would be hoisted up first, in a collapsible litter. We hoped that the skillful medical technicians and the more extensive medical supplies available on board our aircraft might save his life. Speed was of the essence. Once the first critically wounded soldier was safely hoisted aboard our aircraft, one of the on-board medics with medical supplies was next lowered by the hoist on the Jungle Penetrator to organize the rescue effort on the ground.

Rescuing the Wounded

Slowly one by one the wounded soldiers were carefully hoisted up into our aircraft's cargo bay. In that critical high stress situation both pilots were focusing our full attention on keeping the Chinook at a stable hover while monitoring the gages, the radios, and our situational awareness. Our gunners and our orbiting gunship escort kept searching the jungle for any enemy activity in the immediate area. Collapsible litters had been employed to hoist the most seriously wounded onboard the aircraft. A Jungle Penetrator lifted the wounded troops who were able hold on to it. We remained over that critical hostile location for about twenty-five or thirty harrowing minutes. The needles at the end of tubes in the pouches of plasma were inserted into the veins of the most seriously injured who were losing blood. The medical technician that was previously lowered down and the body of the KIA troop were hoisted aboard our aircraft last of all. Once all the dead and wounded soldiers were recovered and were onboard our aircraft, we headed straight for the aid station at LZ Pony.

Later I was told that ground patrol had been the victim of a cleverly devised booby trap. A fragmentation device was strategically placed on a trail, by the enemy, concealed inside a medical kit. When the enemy medical kit was found and was opened it tragically exploded and reaped eight American casualties with one strike.

With all the casualties on board, I felt somewhat relieved as we headed back on the short flight to the 15th Medical Corp field hospital. About two minutes into the return flight, one of our crew members informed us that the first critically injured troop that was hoisted up had just died. I felt all the blood drain out of my face and it made me feel depressed. Life was slipping through my grips as the python squeezed the grips of our Chinook. The medics tried so hard to save each and every soul. Of the eight troops that we hoisted on board two of them were already dead.

During this time, our FM Radio failed, our hoist had blown an oil seal and it was leaking profusely into the cargo bay. Due to the long hover at a high-density altitude our master caution light illuminated. Our right engine nose gearbox was overheating, and the oil pressure was low. However, Major McHaney and I were totally involved and determined to complete that life-saving rescue mission and slay the gripping python. Saving as many soldiers as possible, at any cost, was our mission.

As soon as possible, we landed at the 15th Medical Battalion field hospital pad. We shut down the aircraft to unload the casualties and medical equipment. The living wounded were rushed inside for emergency aid. The American patrol leader, a captain, was taken into the aid station but sadly died about 30 minutes later. The dead KIA soldier's bodies were unloaded last of all. The three dead soldiers would be placed in body bags and flown to grave registration in Qui Nhon for mortuary processing and their last flight home.

As the rotor blades slowly coasted to a halt at 1310 hours, I unbuckled myself from the pilot's seat and slowly walked into the cargo bay. One of the medical technicians saw the grief in my face as I said, "I'm sorry. We tried so hard to save them all." Responding with kindness on his face and in the tone of his voice, the corpsman replied, "It's not your fault sir. The three soldiers who died had no chance of surviving. They all had massive brain damage and they would not have made it anyway. During the explosion they received severe head fragmentation wounds. What you and your crew can be proud of, is the assurance that five of the troops you rescued, will make it." Those comforting words of kindness made me feel a little better as I dwelt in the suffering and carnage of the day. He comforted me and reminded me to be proud that I was part of the rescue operation that day.

On that beautiful day three brave American soldiers died. They were killed in a jungle, in a foreign country, by a booby trap that was disguised as medical supplies. I continued to be thankful that Providence had again spared me from death while at the same time I mourned for those that did not. The luck of those three soldiers had expired and they were the real heroes. I will never forget that harrowing mission and their brave service to the United States of America.

Major Mc Haney and I discovered some time later that we were to each receive a Distinguished Flying Cross for that rescue mission which would become my second DFC in Vietnam.

Distinguished Flying Cross Citation:

Chief Warrant Officer Downing distinguished himself by extraordinary achievement while participating in aerial flight during a medical evacuation in the Republic of Vietnam on 27 January 1967. Chief Warrant Officer Downing, as pilot of a Ch-47 Chinook helicopter, and his crew volunteered to attempt the evacuation of eight wounded infantrymen from a location in dense jungle terrain that afforded no landing area for the aircraft. While hovering the aircraft at tree top level, the constant threat of hostile fire, nearness of trees, and mechanical failure of the aircraft was ever present. Chief Warrant Officer Downing and his crew undaunted and effected the entire extraction by hoist in thirty minutes. The importance of speed was exemplified by the death of one of the wounded while on the ground prior to extraction, and another enroute to the aid station. Much of the credit for saving the lives of six seriously wounded soldiers is attributed to Chief Warrant Officer Downing's courage and determination. His action is in keeping with the highest traditions of military service, and reflects great credit upon himself, his unit, and the United States Army.

Charlie's Tragic Mistake

I heard another interesting story that same day. Not far northeast from LZ English, a listening post had picked up a broadcast from a VC command post located in a "hot enemy" region. Previously, six of our helicopters had been shot down in that immediate vicinity.

To determine the source of the broadcast, several different aircraft at various locations homed in on the broadcast and plotted directional vector fixes to the suspected point of origin. From the radio fixes, the location of the broadcast was isolated to a relatively small area in the jungle. The next step was to insert our troops and surround that area to close in and surprise them. Both the Army of the Republic of Vietnam and our 1st Cavalry troops were engaged in that operation.

Soon after having inserted the troops the enemy position was attacked. UH-1B aerial rocket artillery, UH-1C gunships, and a Chinook "Guns-A-Go-Go" provided precision close air support. The attack amassed a body count of twenty-two NVA troops lying dead in the area. Our aircraft was on standby in the event that additional aircraft support was required. The attack ended about 1700 hours. It was "Charlie's" tragic mistake to send out the radio broadcast and to be caught out in the open. At the end of the day we returned to Lane Field to repair our aircraft and to rest.

The End of January

On Sunday, 29 January 1967, the days seem to be getting longer or maybe it was the fact that I was flying long days. I received more complaints about my mess hall. It appeared that while I was away flying missions the mess crew became lax in their duties. They seemed to not be motivated when I was not present to supervise. I was away flying combat missions sometimes for days at a time. Our commander was more interested in keeping me flying than having me supervise his mess hall. One day he even took it upon himself to talk to the mess sergeant and to chew him out, himself. The commander had the sergeant stand at attention and ordered him to faithfully fulfill his mess responsibilities or he and his mess crew would be relieved of their duty to be reassigned to an infantry unit. The "butt chewing" seemed to work and the quality of the food preparation and the service improved. He had taken care of business and I was encouraged to keep flying combat missions.

It was foggy again and cool that next morning and we were not able to launch until that afternoon. We returned back to An Khe to have our radios and other maintenance squawks repaired. When the repairs were completed we returned to Hammond Field. We accomplished more general "Ash and Trash" sorties to LZ Pony, LZ Minh, and LZ Abbey. We were scheduled for another MEDEVAC but our brakes started leaking and the utility hydraulic system was drained of hydraulic fluid to the point that we were not able to operate the hoist.

A Slick MEDEVAC helicopter had gone down and the crew needed to be rescued. We were down again for maintenance and could not fly the mission. We were hopeful that the aircraft would be repaired that night and that we could fly again the next day. After supper I watched the movie, "*Johnny Tiger*" that took place in Florida and reminded me of home.

We flew "milk runs" which were rather bland routine non-combat missions, on Monday, 30 January 1967. We were on weather hold until 0930 hours due to the low visibility. We had flown aircraft (5120) until the APU failed to start. We again left the aircraft at Hammond Field and caught a ride back to Lane Field. The only interesting mission was the recovery of a downed OH-13S Scout "Snoopy" helicopter from a site near LZ Wedge in the mountains near Hammond Field.

A pleasant diversion arrived in the mail, from my sister, Marilyn. She had sent me more guitar books that would give me a wider variety of songs to practice. On Tuesday, the last day of the month, I only lacked a few minutes of flying time to reach 90 flying hours for that month. I had flown almost 50 hours within the proceeding eight days. That was a lot of time for a pilot flying in a Chinook. I was tired but all things considered I liked what I was doing. The way things were escalating, I anticipated more action and more flying time within the next few months.

My guess was that we would move north to LZ English and begin operations in the An Lao Valley which was a continued enemy "hot spot." Several aircraft had been shot down in that area. There was less talk of some of us being infused into another Assault Support Helicopter Company that was rumored earlier.

The seasonal weather patterns were beginning to change as it was warmer and fairly dry. That was a win for us as it created less mud and better weather flying conditions. It had not rained in a few days and even the U.S. Air Force jets were seen flying missions in the Hammond Field area.

I heard that China was experiencing internal struggles and that supplies to the VC might be cut off, which might turn out to be a fortunate change for us. However, enemy supplies through the "Ho Chi Minh Trail" never seemed to stop coming. It seems that the world situation was always changing. Back home we had heard that three astronauts were killed in a fire at Cape Canaveral which was bad news that made me sad.

My mess sergeant would soon be rotating back to the U.S. and had not yet heard who would take his place. I hoped it would be an improvement. We had a mess hall inspection coming due and I was concerned about meeting the requirements even though the food was good, most of the time. The month of January came to an end.

A Routine Early February

On Wednesday, 1 February 1967, I was one month closer to heading back home. Time seemed to be flying by and I was glad. We ran out of inspection time on our aircraft and had to return to An Khe. I was thoroughly tired and hoped to get a couple of days off. The sun beamed with a welcome invitation, and I wanted to work on my suntan and catch up on my letter writing and my journal entries. There were still some rumors about some of us being infused into the 213th ASHC but I just couldn't see that happening.

I continued to ponder what I would do if I returned home in one piece. I was still practicing the new music on my guitar and reading several of the books that were sent to me. In routine evening fashion, the outgoing artillery continually pounded away from An Khe as I ate supper and went to bed early.

There had not been much activity for me on Thursday, 2 February 1967. I lounged around and rested. I took a nap that afternoon, but soon realized that I was still exhausted. After chow that night I watched a science fiction movie that didn't make any sense. The next morning I spent quietly preparing my field gear for the next mission.

On Friday, at 1530 hours, Lieutenant Duff and I were paired as the pilots and together boarded aircraft (141) and flew to Hammond Field. LT Duff was the recent replacement for Captain Wade who had been sent to a hospital in Japan after our crash. This was the first time that I had flown with LT Duff. He was a young slender and serious officer. I instantly liked him. By that time, I was approaching 2,000 flying hours and had flown in combat missions for over six months. On that mission I was the most experienced pilot. After we accomplished normal missions for 3.25 hours we returned to Lane Field. I felt comfortable flying with LT Duff knowing we would most likely fly more the following day.

There was a rumor based on an INTEL report that Lane Field might be attacked that night. I had seriously doubted that it was a possibility considering Lane Field was a relatively secure and well protected area. LT Duff had attended a security briefing and there would be no telling what kind of games we would be playing that night. We did have automatic weapons and a gunship there on standby in case of an impending attack. I could have manned a M-60 machine gun if required. Due to the INTEL and possibility of an attack, it was decided that our aircraft would be dispersed to our airfield at Qui Nhon.

As I expected, on Saturday, 4 February 1967, the VC had not attacked Lane Field. However, we experienced a miserable night sleeping on the ramp inside our aircraft at Qui Nhon. I slept on a section of the red passenger seats and used the pilot's seat cushion as a pillow. At least there was plenty of room for our crew to stretch out enough to sleep in our unloaded Chinook. I could hear the C-130s taking off and landing all night. Much needed cargo was flowing to Qui Nhon. Our aircraft was parked so close to the runway that it sounded like the airplanes were coming right up our cargo ramp.

In another shift of fortune, my good friend, Major Max K. Mc Haney had assumed command of "C" Charlie Company the day before. Major Fountain would be promoted and be moving up to the Aviation Group level. Major Fountain was a great commander. I had also come to know Major McHaney as an outstanding company commander. Major McHaney moved out of our tent and into the commander's quarters. The Major made an impressive speech in the "O" Club when he assumed command and had my complete respect.

Aircraft (141) developed more maintenance problems that morning. The accessory gear box (AGB) motor failed which caused the number two engine to hot start with a high exhaust gas temperature (EGT). The aircraft would be down for repair for several hours. After the repairs were completed we only flew for one hour. We returned to An Khe to disperse the aircraft for the night.

After we landed at An Khe I was exceedingly thirsty and headed straight to the "O" Club for a soft drink and to visit with some of the other pilots. I was sitting there not paying much attention to what was going on and looked up to realize that the Group Commander was presenting awards. My friend CWO-3 B.K. Evans said, "Jim, go up front they are reading a citation for you."

I was completely surprised since everyone thought that I was still at Lane Field. I heard my name as the citation was being read. The citation was for my first DFC while I was flying a Slick emergency resupply mission with the 229th AHC on 21 September 1966. That award caught me by complete surprise and I swelled with pride with satisfaction knowing that in fact, I was living out the greatest version of my boyhood dream. I walked back to my tent in solitude as it was a much quieter evening than the night before in An Khe. As I lay down for the night I thought about that night's DFC presentation and knew it was another night in Vietnam that I would never forget. I rested well in my own bed, with pride and gratitude, and it felt good.

Sunday, 5 February 1967, was another good day. The weather was beautiful, the sky was blue and clear, and the sun was warm. Even though I had received my first coveted DFC, my mind drifted back home. I wished that I had someone special to share life with. Maybe that would come later. I did recall that Carol had caught my eye in Bible class and wondered if she was someone to ask out upon my return home. God had a stronghold on my life and my DFC was evidence of that. The task at hand was to do the best I could while I was in Vietnam and felt confident that God would take care of the rest upon returning home.

LT Duff and I flew a ladder mission into Happy Valley. Troops climbed up and down the ladder that was extended from the rear ramp. We hovered in that exercise for about one hour. We became adept at maintaining the Chinook at a stable hover. It took a good deal of skill and concentration as we took turns at the controls during that demanding mission.

On Monday, 6 February 1967, we launched out to recover a downed Slick. When we arrived at that location the problem was only a failed engine N1 Indicator. The Slick crew elected to ferry the aircraft back to An Khe. We did not accomplish much flying time that day.

LT Duff and I flew aircraft (111) from An Khe to Hammond Field on Tuesday. The demand for missions were increasing and we flew about 7 hours that day. More missions were scheduled into the LZ English and the Happy Valley area. We sling loaded 105 Howitzers with a piggy load of fifty rounds of Scorpion ammunition into LZ Keller which was located just east of LZ English.

We knew that it was a hot area since two helicopter gunships were assigned to escort us to the LZ. No ground fire was encountered on that mission. In fact, "Charlie" had become afraid when these deadly accurate gunships, with the four machine and rocket pods, were escorting our helicopters. They did not dare mess with us.

On Wednesday, our sorties were focused on resupply missions into LZ Puller, which was located slightly west of the infamous LZ Bird. There was a Tết Truce ceasefire in effect, so all was quiet for the moment. We had learned from the LZ Bird incident that the enemy could not be trusted and might still break the truce. I practiced more instrument training that day. We accrued a total of 6 routine hours. That day was my older sister, Clara's, birthday, and I had hoped that she was celebrating with her family in Oregon.

Thursday, 9 February 1967 was an easy routine flying day. That evening we enjoyed many hues of blues and purples in the sunset on our flight back to An Khe. As we flew above the rising cumulus cloud layer, the sky looked like an art piece in an expensive gallery and was truly majestic. Vietnam was a beautiful country wearing the scars of blanket bombing and shell craters. We logged a total of 7.1 long hours that day. I stayed tired and my "butt" felt like concrete. I practiced some actual instrument and hood time on the flight back to An Khe. Upon returning I was too busy with my mess hall duties to either play my guitar or to read.

Friday was a rest day between missions. I finally found some time to read while sitting out in the sun with my shirt off. It felt good to soak up the sun and continue working on my tan. Later I worked on several new chords on my guitar and sang along to one of the new songs

I had learned. Singing seemed to help relieve my stress and made me feel better about the world. Back home my younger sister, Marilyn, and I, liked to sing together, and it always seemed to bring about joy. I thought about home and family when I was playing and singing. I continued adding to my journal eager to share my happenings with everyone back in the states.

I had become relatively happy being able to fly even though the missions were becoming hairier, scarier and death-defying acts rather than recreational aviation. I was building flight time and I believed my combined flight time would help secure a good job in the field of aviation when I got out of the U.S. Army. And, I knew that I was contributing to the war effort in Vietnam and was committed to seeing it through to the best of my ability. Rescuing people and saving lives was most rewarding and made me feel proud. For me, it was better to heal than to kill - and more than anything I did not want to arrive home with any blood on my hands, if I could help it.

After resting all morning, CWO-4 Ness and I, took aircraft (118) to Hammond Field on Saturday, 11 February 1967. He had an exceptionally long career in the U.S. Army. He told me interesting stories of flying when he was in Africa. After I had returned to the U.S. I heard that he had been shot in the foot, which ended his long flying career. CWO Ness and I would be supporting our "A" Alpha Company call sign "Long John." We ended up flying about 4 hours on the first day. Our missions consisted of hauling troops to LZ English and then sling loading artillery and ammunition into an ARVN camp north of LZ English. The ceiling was low and we traveled low level, under 500 feet AGL, most of the way.

While flying I could see our U.S. Air Force jets pounding a town to the east of our location on the coast. That was followed by artillery fire into that same area from LZ English. Spark gap gunships and aerial rocket artillery were later engaging ground targets in that same area. Intelligence reports had informed us that a NVA battalion size unit was hiding somewhere in the area near Bong Son.

An attack was expected to occur at LZ English either that night or the next night. It seemed a shame to destroy the beautiful countryside by dropping bombs and firing artillery shells. There were pristine palm trees, grass huts, fishing boats, green lagoons, and flowing streams as beautiful and picturesque as a travel post card. That was as good as any picture I had ever seen of a South Sea Island paradise. It was a shame that by contrast, we were trying to kill each other. In the aftermath of the attack, I saw palm trees that were splintered and huts that were burning, shell craters and bodies were visible in the villages. Cattle had returned to rot in the fields as the python ravaged the innocent in its heyday.

We spent a good bit of time hauling out troops into blocking positions further north of LZ English. The plan was to assault that area the next day and to drive the NVA into a trap. We had the advantage of rapidly deploying troops by airlift while "Charlie" had to travel more slowly on the ground at night. The weather was still bad with low hanging clouds that forced us to fly at a dangerously low altitude. We were constantly monitoring which LZ was firing artillery and where shells were impacting. Flying low made us more vulnerable and easier for "Charlie" to hit us.

I heard that Nancy Sinatra, in her recent hit, "*These Boots were Made for Walking*", was visiting Hammond Field that day and was disappointed that I missed seeing her. But we were in the middle of a war, and I still had missions to fly. We logged 3.8 hours on that day.

LZ English Maintenance, Repairs and Missions

Sunday, 12 February 1967, was the worst day that I had experienced in some time. We continued to support "Long John" or "A" Alpha Chinook Company. We were moving the troops from LZ Abbey and LZ Putter to a new area northwest of English in the mountains. That was also an extremely dangerous area where several aircraft had been lost.

To start with, the weather was terrible with the cloud layer lower than usual. We were barely able to squeeze through the An Khe pass and we traveled low level most of the day. Another scary problem was experiencing unreported artillery projectiles exploding northwest of LZ English. We contacted the artillery net and they were not aware of any active artillery fire in that area. I assumed that the fire originated from LZ Keller, which was located due west of LZ English.

After the last sortie into LZ Putter, we hooked up another load and headed for LZ Sand. Over Bong Son we lost all pressure to the number two hydraulic flight control system. The master caution light and the emergency warning panel lit up like a Christmas tree. We decided to declare an emergency and land at Bong Son. We radioed Two Bits tower for landing instructions. The stability augmentation system from the failed system was causing all kinds of severe inputs into the flight control system. We had to overpower the flight control inputs long enough to drop off the sling load and land at Two Bits.

After safely landing and parking the aircraft, our crew chief found a ruptured hydraulic line in the closet area. Red foul-smelling hydraulic fluid, under 3,000 PSI, had spewed out all over the area near the cockpit. Considering the events that had unfolded, I was incredibly happy to be safely on the ground. Another Chinook (070) was also down at Two Bits for a failed transmission. The accessory drive gearbox

(ADG) had seized up. Our maintenance crew cannibalized the hydraulic line from Aircraft (070) and recorded the removal of the line in the aircraft maintenance forms. The line was replaced, the fluid level was replenished, and the air was bled from the lines. The spilled hydraulic fluid was cleaned up and we were ready to continue flying missions.

Aircraft (070) was to remain at Bong Son and we loaded the pilots on board and returned to Lane Field. Thus, our high stress day was defined by bad weather, the vulnerability to ground fire, an unknown origin of artillery fire, a flight control hydraulic system failure, and an emergency landing. We were all exhausted and weary but we had gotten through it. I expected that the weather would be bad again the next day.

We were delayed a good part of Monday, 13 February 1967, as more hydraulic repairs were being made on our aircraft. After the field repairs, we returned the aircraft back to An Khe. No more maintenance problems were encountered. After that we flew aircraft (141) back out for more missions around LZ English. I expected mortar attacks at LZ English at any time which was formerly an NVA stronghold; and, it would take a great deal of effort in order to drive "Charlie" completely out of that area.

Tuesday was Valentine's Day, and for a moment my thoughts drifted to what it would be like someday having my own wife to share it with. Like Uncle Vernon and Aunt Carrie, Mr. & Mrs. Mosley, and Ron and Lois Bastien, I, too, wanted the same kind of deep abiding love and family of my own, someday.

We were down much of Tuesday for maintenance as the maintenance crews worked on our aircraft (141). Chinooks required a good deal of maintenance effort to keep them flyable and the repairs seemed endless. The oil pressure indicator on the forward transmission had excessive fluctuations but luckily we were cleared for a one-time flight back to An Khe.

Our base camp would be moving out of Lane Field on the next day so we carried a load of food and supplies from the nearby ration distribution point for our mess hall back to An Khe. The field mess hall would then be set up at a different forward location.

That evening at An Khe there was a live Korean floor show at the "O" Club and, as it turned out, it was entertaining enough to keep my attention the entire show. Later that night after the show had ended my thoughts shifted onto more serious things. I had great anticipation for going home laced with anxiety of what I would do next. During my time in Vietnam I received numerous letters from friends who wanted to hook me up with different girls. I was not really interested in just any girl, I wanted Miss Right or the one right, for me. I knew that God had already chosen someone for me and, as Providence always transpires, I knew I would know it when I saw it. I shifted to first things first knowing that finding a job was more important than landing a date. Closer to the end of my tour I would start inquiring about flying jobs.

The only mission on Wednesday, 15 February 1967, was to fly to LZ English. We remained overnight on RRF duty. Outgoing artillery and flares were fired all night long and that made it a long night. We remained on alert in case of an attack as I slept on the seats in the cargo bay.

Thursday was another long flying day. We logged 7.2 hours. Sorties were flown to LZ Sand, LZ Santana, and LZ Tom. On one of our sorties our aircraft was fired upon between LZ Santana and LZ Tom. That was the first time that I saw tracers pass in front of the cockpit, which was worrisome, since the enemy gunners were starting to lead the aircraft with their fire. It wasn't a position I wanted to be in.

As we departed that area, the ground troops were in contact with the enemy. I knew there would be heavy fighting near LZ English since there were many determined NVA soldiers fighting back in that area. Due to the possibility of enemy mortar fire only a few aircraft were permitted to remain at LZ English overnight. More of the aircraft were dispersed to An Khe for the night.

Officer of the Day

I relaxed during the day on Friday, 17 February 1967, but I had the Officer of the Day (OD) duties that night. The OD's duty was to assume responsibility for security and guarding the area. In this assignment we wore a distinctive arm band labeled OD in large white letters and carried a loaded 38-caliber side arm. I felt like an old western sheriff or marshal making his nightly rounds. There was a published OD checklist to follow. The primary duties were to maintain order among the enlisted troops and ensure that no one was carrying firearms or exhibiting threating or violent behavior while they were drinking in the enlisted clubs. The non-commissioned officers (NCO) and especially the enlisted men's (EM) club were where excessive drinking could easily precipitate arguments and fights.

An additional duty as OD was to supervise the posting of guards in our company area during the night. That evening there were no major disturbances and all proceeded relatively well. After the clubs closed on Saturday the entire camp became quiet and I finally got some sleep at my duty station at 0300 hours for an hour or two. Once my OD duty ended at daybreak I returned to my tent and slept until noon. After that, I ate lunch, read, played my guitar and prepared my field gear for the next mission. I was scheduled to return to LZ English the next day.

Shower Runs

On Sunday, 19 February 1967, I was paired up with Captain Carl Dunn and we flew aircraft (141) to LZ English. Captain Dunn had been in my Chinook transition class back in Alabama at Fort Rucker. He seemed to always have a good sense of humor and had the ability to make everyone else laugh too. He was fun to be around, so naturally I was glad that he was assigned to our battalion headquarters as a staff officer. Battalion staff officers were periodically scheduled to fly with the different company units to stay current in the Chinook.

On Sunday we accomplished a different mission. We flew "shower runs." On shower runs, we delivered troops to designated shower points so they could (literally) take showers. Water pumps with makeshift showers in tents were located on the banks and offered troops a chance to clean up after days on the ground. We picked up ground troops in the field and dropped them off at a guarded shower point on a sand bar on the north bank of the Bong Son River. The "shower runs" consumed much of the day so we did not log much flying time. What seemed mundane in flying offered relief and much needed revitalization for our troops.

The local villagers always came out in aggressive salesforce style to sell the troops items ranging from fresh fruit to local artisan-made items, with one intent, getting our money. Local barbers were giving shaves and haircuts which was perfect timing for me, so I conveniently got a haircut while I was waiting for the next shower run exchange. Even while getting a haircut, I never let my guard down and continued to be vigilant since a common trick of the VC was to teach children to explode grenades in a group of our troops. I had my 38-caliber pistol in my holster and I was very aware of my surroundings. What saddened me immensely was that it did not seem to matter to the VC that the children were killed as part of their warfare.

As we parked on the sandbar at the Bong Son River during one of our shower runs, our aircraft door gunner told me several stories of his previous experiences as a ground troop in the 1st Battalion Artillery of the 7th Cavalry. He had extended another year to fly as a door gunner. He went into great detail sharing the infantry's hardships while on patrol in the jungle. They slept in all types of difficult conditions in the rain, in the jungle, in the mud, and in the dirt. While on patrol, his unit encountered snakes, mosquitos, various other insects, and leaches from the streams and marsh areas. He explained to us his firsthand experiences of how the VC liked to set up all different kinds of ambushes and "booby traps." The enemy enjoyed mutilating our soldiers and were able to effectively hide themselves undetected in caves and tunnels everywhere. It was during that conversation that I gained an even deeper, and more profound respect for our brave ground troops for what they had to endure in the jungles of Vietnam. I continued to listen and learn from that intensely serious conversation and the depth of emotions that he shared in describing it all.

We continued to fly routine sorties. Defensive artillery continually fired most of the nights that we remained at LZ English. On Monday, 20 February 1967, during the night at LZ English, a few enemy mortar rounds impacted nearby in white flashes. Our UH-1B ARA alert ships quickly located their position and fired rocket salvos into that area. The mortar attack immediately ceased.

The night prior I saw some of my old friends from "A" Alpha Company of the 229th Battalion. They still wanted me to come back and fly UH-1Ds with them. I was flattered and shared that my commander assured me that was not going to happen. His answer was not only "no" but "hell no." The commander assured me that my assignment flying Chinooks was far more important.

While chatting with my old UH-1D friends they caught me up on their recent activities since I had departed from their unit. They still had their signature shaggy mustaches and seemed to enjoy the tiniest bit of rebellion as an earned right of war. They explained to me how it was their UH-1D Slick pilots, who air assaulted LZ Bird on the night of, 27 December 1966, while it was under heavy enemy attack during the Christmas truce. Their unit bravely inserted the ready reaction force on the perimeter of LZ Bird. One of the young pilots smiled as the story was told of how his UH-1D was riddled with bullet holes as he approached the rice paddy at LZ Bird.

Mercifully, no one in the aircraft was hit and they lived to talk about it. They went on to share that, as the ground troops exited the aircraft and scrambled for cover, the crew of the downed Slick was rescued by two of his brave fellow pilots. It dawned on me that it was that very Slick, with the blue triangle insignias painted on the pilots' doors, that our Chinook crew had recovered later that morning from the rice paddy. That incident struck me as a profound coincidence and signified that we still were part of a team that could count on each other like brothers. The Grim Reaper seemed to snatch many heroes in Vietnam, while this crew was spared to live and talk about it. We were all connected in many ways.

I remembered that, even then, as I lifted that downed Slick from the muddy battlefield, I knew that the bond was still there. I had just moved on to flying a larger and a more sophisticated helicopter with more experienced pilots. Until that point in time none of their Slick pilots had been killed. That made me feel good and I was immensely proud of those brave young men.

Airstrikes in Progress

Our Chinook missions that day were to mostly resupply LZ Sand and LZ Santana with ammunition. As I flew I observed villages burning everywhere in the immediate area. Airstrikes were in progress all around us. I observed several Slicks in "V" formations being escorted into hot LZs by gunships. I was sure that some of my friends were flying in those combat assaults. I offered a silent prayer for their protection. As I recall, no aircraft were lost that day, for which I remained very thankful. It was always difficult to lose good friends to the coiling grip of the python.

Consequently, at that time I had developed a "case of the runs" or major dysentery due to all the recent combat activities. All that I had been eating were cold "C" rations for days-on-end. When we landed, some of the villagers were selling cokes and beer not a mile away from where we had been burning villages and killing VC. The villagers acted as though they couldn't have cared less; the ambiguity did not seem right to me, as humans lay strewn across fields like rotting cattle.

For pilots, that war seemed to be more like an extremely dangerous game. We got up in the morning and flew combat missions. At the end of the day we ate hot food, took hot showers, and watched movies. As General Hamilton Howze had foreseen: the helicopter revolutionized warfare. The helicopter had taken much of the hardship and the pain out of warfare. If someone were wounded, a helicopter would rescue him and rush him to an aid station. We delivered ammunition, hot food, and beer to the troops in the field in sharp contrast to previous wars.

The VC did not have it so well. They hid themselves in their deep damp holes with little food and comforts. Yet, with unwavering persistence, they were determined to win that war. The VC had been masters of ambush techniques and sinister "booby traps". They felt safe in the jungle and were willing to annihilate at any cost. They had been effectively hidden while VC snipers picked off our troops one at a time. The United States military was characterized by our helicopters flying in the air while the VC dug into the ground with their shovels.

On Tuesday, 21 February 1967, CWO-2 Smith and I launched out to LZ English flying two hours. Most of the day our aircraft was on standby awaiting emergency resupply or rescue missions. Our troops were engaging the VC troops everywhere in that area, it continued to be very dangerous.

The weather was good for a change that day at LZ English. The sky was clear with no rain. After chow I read, made journal entries and went to bed early. Our aircraft was on standby again on Wednesday, but we did not fly. We returned to An Khe at the end of the day.

Moving to the Bachelor Officer's Quarters

On Wednesday I experienced another milestone. I moved from a tent into a new semi-permanent bachelor officer's quarter. The rooms were small but nice. As time progressed temporary wooden buildings were being built for us to stay in. We had screen doors to keep the bugs out and concrete floors. The first few feet of the walls were constructed of concrete 6 inches thick. This reduced the risk of being struck by shrapnel during mortar attacks. The remainder of the walls were louvered boards that were covered with screen. The roof was made of corrugated galvanized panels. The BOQ was a big step up from our tents and I started setting things up and moved my refrigerator in there.

Our BOQ that I help construct 1967.

I shared the room with CWO-3 Elmer Anderson. He was a highly intelligent and interesting person, and I thoroughly enjoyed many good conversations. He was something of an introvert, but we seemed to mesh and easily became good friends. When I was not busy flying, I enjoyed contributing to the building projects spending many hours painting the newly constructed buildings.

We managed to fly 2.5 hours on Thursday. We flew routine out and back missions from LZ English. It was another beautiful cloudless day, one where we could see forever. The whole valley filled with palm trees was a brilliant emerald green as the sun beamed to magnify the intensity in the color of the foliage. It would have been a perfect scene had it not been for the smoke off in the horizon, north of LZ English, from burning villages. The still air rippled from the shock waves of heavy artillery fire. The sweet smell of the grass in the morning was later overpowered by the odor of artillery gun powder that drifted our way. It seemed that I would not get as much flight time in February.

An O-1 and B-52's

There was one story that I had heard of an O-1 Birddog (a two-seat fixed wing observation aircraft) that was flying along in an area where there was a high concentration of VC. There had been a high cloud layer, but no other aircraft could be seen in the area. A VC farmer desperately wanted to fire at that small, unarmed airplane. After scanning the sky, from horizon to horizon, for other aircraft, the VC picked up his rifle that lay hidden in the brush. He carefully took aim at the O-1 and fired.

The O-1 pilot saw the muzzle blast and headed straight for the VC position in order to report the enemy location. Now what the O-1 pilot and the VC farmer didn't know was that several B-52s were in formation high above the cloud layer and they were on a radar controlled "Arc Light" on a carpet-bombing mission of that very VC infested area. As the O-1 passed overhead the location of the farmer, the B-52s released their bomb loads. Shortly after "bombs away", violent explosions could be seen erupting all over the entire valley creating a new field of rotting cattle. The VC probably thought to himself, "If those explosions were caused by that small aircraft, then please don't send a big one."

I received several letters from home on Friday, 24 February 1967. My folks had put my photo in the local newspaper in recognition of the recent DFC that I was awarded. This action assured me that they were indeed proud of me. A small nod of recognition can be better than a roomful of applause. I did not fly that day. I sat out in the sun and played my guitar.

Later we were briefed on the gravity of the combat situation north of LZ English as enemy troops were on the move in that area as our combat efforts had forced the enemy further north.

More Maintenance Problems and More Stress

Recent intelligence reports indicated that 2,000 NVA troops and possibly another NVA division were massing north of Bong Son between Duc Pho and Ba To. That was another hot area that we eventually would have to attack. As we were flying missions, our aircraft had to pass over the An Lao Valley knowing full well that heavy weapons were positioned there. We were to receive a final briefing at LZ English once we landed. The safest choice to travel in that dangerous area was to fly at altitudes above 3,000 feet where we were normally immune from small arms fire. However, there was still the possibility of colliding with Air Force jets or being hit by unreported artillery fire.

On Saturday, 25 February 1967, we flew to LZ English but everything seemed to be on hold, so we did not get to fly very much. We returned in the evening back to An Khe. We flew back to LZ English again on Sunday. Not much was happening and we only logged two hours of flight time. Monday, we flew four routine hours and at the end of the day we remained overnight at Qui Nhon.

It was the end of the month, Tuesday, 28 February 1967, when we encountered a series of maintenance problems. Three of our forward rotor tip caps were damaged when we descended into a very small landing area where there were many trees. Cutting tree branches with your forward rotor blades definitely increases the "pucker factor." Leaves and small branches were scattered all over the LZ by our rotor wash as we landed. After accomplishing that mission the number two Engine Fuel Control Unit (ECU) failed and it would not permit the engine to move to the flight position or full power. We also encountered other minor maintenance problems but we did manage to fly the aircraft back to An Khe on that highly stressful day; it was a relief when we made it safely home.

About that timeframe, Major General John J. Tolson assumed command of the 1st Cavalry Division. His tour of duty was listed online as March 1967 to August 1968. He was the third commander listed after Major General Hugh Exton.

Stress, Sorties and Sandbaggers

A new month began on Wednesday, 1 March 1967. I slept late and I was then assigned the task of inventorying the consumable alcohol supplies in the "O" Club. Of most concern was to verify the current alcoholic beverage inventory. One common issue in Vietnam was that some club managers were falsifying inventory records and pocketing money. Thankfully, the accounts in our "O" Club balanced after the inventory was completed.

Thursday was another lax flying day. That morning I played my guitar, read a portion of Michener's "*Caravans*", and read the "*Book of Romans*" in my Bible. For the past few weeks the Chinooks had not been flying much. I received letters from home that helped keep me connected and hope alive for the future. That afternoon I flew 2.5 hours. Most of the sorties were flown from LZ English to nearby LZs. Boredom was setting in and I became restless again from the lack of flying.

As the battle area locations continued to migrate north of Bong Son and LZ English, much of the logistics operations moved from Hammond Field north to LZ English. There was a short runway at LZ English and CV-2 Caribous and Air Force C-123 aircraft were the only cargo aircraft capable to land and unload on that short field. LZ English became a new forward distribution point as the 1st Cavalry Division pushed further north. After offloading cargo from the cargo aircraft, loads were reorganized and prepared to be distributed to the forward areas by helicopters. Our Chinooks assumed much of that mission.

Friday, 3 March 1967, was another slow day. We flew out to LZ English but our flight time was minimal and I was completely bored. Saturday became a little more exciting as we began the day by flying in a combat assault. The Slicks from the 227th AHB inserted the first lift of troops into LZ Purple, which was northwest of LZ English. Next a combined total of 1,200 ARVNS needed to be airlifted there. The first wave of troops on the ground secured the area. Because of the sheer volume of ARVNs that needed to be moved, Chinooks were utilized since we could carry thirty-three combat troops at a time with each sortie. After that day's missions, we spent the night at Qui Nhon.

Sunday, 5 March 1967, was another slow flying day. The combat situation was progressing slowly. We spent the night at LZ English on RRF duty. Monday proved to be another very slow day, so to pass the time I finished reading, "*Caravans*." I thought the book was very interesting. We remained overnight at Qui Nhon and flew a few sorties on Tuesday. There was a lack of coordination, which promoted dangerous situations. We had been experiencing unannounced friendly artillery fire that was exploding near our flight path and had no communication with the Black Hat controllers on the ground when we dropped off our loads which caused a good deal of anxiety.

Upon returning to An Khe we were briefed on a possible incoming artillery alert which made for a very stressful day. I slept late on Wednesday and a group of us drove downtown. I did some shopping and purchased some ribbons for the medals I had earned, for wearing on my dress uniform. That evening there was a party and a floor show in the "O" Club. Caviar and other luxuries were served. I didn't eat the caviar but the boiled shrimp and grilled steak hit the spot for me. The floor show was well received. I was forced onto the stage and sang a song with the cast. In the audience several of my pilot friends were whistling, hooting and hollering; "Don't give up your day job!" It was fun for a change, and it is always helpful to be a good sport.

On the afternoon of Thursday, 9 March 1967, we flew another Chinook to LZ English. We logged about 2 hours at the end of the day. The weather out of An Khe was bad and we took a longer alternate route to LZ English to avoid ground fire. I found more books to read and stowed them away in my area of the BOQ. I truly enjoyed reading and having intelligent conversations like I shared with my sister, Harriet, but most of my friends were more interested in drinking to pass the time.

I hoped that I would have more interesting friends when I returned home. On Friday, 10 March 1967, we flew about 4 hours. The sorties were routine resupply missions to replenish cargo for the various LZs. In my off time I strummed the strings of my guitar for a bit before settling in to read. The pilots still called me "Tiger" since I liked to fly as much as I possibly could. Every unit seemed to have their own "Tiger", so I was labeled "C" Charlie Company's "Tiger."

Lucky for me and my desire to accrue flight time, there were many "sand baggers" who gladly gave me their scheduled missions to avoid combat flying. There were only a few pilots in our unit that were accruing as much flight time as me. I kept thinking more flight time might help me land a better flying position once I got home. Many of the missions could have been my last and every pilot understood the reality of being hit or their aircraft coming apart in flight, but the other pilots would say; "That was why we get flight and combat pay."

On Saturday, 11 March 1967, the 1st Cavalry troops encountered a large group of VC southeast of LZ English. Several VC were killed and many more were captured. Four helicopters were shot down during the combat assaults. Our Chinook was not directly involved in that operation and I still managed to log more instrument time. As a change of pace from my usual guitar playing and reading, I decided to carve a head out of a piece of wood for the lack of something better to do. Keeping my hands busy and my mind creative seemed to anchor me and keep me calm. I fastened a makeshift lanyard to it and wore it as my Hammond Field tribal necklace. Years later I still have that memento among all the others.

Carved face and our hex tents at Hammond Field 1967.

Chinook Bomber Pilot and Napalm Missions

For another new experience, I was being trained as a bomber pilot. The Chinook crews were being prepared for a new mission of dropping drums of napalm from the air. Two missions had been flown so far. The purpose of the napalm missions was to burn houses, stores of rice, and other things of value that could have help sustained the enemy.

An aluminum rack with built in rollers was installed along the cargo bay and the rear ramp, as the delivery system. Fifty-five-gallon drums were placed upright on the roller track and secured by tie down straps. On each drum, an extremely high heat producing thermite grenade, was taped to the top, and a length of safety wire, was attached to the pin of each grenade as a lanyard. Upon command from the pilots, the crew would roll each drum out the back of the aircraft and at the same time hold on to the safety wire lanyard. Seconds after the pins came out of position on the thermite grenade, the grenade would start to burn and quickly burn through the thin metal of the drums to ignite the napalm. The pilots who flew these missions would jokingly say that we were B-47 bomber pilots. It took some practice to hit a specific target with any accuracy using the napalm drums.

Watching a C-130 Hercules Ablaze

I did not fly at all on Sunday, 12 March 1967, and even slept in late followed by lounging in the sun and reading. At about 1530 hours a C-130 Hercules ran off the north end of our runway at An Khe about 100 yards from where I was sunning myself in a chair. The aircraft had aborted the takeoff roll once, but then decided to apply full power again and continue with the takeoff. This was a big mistake because the C-130 did not achieve takeoff speed and it ran clear off the end of the runway. There were many large stumps at the north end of the runway and that C-130 bellied in hitting several of the stumps. One side of the main landing gear caved in, and the aircraft tilted sharply to its right side. At that point, the propellers on the number three and four engines struck the ground. The elevated number one and two engines on the left wing continued to run.

The number one and two engines were promptly shut down and everyone inside safely evacuated the aircraft. A fire started to burn on the damaged number three and four engines on the right wing. A fire truck showed up within a few minutes. Like a slapstick Saturday morning cartoon, the firemen aimed the hose at the growing fire, but nothing came out. The fire then penetrated the ruptured right wing fuel tank and the C-130 became engulfed and fully ablaze. There was no way to contain the massive fire. A crowd gathered and we all watched as the C-130 incinerate to a charred shell and ashes. The C-130 was a total loss. After the fire simmered and stopped, I took photos of the charred remains.

The C-130 pilot claimed that a Chinook was hovering near the runway, which caused the C-130 pilot to lose control. I doubted that was really the cause of the incident from what I had just witnessed, but I didn't want to spread rumors.

Our latrine "crapper" was placed about fifty yards from where the C-130 had come to rest. There was a tin roof and flimsy frame for our outhouse that was covered by rice paper. It became the standard practice that if you were in the "crapper" and you heard a C-130 taking off you were cautioned to look through the rice paper to ensure the aircraft was not heading directly for you. This gave a whole new meaning to, "You did not want to be caught with your pants down," quite literally.

The Ides of March

We flew out to LZ English Monday morning on 13 March 1967. We flew two sorties of combat assaults after the Slicks inserted the first few waves of troops into a new LZ. For the most of our day we remained on RRF standby duty and only logged 2.1 hours. My flight time for February was radically reduced and my ambition was exceeding my reality, by far. I wanted to continue my instrument training and anticipated gaining as much flying experience as possible.

After we returned, I ate supper, read for a while, and then watched a movie. The following day, Tuesday, flying turned out to be better with 2.0 hours of flight time. The missions were routine and uneventful but I was able to log some instrument time. After departing An Khe we received a radar vector and shot a ground-controlled approach into LZ English. I had become fully confident with my instrument flying and understood that I might could have crashed for other reasons, but I had been determined it would not be due to bad weather conditions and disorientation.

It was still difficult to have an intellectual conversation with most of the people as drinking and a discussion of sex appeared to be some of their top priorities. I knew that I wanted more out of life than that. My crash on 18 December 1966 I interpreted as a wake-up call. I believed I was spared to focus on higher things. I was keenly aware that drinking and sex did not make one a better pilot. And like in Ecclesiastes, "There is a time for everything," and that certainly was not the time for me to be distracted by anything that shifted my focus from staying alive or my spiritual upward spiral in life.

Not all the men let loose, some good men remained true to their wives. When I returned home, I wanted to be honorable and demonstrate integrity in hopes of attracting a noble and faithful Christian wife of the same morals. Up to that point, my focus in life was to recover from my harsh upbringing, and to become a good pilot. Since I joined the Army in 1963 my flying had been extremely rewarding and a personal confidence building experience. I was finally developing self-esteem and knew that God was forging me into somebody of honor and accomplishment. I reflected on the gains in my life as a combat U.S. Army pilot and I was very thankful that God forged me even with intense fire.

Wednesday, 15 March 1967, was "The Ides of March." Julius Caesar was stabbed to death in the Roman Forum on this day in 44 BC. On that same day in history, we flew back out from An Khe and flew 3.8 hours of routine resupply missions. Little was happening so I took a nap on the troop seats in the back of the Chinook when we were parked and on RRF standby. On our last flight back, we sling loaded a Slick from Bong Son to An Khe.

Back at An Khe, Zudi, a stray dog that hung around our company area gave birth to six pups. There seemed to be an epidemic puppy population explosion; and, there were all too many stray dogs hanging around our area. They were playfully entertaining; but, if they were to survive, I knew we had to find new homes for some of them.

Zudi and her pups 1967.

James & Zudi's pups 1967.

A Social Experiment of Caged Rats

Our sister "B" Bravo Company had taken the responsibility for our field operations and I was fearful that it might decrease our flying missions even more. I was rapidly getting bored with the slow pace and was emotionally ready to go home.

Not much was happening on Thursday, 16 March 1967. CWO John Greene received another care package from his wife and he prepared his signature, invitation only, chili for the cookout. As the mess officer, I was expected to provide the ground beef and cheddar cheese. To add to the entertainment and festivities, there was a group of three skaters from England due to perform floor shows that night. There were two women and one guy. John invited the three skaters to his chili cook out which was a welcomed change to the routine roast beef and potatoes, and our English guests were quite a novelty. We stayed up telling stories and messing around until a little after midnight. I didn't normally stay up that late, but I did not have to fly the next morning and I really enjoyed my time with friends and guests.

Friday, 17 March 1967, was another day without any flying and it was boring. After flying with tracers, dodging artillery, and watching C-130s explode, my boredom seemed to be more frequent. I enjoyed the high-octane challenge of saving people and successfully completed missions. I frequently tried passing the time by reading and playing my guitar but even that slowed the time rather than speed it up.

I woke up on Saturday with still no scheduled flying. They were only flying one platoon at a time and ours was not on the schedule. I sighed and walked away dejectedly knowing that we might be idle for a few more days. I did get 0.8 hours on a test flight with the new maintenance officer. At the time, I did not know that it would be the first of many career maintenance test flights to come.

When our other pilots didn't fly they turned into a bunch of heathens which was probably another reason why I didn't enjoy downtime. They talked about sex disrespectfully, and drank heavily, that it was difficult to even relax in such a toxic atmosphere. I felt my anxiety increase watching what felt like a social experiment of caged rats. The carousing and debauchery continued day after day until we finally started flying again.

There was no scheduled flying on Sunday, 19 March 1967. I sat out in the sun adding to my tan and read in a somewhat more serene setting. Since I was on standby it was not convenient for me to attend religious activities. I missed attending church service and having deep philosophical conversations about the Bible and our existence as spiritual beings. On occasion I did have religious discussions with the Catholic Chaplain who stayed in our company area. He was of the Jesuit Order and a remarkably interesting person. I enjoyed our discussions and his perspective on life, history and spiritual concepts. He provided services for the Protestant soldiers anytime a Protestant

Chaplain was not available. Often, the fearful ground troops, wanted to be "Right with God" and attend a religious service before they left the security of An Khe. They were fully aware that the Grim Reaper could have a heyday if they encountered the enemy in dangerous field landing zones. Occasionally I had discussions with some of our pilots but most of them were not interested in having spiritual or deep conversations.

That evening was the live floor show at the "O" Club. The skaters who had eaten chili with us had set up and practiced and were ready to perform. Sadly, the show really wasn't very good, in my opinion, but it was still a change of pace and I had enjoyed socializing with the skaters the night before.

Monday, 20 March 1967, you guessed it, was another slow day. In routine Downing fashion I slept late, worked on my tan for a few hours and read. Our platoon was scheduled to begin flying on Wednesday. I had hoped that it would keep us busy for a change. Until then, the pilots were endlessly drinking and preoccupied and still talking about sex. At least the weather was warming up and spring was about to begin. Springtime always brings about regeneration and revitalization, which I was hoping for after winter in Vietnam had proven to be such a traumatic period for me. I was still very thankful to be alive.

I was proud of my final tour of duty in Vietnam. In that time of transition, change was in the wind as I had become "my own man." I was no longer a child to be controlled by my parents but rather a man with a purpose longing to make a difference.

After all these years later, in looking back, it was my time in the U.S. Army where I developed a spirit of overachieving. My nickname, "Tig" carried an even deeper meaning for me than just picking up more flying time. It built an unwavering faith in God, knowing that He was the One that helped me charter a new way of life from a child of trauma to a man of greater purpose. I had much to prove to myself and to the world and, God's guidance in Vietnam, afforded me that gift. By overcoming my fears and growing my love for God, I wanted to honor Him. God had made Himself known to me, as He placed His hands between me and the grasp of the Grim Reaper, on all too many occasions. Immediately after we hot refueled and shut down the aircraft on Saturday, 28 January 1967, a group of medical personnel troops came running over to our aircraft. As fate would have it, we had, unknowingly, arrived in a dangerous forward area at the time that an urgent life-saving medical evacuation (MEDEVAC) rescue mission was desperately needed. We were then briefed that a patrol of American ground troops had been ambushed and had suffered fragmentation wounds at a site near Happy Valley. It was reported that there was one KIA and seven wounded in action (WIA) at that location. There was no area large enough there for a rescue helicopter to land. Only the Chinooks in our division had rescue hoists installed. Therefore, only our CH-47 aircraft was available at the scene with the necessary rescue hoist equipment. The brave Major McHaney willingly accepted the mission. The major said to me, "Well 'Tig' we have a hot one." He knew that he could count on me, in the most dangerous circumstances, especially under pressure. I respected and trusted him enough to follow him into the deepest valley.

Springtime in An Khe and Hong Kong

Winter had finally passed, Tuesday, 21 March 1967, marked the Spring Equinox and the 1st Cavalry Division "Spring Campaign" had already been set in motion. It was time for us to employ our own deadly Two Step Viper. As springtime arrived there appeared to be more increasing activity and determination to continue, with renewed vigor, our own campaign against the enemy. The "search and destroy" mission strategy was about to be intensified against the enemy for what they had done at LZ Bird during the Christmas truce. The VC and NVA appeared to be immune to their own rotting cattle and causalities of war as they were equally determined to resist our advances. They were feeding the python, to strengthen its ability to suffocate and kill its prey, even more swiftly.

> *That spring, the time when kings usually go off to war, Joab led the army out and ravaged the Ammonites.*
>
> *-1 Chronicles 20:1*

Like Joab leading the army, LT Duff and I headed out to LZ English. We waited at Two Bits Airfield at Bong Son until the fog lifted to be cleared for the remaining flight into LZ English. We flew 2.9 hours of routine sorties that day. That night we stayed over in Qui Nhon. The spring weather was volatile with high winds. The earth heated during the day which produced daily low clouds with heavy fog in the mornings that restricted visibility.

A UH-1B Gunship Exploded in the Air

There was more combat activity on Wednesday, 22 March 1967, as we sought to "seek and destroy" the enemy forces. Additionally, there was more combat movement in the area around LZ English than I had witnessed in many weeks. The whole valley north of LZ English was being constantly pounded by field artillery fire, by Chinook "Guns-A-Go-Go", and by tactical air command jet strikes. Smoke from many villages drifted in over LZ English. Our first sortie was to extract artillery pieces from LZ Sandra and deliver them to LZ English, which was code named "Red Leg". The next sortie was a "Blue Leg" extraction of troops from LZs east of LZ Santana. The VC were hastily moving north, and we were re-positioning our artillery and our troops to sustain our engagement with them.

At about 1710 hours, LT Duff and I witnessed a UH-1B gunship explode in the air and fall to the earth about a mile or so west of our position. That sight made me feel sick. Two Step Vipers were infiltrating from every direction and the Grim Reaper was having a heyday. It was difficult for me to see that tragedy unfolding as I prayed for the lost aircrew members and for us to have the strength to accomplish our own daring missions that might lie ahead. The UH-1B had been hovering there about 100 feet above the ground. We also noticed that artillery rounds were impacting in that area especially all around the aircraft. Our immediate assumption was that the aircraft was hit by friendly artillery fire. Within a few seconds the remains of the shattered helicopter furiously burned as thick black smoke billowed from that location among the palm trees. The hanging Two

Step Vipers had lunged and pierced another aircraft and crew in the blink of an eye. It happened so fast that the crew never would have known what had even hit them. Within seconds we broadcasted a blanket radio advisory on the emergency UHF channel. A minute or two later we saw another UH-1 arrive and hover over the crash site in anticipation of saving lives. I knew immediately that there was no chance of survivors as, I'm sure, the crew in that UH-1 quickly realized. In the pit of my stomach, I felt a sensation of bereavement and dejection as it was another senseless loss of an aircraft and crew. Two Step Vipers were spring-loaded and viciously anticipating new prey.

In the springtime, new life and new growth is expected, however, in this combat situation, in a flash, we witnessed death and the loss of lives of these brave American air crewmen. I suppressed my deep emotions to clear my mind and focus on the present mission. It immediately reminded me of the importance of knowing where artillery was firing from and where it would be impacting. This was warfare, and to survive it would require us to outsmart and outmaneuver the deadly VC Viper. I became hyper-vigilant in that moment, fully aware that not maintaining situational awareness could cost me my life and the lives of my crew. With much relief we survived "Red Leg" and "Blue Leg" missions to return unscathed, physically, back to our LZ. As I exited the Chinook my feelings of bereavement for the loss of the U.S. Army crew flooded forward and I was smitten with the continuation of feelings of dejection and bereavement. Combat losses were becoming all too routine.

Passing Time Between Sorties

At times between sorties, I liked to talk with some of the ground troops about life in the jungle. They really appreciated the helicopters supplying them with ammunition, medical supplies, beer, food, and other supplies. The prized choices of "C" rations were peaches and pound cake. The more experienced troops liked to make a stew out of several different cans of "C" rations. Personally, I liked the "pecan cake rolls" and the "beans with franks" because that meal could be eaten cold.

The M-60 ground troop gunners complained about having to lug the heavy guns through the jungle. Through our conversations I tried to encourage the ground troops; I always believed that they were the true heroes of the Vietnam War. We flew 5.3 hours that spring day.

We spent another night at Qui Nhon on Thursday, 23 March 1967. It was a light flying day as we flew one combat assault and flew a heavy welder back to An Khe. We logged 2.4 hours. It felt good to be back to my current home base to get a shower and catch up. I had not received much mail lately, but it always gave me hope and anticipation to check. That evening we enjoyed another social event of CWO John Greene's, signature chili. As usual, I supplied the ground beef and the cheddar cheese. The chili was unusually hot and spicy, but it was a satisfying reminder that we were grateful to be alive to appreciate the small things in life. After eating that hot "afterburner level" chili, we joked the next morning; "You'll need to crap in the creek to keep from setting the woods on fire." In reality, the latrine became a revolving door all night and well into the next morning.

Proud of our Concrete Patio

Our building program progressed as we added a concrete patio. Beginning with the arrival of "*The Second Team*", there had been much building progress accomplished since I arrived in Vietnam in August of 1966. In addition to helping on our building projects I began counting down the days until I left for home. That day I had 72 more to go. I shifted my plans to focus on starting a new life back home and invested some time exploring civilian flying jobs that might be available back in the United States of America.

On Friday, 24 March 1967, to ease my mind I played my guitar for a while and allowed my mind to wander aimlessly as I sang a few of my favorite songs. I enjoyed working together with a team and didn't want to be alone, so I walked over and pitched in and helped work on the concrete patio; I hoped that my contribution would make life in Vietnam more comfortable for the incoming replacements, even though I only had 72 days left to use it. I liked the thought of leaving things better than when I had arrived as they would face the same agony of war that I did. Sometimes something as simple as a concrete slab and wooden walls were enough to make life a little easier. The manual labor was cleansing and it shifted my focus for the day which felt good. I was glad that I was part of something constructive.

That same day I had heard that I would be going on a five-day "rest and recuperating" (R&R) trip to Hong Kong at the end of the next month. There had been an opening in the quota and I was lucky enough to be selected. By the time I flew another month and went on R&R to Hong Kong, I would be returning as a "short timer". With excitement at the thought of an R&R in Hong Kong, I could hardly go to sleep. I felt both energized and optimistic as I started looking forward to the closing weeks of my tour of duty. I had a scheduled flight to Hammond Field the next day so it was a relief to finally fall asleep on a happy note.

On Saturday, 25 March 1967, we flew to Qui Nhon, to LZ English, then back to Hammond Field. For the remainder of the time, we sat on

RRF standby at Hammond Field until 1600 hours. After our shift we headed back to An Khe. That evening we poured the first section of concrete on our patio. Our company area was shaping up nicely and we were all very proud of our construction projects.

Cobra Coiled Around the Scorpion

I flew out to LZ English on the next day and we remained overnight at Qui Nhon to keep the aircraft dispersed. If I was lucky, I would be away two nights and three days. I was thankful that everything was going so well. I had learned a great deal about aviation, helicopter warfare, and about myself since I first arrived in Vietnam. I was becoming a stronger person at that time and evolving into a more independent individual. I hoped the good Lord would not give up on me. I started asking around and reading as much as I could looking forward to the Hong Kong R&R. One of the guys told me that Hong Kong was a good place to have civilian clothes tailor made. I liked the thought of a custom fitted suit, and hoped that I could arrange a fitting during the few days on my R&R.

On Sunday we participated with other Chinooks in an "Artillery Raid" which was a newly developed tactic. We were to airlift a 105 Howitzer battery or Scorpion onto a hilltop near a VC infested area. The purpose of that "Artillery Raid" was to catch "Charlie" by surprise. The intent of that mission was to quickly insert an artillery fire base of 15 Howitzers onto a selected LZ hilltop.

That LZ had not been previously occupied by either us or the NVA. Various RECON techniques confirmed that "Charlie" was not within immediate striking distance to attack that hilltop LZ. From that hilltop, our artillery fire could easily reach many of the locations where the enemy was hiding.

With a helicopter gunship escort, the first Chinook in the raid was to land and insert a security force and the gun crews on the ground first. As the first Chinook departed the LZ, the remaining Chinooks would drop off the "Scorpions" at about one-minute intervals. After the final Chinook departed the area, the first artillery piece was ready to commence firing at nearby suspected VC locations.

There was one odd incident that took place during that artillery raid. In the hook up area, a large cobra snake had become frightened, took refuge, and coiled around a structural member of one of the artillery pieces, (Code named Scorpion). During the cargo hook up process, the crew chief reported to the pilots, "Sir, a cobra has just coiled itself around the Scorpion." Thus, the snake made a terrifying air journey to the LZ. On final approach into the LZ one of the pilots called the ground controller, Black Hat, and said, "Beware there is a cobra on the Scorpion." The ground controller keyed the FM radio and asked, "What is a cobra"? The pilot replied, "It is a very poisonous snake about eight feet long." In retrospect, it was a funny story, but at that moment there was no time for laughter, it required extreme caution.

Immediately after the sling load was released the frightened cobra was dispatched by the ground troops. The story of that Vietnam incident was told many times over always followed by laughs and cheers and comical hollering. After dropping off the Scorpion we flew more routine resupply missions logging 6.0 hours that day.

Crying Bird Missions

We flew more resupply missions on Monday, 27 March 1967. That evening we saw an outstanding floor show with an international cast of a Frenchman from Paris, an American guy from California, and a young woman from Tokyo. The woman had a beautiful voice, and the others were entertaining enough, too. I really enjoyed the down time and letting my mind be filled with creativity and entertainment while watching the show.

On Tuesday we went on a Chinook scrounging mission for our building projects. We were able to obtain twenty bags of concrete from the U.S. Air Force at Qui Nhon. We logged only 1.0 hours. That evening I watched the movie "*The Ten Commandments*" starring Charleston Heston. It ended the same way as it did as the first time I saw it in high school and I enjoyed it equally as much. It reminded me of my personal covenant with God and God's covenant with His people. I fully understood the importance of not just knowing, but also following the Gospel. I felt at peace knowing that I was following the Gospel to the best of my ability, even in times of war, and in return God was guiding my personal path through Providence.

On Wednesday, 29 March 1967, we returned to LZ English. We flew two, 2-Chlorobenzalmalononitrile (CS) gas missions. These were referred to as "Crying Bird" missions. In simple terms, we were flying tear gas missions (CS) and dropping it on the enemy. To accomplish this, we used the same roller rack as the napalm drop missions. Thus, we flew more "B-47 bomber" missions. That day our "Crying Bird" missions were deemed a success and we encountered no problems in the delivery.

A few days later other Chinook crews were dropping CS gas on the west side of LZ English, and their "Crying Bird" drop site happened to be up wind. About an hour later after dropping the CS, a prevailing wind caused the tear gas to drift over LZ English and all of our eyes started burning and turned fiery red. About the same time a more serious CS gas incident occurred when one of my CWO friends was onboard another aircraft. One of the fifty-five-gallon CS gas drums ruptured before it exited the cargo bay. As all Chinook pilots knew, because of the "Bernoulli Effect", air was sucked forward and exited out the pilots' windows and the concentrated CS gas permeated the entire aircraft and disabled the whole aircraft crew.

Thankfully, my friend, without hesitation, grabbed a gas mask in the cockpit and managed to put it on before becoming debilitated. With his eyes and skin burning he was able to make an emergency harrowing landing at LZ English to evacuate the crew and provide them much needed relief. The immediate response was to take care of the crew but the helicopter would also need some attention to get that Chinook flying again. With gas masks on, maintenance personnel removed the CS gas canisters and all the insulation fabric that was installed in the cockpit and cargo areas. The inside of the aircraft was then thoroughly washed down. The CS gas had permeated the aircraft so densely that it could not be entered by unprotected crew members for months. A crew, all wearing gas masks, flew the aircraft back to An Khe. The aircraft was parked distinctly away from the other aircraft on the "Green line." Eventually that aircraft was used to cannibalize parts until the CS gas would finally dissipate, over time. I'm not sure if that Chinook ever took flight again because it was still parked at An Khe when I left Vietnam over two months later.

March's End and April's Beginning

Thursday, 30 March 1967, began with an artillery support mission at Hammond Field. As we hooked up to the "Scorpion" 105 Howitzer with a piggyback load of 50 rounds, the number one engine bleed band started popping and the number one torque indicator needle started spinning. The engine sounded as though it was coming apart. We aborted the hookup and the entire mission until the engine could be repaired. That normally required the change of the engine fuel control and the adjustment of the engine bleed band actuator. That evening I was assigned the task of Assistant Officer of the Day (AOD). I was awake throughout the entire night listening to the communication radios for emergencies and "minding the fort." I only logged 0.5 hours.

The missions for the month of March ended on a Friday. That afternoon we flew out to LZ English flying a total of 3.3 hours. We stayed the night at Qui Nhon, and to our surprise that evening, we enjoyed an unexpected fine lobster dinner at the "O" Club.

Saturday, 1 April 1967 (April Fool's Day), was a good flying day as we logged 7.8 hours despite minor maintenance problems on our aircraft (902). I hauled loads for several different units ending the day in Qui Nhon, with a splitting headache from eye strain. I curled up in pain and went to sleep in the back of the aircraft.

Taking on Enemy Ground Fire

I experienced another "first", on Sunday. At 0700 hours two small-arms rounds hit our aircraft as we were sling loading a bulldozer track and blade into an LZ just east of LZ English. We were informed that the area was secure and not to expect any enemy ground fire. That certainly wasn't the case because I heard close proximity automatic gun fire over the sound of the aircraft. I keyed the intercom and asked our gunners, "What are you firing at?" The response was, "It's not us sir, that is incoming." Since we could not detect any tracer fire, we suspected that it was probably coming from an enemy AK-47 automatic rifle. We had no idea where the fire was coming from. A sniper was probably well concealed in a hole that could not have been far away.

After dropping off the load we returned to LZ English to formally inspect the aircraft for damage. One round had struck the right aft wheel well. Another round had entered the bottom of the aircraft and then exited through the internal cargo bay floor not far from the cargo hook door. The trajectory of the round continued through the handle of the crew chief's broom that was placed behind the left seats webbing. The projectile then exited through the left fuselage skin of the aircraft.

A scan of the instrument panel did not detect any problem with any of the aircraft systems. Apparently, nothing vital to the aircraft operation was penetrated and there were no visible hydraulic leaks. When the shots were fired the crew chief was positioned face down on the cargo floor and his legs spread eagle as he observed the external load. At the time the crew chief was not wearing his flack vest. I knew this lack of standard procedure could easily have proven deadly.

I always insisted that the crew wear their flack vests while we were flying so the fact that he wasn't, was also concerning. Luckily for him the round missed his body, but only by one or two feet, just barely out of reach of that Two Step Viper. That was a big wake-up call and spiritual encounter for that crew chief. Since that incident, he was always seen wearing his flack vest on every flight that followed.

That was another happenstance in war where I felt that we were spared from the Grim Reaper's playful schemes. I was thankful and gave praise to God, that no one died on my watch, that day. That incident was the only time in Vietnam, that an aircraft that I was flying, was ever hit by enemy fire. Many others had not been so fortunate.

After checking out the aircraft for further damage we continued flying missions. We flew two artillery lifts and other resupply sorties logging a total of 8.3 hours. On the last leg of the day we sling loaded a damaged UH-1D back to An Khe and stayed the night there. It was a long tiring day both physically and emotionally.

Resupplying, Mortar Attacks, and Building Projects

After the long day before, I was off on Monday, 3 April 1967. I slept late and I tried to stay busy finding things to do with an increasing awareness that I was thinking more and more about what I would do when I went home. My plans for after the U.S. Army were consuming my thoughts and were becoming pervasive.

Other than the flying dangerous missions, I had become thoroughly bored here. Maybe it was because I had accomplished in myself that which I had set out to do. I felt confident and skilled as a pilot, I risked my life for my country, and I had contributed to the Vietnam War effort. I was "my own man" and simply ready for more out of life than flying in this war.

I flew 3.0 hours on Tuesday. We flew a few local resupply sorties to the top of Hon Cong Mountain, which was located on the west side of Camp Radcliffe at An Khe. Powerful communication radio towers and radio equipment had been installed on the top of the flat mountain which made a significant difference when sending and receiving military communications all over Viet Nam and receiving TV and radio broadcast from Saigon. Later I prepared my field gear, hoping to return to field operations the next day.

On Wednesday, 5 April 1967, the temperature was rapidly heating up. We made one trip to LZ English and remained on standby. That evening we returned to An Khe. I helped pour more concrete on our patio. It felt good to help and stay occupied. Building and pouring concrete was routinely comforting in many ways and at least I didn't have to worry about tear gas or cobras coiled on a Scorpion.

Our mission on Thursday was to ride out to LZ English and recover a Chinook that was left there due to maintenance problems. I ended up only flying 0.9 hours. Upon returning to An Khe I helped pour more concrete. We seemed to be making progress with our "C" Charlie Company building program.

On Friday, 7 April 1967, we were ordered to go to "the field" for two days or so. We would be based at Hammond Field which had turned into a dust bowl in the hot dry weather. Dust posed a big problem making it necessary to take additional steps and precautions. The aircraft parking and our cargo hook up areas were heavily sprayed down with "Pinta Prime" which was an asphalt and oil-based solution that kept the dust from billowing while aircraft were hovering to hook up sling loads. Like being in fog, thick dust could also create an instrument flight rule (IFR) condition in the event that we could not see the ground. Hovering in that condition could quickly become dangerous and even lethal with disorientation. We flew 7.3 hours that warm day.

About that time, the 1st Cavalry Division was starting a big move up north into the Duc Pho area as we forced the enemy to flee northward. The Marines at Duc Pho were pulling out and we airlifted some of our units to establish a forward 1st Cavalry Division base as an enemy blocking position. It was a warm and quiet night at Hammond Field.

On Saturday, 8 April 1967, we were busy moving more troops and equipment north to Duc Pho. Everything was going well until the housing on the number one engine start motor, cracked. We were down for a couple of hours awaiting a part. That evening we flew back to An Khe logging 5.2 hours.

I was sleeping soundly a little after midnight on Sunday, 9 April 1967, when I was abruptly awakened by the sound of incoming mortar fire on the "golf course." Several aircraft on the "golf course" had been hit. Chinook (108), the last aircraft that I had flown, was punctured by

1,200 fragments of exploding mortar shrapnel. I looked up and thanked the Lord that I had not been sleeping inside the aircraft. Our standby gunships and aerial rocket artillery quickly responded and fired into the enemy mortar positions. It must have forced them to retreat because the mortars went immediately silent. I went back to bed a little shaken from the mortar attack that was reminiscent of the attack when I had been first assigned to "A" Alpha Company of the 229th AHB at the south end of the "golf course".

Around sunrise I was awakened for a mission back out to LZ English. After we flew for about six hours, a seal on the aft transmission started leaking. We flew back to An Khe after logging 6.7 hours. I had mixed emotions as my good friend Web Manual had completed his tour of duty and was headed back home the next day. I had learned much from him and developed a brotherly bond. I hated to see him leave but I was happy that he was going back to his home in Tampa, Florida. I hoped to see him there in June.

I was off on Monday, 10 April 1967. I spent a good part of the day helping pour concrete and painting on our company building project performing the duties of a construction worker. Since the recent mortar attack, we had been dispersing our aircraft in the evening into a grassy area that we called the "Green Line." The crew chief and I flew one of the Chinooks to the "Green Line." Dispersing an aircraft to the "Green Line" was the only time that one pilot could fly a Chinook solo in Vietnam. I was picked up by one of our Jeep drivers and logged 0.3 hours in my journal when I arrived back at camp.

Our crew flew aircraft (118) to LZ English early the next morning. Our missions on Wednesday, 12 April 1967, were to fly routine loads from LZ English to our forward base at Duc Pho. The aircraft developed a slow leak from the aft swash plate, so we needed to fly the aircraft back to An Khe the next day. We logged 5.0 hours of flight time. We flew our "sick bird" back to An Khe early Thursday, 13 April 1967. I spent most of the rest of the day lending a hand on the building projects in progress.

On Monday, 17 April 1967, we finished installing the roof on one of our bachelor officer's quarters. The BOQ was just about finished and looking good. I received a few letters from home which was refreshing especially since it had been quite some time since I received any mail. Everything seemed to be going fine back home and I treasured every comforting word of encouragement. Friday, 14 April 1967, was another exciting flying day flying two combat assaults. One sortie was into LZ Hancock and the other was into LZ Hatch. That reminded me of the days that I was flying Slicks with "A" Alpha Company of the 229th AHB. One never knew what to expect when assaulting a new LZ. The Chinook was a much bigger target than the UH-1Ds. We logged 8.8 hours of combat assault flying time.

There was nothing like starting your day with an inflight emergency in Vietnam. On Saturday, 15 April 1967, we left Hammond Field and headed out on an artillery lift. I smelled smoke but did not pay much attention to it. As we broke ground, I noticed the number two engine rectifier load meter was reading zero. The number one engine rectifier load meter was reading abnormally high, and it was fluctuating. By then the flight engineer reported that smoke was billowing out of the main battery compartment on the right side of the aircraft. We declared an emergency and landed at Two Bits Field at Bong Son, just in time. The battery had been overheating and was about to burst into flames. We immediately shut down the aircraft and let the battery cool down. This had become a serious electrical malfunction to repair. The aircraft battery and the number two engine rectifier were changed. Luckily, none of the electrical wiring ended up being damaged. We flew back to An Khe logging 6.5 hours despite the electrical malfunction we had encountered. I was off on Sunday and slept late. Later in the day after I had been up and about, I painted two patio tables and then I read for a while. I went over to the PX area and bought a shirt, more camera film, and items for my upcoming R&R to Hong Kong. I thought it would be good for me to be out of Vietnam for a while. I was grateful for the opportunity and happy to be exploring more, abroad. That evening we were rather relaxed and made a casual social event out of cooking a pot of chili.

On Monday, 17 April 1967, I painted all day long on a mission to complete the new building. As we were painting a variety of different people kept dropping by our company area to admire our building project. We were the most happening thing in camp and were all proud of what we had accomplished. I had many painting jobs as an enterprising teenager and not only enjoyed it as a monotonous escape, but I also was skilled at it. The compliments and appreciation went a long way, and I felt good leaving something better for the next team. Late in the evening I relocated a Chinook to the "Green Line" which only logged 0.3 hours.

My Friend, Bob Bradley

It was in January of 1964 at the church in Ozark, Alabama, when I first met 1st LT Robert Neil "Bob" Bradley and his wife, Virginia. I had just arrived at Fort Rucker from Fort Wolters, Texas, after completing my primary helicopter training. Bob was a rated U.S. Army Aviator and had instructed some of the pilot ground school courses at Fort Rucker. Like a magnet, we were drawn to each other not only through aviation, but also through our values. Immediately we became friends. He was farther along in his U.S. Army flying career and I looked up to him as a mentor and as an example of what I, too, wanted to become.

The Bradley family often invited me into their home on base housing. At that time, they only had their daughter, Robin, who was born while I was at Fort Wolters. As I remember, she was born about the time President John Kennedy was shot in Dallas. After I completed my advanced helicopter training at Fort Rucker in June of 1964, Bob and I served together in Korea a few months later. On Tuesday, 1 September 1964, I saw 1st LT Bob Bradley for the first time in Korea. As a commissioned officer Bob was assigned for a tour of "ground duty" north of the Imjin River at Camp Young in the Spoonbill area. That 1st Cavalry Division Camp was located not far from the dangerous Demilitarized Zone (DMZ). Should the North Koreans launch an attack from the north his company would be in the first line of defense against the invasion. Since this was not a flying assignment for him, I made a special effort to ensure that Bob logged four hours of flying time each month for him to collect his flight pay. I was, then, in a position to help repay a little of his kindness to me.

Whenever we had the opportunity, Bob Bradley and I attended chapel together. About that timeframe I heard that a small group of Christians, from our church, traveled to our headquarters at Camp Howze, from Seoul every Sunday. LT Duggar and a few others made the twenty-mile bus trip to meet with the church group frequently in the Camp Howze Chapel. They, too, were spiritually guided and dedicated Christians.

On 28 June 1965, my friend, 1st LT Bradley, came down to Stanton Field to take his annual written exam. After my day had ended flying General Exton, I returned to Stanton Field (A112) and noticed that Bob

Bradley was there. It was a welcomed surprise. We ate dinner together, talked and then flew back to Camp Young. Bob was at the controls of my OH-23 Raven as we flew back as the sun had set and just before dark. According to the Armistice Agreement, helicopter operations were prohibited across the Imjin River after dark so we had made it just in time. Both of us had been homesick and our friendship felt more like we were brothers. We got together and connected every chance we could, respecting one another as men of faith who were trying to do what's right.

After I returned from Korea, my old friend, Captain John Chutter, General Exton's Aide-de-Camp, invited me to visit his quarters at Fort Benning, Georgia. I left Fort Rucker at 0700 hours and drove to his home. It was good talking about General Exton and our exploits in Korea. I explained to him that I had been in CH-47 training and that I would soon leave for Vietnam. I had a profound respect for Captain Chutter. He was a straight arrow and I loved him like an older brother. On the same trip to Fort Benning, Georgia, I was able to visit my good friend and my brother in Christ, Bob Bradley.

Captain Bob Bradley and his wife, Virginia, had also been stationed at Fort Benning. I vividly recall Bob holding his newly born second daughter, Dawn. He was beaming with pride; he and Virginia were such a positive example of what I had hoped to experience someday in a family of my own. Bob had been promoted to the rank of Captain and was set to receive orders for Vietnam. As far as I know, that was the last time that I ever saw Bob Bradley.

My Saddest Day in Vietnam

On the night of Monday, 17 April 1967, I heard the sad news that my dear friend, Captain Bob Bradley, was killed on, 21 March 1967, nearly a month prior. The loss of Bob emotionally impacted and devastated me more than any loss I had suffered in my life. It was one of the saddest days in my life. I felt as though I had lost a close family member. He was one of the finest gentlemen and Christian friends that I had ever met. I was overcome with deep mournful grief that day. Years later I found this entry describing the deadly event that took his life.

> *On March 21, 1967, this aircraft [UH-1D Tail number 64-13645] from the 498th Medical Company (Air Ambulance) was on a rescue and recovery mission for medical evacuation in Long An Province (III Corps). While hovering at 100 feet over the pick-up zone, the helicopter was hit by a single round of small arms (AK-47) fire which entered the cabin area and caused the aircraft to crash. The pilot, Captain Robert N. Bradley, and a crewman, SSGT Tennis C. Ferrell, suffered fatal injuries in the crash. Two other crewmen were injured. The crash destroyed the helicopter.*
>
> *-Vietnam Helicopter Pilot's Association*

On the first day of spring, that March day, the world suffered a great loss as Bob Bradley's death was one of the single most tragic events that I encountered during my tour in Vietnam. My crash on, 18 December 1966, and the death of my friend, Bob Bradley, forever changed me. The life of Bob Bradley was always one of inspiration and joy. He was happily married with two small children, and he was an excellent pilot. He was a good Christian without any hypocrisy. He lived the life that I had hoped for, and I looked to model my future family after his, someday. I simply closed my eyes and heard the lyrics to a church hymn that Bob and I had sung together many months before his tragic death. The words from this 1868 spiritual hymn, breathed comfort in a time of deep despair. I knew someday I would most certainly see him again in the sweet by and by.

In the Sweet By and By
There's a land that is fairer than day,
And by faith we can see it afar;
For the Father waits over the way
To prepare us a dwelling place there.

Refrain:
In the sweet by and by,
We shall meet on that beautiful shore;
In the sweet by and by,
We shall meet on that beautiful shore.

We shall sing on that beautiful shore
The melodious songs of the blessed;
And our spirits shall sorrow no more,
Not a sigh for the blessing of rest.

To our bountiful Father above,
We will offer our tribute of praise
For the glorious gift of His love
And the blessings that hallow our days.
-Sanford F. Bennet

Now as an older man I still ask God the question, "Why wasn't I taken in his place"? He was good, he was kind, he loved God and he loved his family. His faith and obedience made him equally deserving to remain alive, even, if not more so, because he had a family of his own that needed him. For much of my life I have pondered the reason why Bob Bradley's name had to be engraved in granite on the Vietnam Memorial Wall in Washington, DC, instead of my own. After much pondering and soul searching, I realized the answer to my own question, Bob was ready to be taken, and I was not. God had prepared his dwelling place and was ready to meet him on that beautiful shore. It was God's will, not mine. To me it is still a great mystery. It brought me great comfort to know, that Captain Bob Bradley, would experience the earthly sorrow of war, no more, but instead experience the glorious gift of God's love. He was a Christ-like example for me to follow. I believed that God had preserved my life because I still had much to learn and carry out. After his tragic death, I lived to honor his memory in every aspect of my life. For a time, my life was intertwined with Bob Bradley in Alabama, Korea and finally in Vietnam, and for that I will always be grateful. To this day, not many days pass between my thoughts of Bob Bradley and the impact that he made on my life.

In the "Great Beyond" I would be honored to be his copilot.

Hong Kong Bound

Tuesday, 18 April 1967, was an exercise of futility. We tried to take supplies to the top of Hon Cong Mountain on the west side of Camp Radcliffe at An Khe. However, the uplifted warm damp air kept the top of the mountain obscured by thick clouds and there was not enough visibility to land. We finally gave up on the mission and only flew 1.2 hours.

That day was another company milestone. The new BOQ buildings had just been completed and our old tents were struck and removed from sight. It felt good to get rid of the old to replace it with something much more substantial. In the same way, it was the beginning of another cycle in the mystery of life. I felt sorrow and became more self-aware of my own changing goals and ambitions.

Since I joined the U.S. Army in 1963 my prime motivation had been to overcome the past struggle with my parents at home and to earn my own place in the world. My flight training, my tour in Korea as the General's pilot, my becoming a flight instructor at Fort Rucker, Alabama, my Chinook crash, the loss of a good friend, and all the experiences during my tour of duty in Vietnam, had inspired me to always be thankful and to continue to seek a higher path.

Wednesday, 19 April 1967 morning - I helped paint the final brushstrokes on another new BOQ building. That afternoon the weather was somewhat clear and we flew the Hon Cong Mountain resupply mission. On the last sortie 7,000 pounds of concrete blocks were loaded internally into the cargo bay. On final approach to the pinnacle, the transmission low oil pressure light illuminated. It turned out that a failed pressure transducer was the problem. Although everything fared well, that still made my heart pound. I was fully aware of my mortality during those 1.3 flying hours, and was thankful to God once again.

With great anticipation on Thursday, 20 April 1967, I put on a khaki uniform and was driven to the An Khe airfield. I began my trek to my R&R in Hong Kong, China. I caught a hop on a C-130 Hercules to Cam Rahn Bay. I spent the night at the R&R Center while the weather was overbearingly hot.

On Friday morning I crossed paths with Captain Bill Harding. He was a lieutenant at the 3rd Brigade. He had been the 3rd Brigade's Aviation Unit's Commander in Korea when I first met him. LT Harding and I were the only assigned pilots in that small unit while on my first assignment in Korea. I took a liking to him rather quickly because he was always at ease and just enjoyable to be around.

Captain Harding was in a particularly good mood because he was on his way home to the United States of America. It was good seeing him and reflecting back on the good times we enjoyed together while in Korea. That afternoon we boarded an ancient propeller driven DC-6 for a three-hour flight to Hong Kong. The last DC-6 was built in 1958. The DC-6 cruised at 211 knots. Since I was a pilot, the flight crew invited me to spend some time in the cockpit. They were older pilots and had thousands of flying hours. While up in the cockpit they were admiring my award ribbons and especially my Distinguished Flying Cross. I enjoyed their company and was honored by their kindness; it was a remarkably interesting visit with the pilots. They were interested in how the war was going and I was able to fill them in on the war efforts. I often wondered if I wanted to become an airline pilot someday too.

After lunch, a very attractive blond flight attendant arrived at my row to serve coffee. Just as she leaned over to pour a cup of coffee to the soldier sitting in the seat next to me, someone passed by in the aisle and accidentally bumped her. It jolted her just enough that she accidentally poured hot coffee on my left thigh. It was scalding hot and it made me wince. Later I noticed that my thigh was red but thank goodness it was not blistered. I thought to myself, "Of course, I meet a pretty blond flight attendant, and within minutes, I already got burned. That was par for my love life."

Arriving in Hong Kong

After landing in Hong Kong, we were met by busses and taken to a military welcome center. A U.S. Army captain dressed in civilian clothes provided a general briefing on how we were expected to conduct ourselves while in Hong Kong. We were cautioned, yet again, about the "Ugly American" image. Warnings also included places that were strictly off limits for us to go. As a perk for winning the R&R selection, the military paid for the flight to Hong Kong and for the hotel room. After that first general briefing, the females in our group were invited to wait in the busses.

Now separated from the ladies, we received a briefing on the "wiles of evil women" who were after the soldier's money. We were warned about contacting social diseases and what medical facilities to call if anyone became ill or was injured. After the briefing we boarded the busses and were dropped off at our respective hotels.

My room was in the President Hotel. After living in the jungle, my new quarters were plush and luxurious. I enjoyed the luxury of having a bathtub and hot running water. I walked around the area near the hotel and enjoyed the simplest things that I took for granted prior to living in war conditions. The people appeared sophisticated and constantly in a hurry. The young women were professionally dressed, trendy and nice looking. Taking a closer look, I soon realized that anything was available for a price. Chinese people, seemingly, would eat anything. It took a while to get used to the traffic because they drove on the opposite side of the road compared to the United States. While getting accustomed to this new environment I focused on some of the things I wanted to accomplish on my R&R. I located a nearby camera shop and dropped off my camera to get it repaired so that I could capture this new adventure in Hong Kong. The local camera repair technician informed me that I could pick it up the next day.

My focus on Sunday, 22 April 1967, was to attend my fitting for tailor made custom suits. The military had arranged a contract concession for the soldiers, to buy suits, while on our short R&R. The pace of the fitting was fast, I ordered $280 worth of suits including a tuxedo and a white dinner jacket. I thought it was novel and would be cool to return to St. Petersburg, Florida, owning my own tailored made suits and tuxedo. I wanted clothes to match my new image. I picked out the material and was measured. As a courtesy, they provided me with a loaner suit that I could wear while in the city. Since I had to wear civilian clothes, I took advantage of "dressing to the nines" as I toured Hong Kong with one of my enlisted friends. While out driving, as we reached high atop a hill, I looked to the right and saw the Hong Kong airport runway. It seemed to be the perfect spot to pull over and take a picture, so I posed in my best "James Bond" fashion.

The shop worked tirelessly through the night as part of the process for a quick turnaround. The next day I arrived for a fitting, final alterations and returning my loaner suit. The following morning the final alterations were complete and my custom tailor-made suits were packed in shipping containers designed for longer international shipping. Nearby, there was a military Army Post Office (APO) and I successfully shipped my new suits back home to Florida.

Overlooking Hong Kong Airport.

Shopping, Sightseeing and Touring

Daily, several of us would attend floors shows, night clubs, the movies, or turn into tourists participating in the sights and local tours of Hong Kong. I even saw the movie, "*Cheyenne Autumn*" with Richard Widmark, Carol Baker, and James Stewart. On one tour we ate dinner in an authentic Chinese restaurant and enjoyed the smells and tastes of foods and customary interactions I had never experienced before. After dinner I ran into a shopping area and purchased some watches and gifts for my family back home.

While browsing in the large shopping plaza, a beautiful string of cultured pearls caught my eye, they were simple, yet I was drawn to them. For some reason, I felt compelled to purchase that string of pearls. I did not have any girl in mind, but I thought to myself that it would be a perfect gift to wear with a white wedding dress, someday, if I ever found a girl to marry. And I just happened to have purchased a tux that would complete a future wedding day. I may have been caught in the moment as I was wishing to find a good wife when I returned home. I moved on my instincts that day and purchased that brilliant strand of pearls. The saleslady packaged them up in a black velvet box, wrapped tissue paper around it and placed it in a fancy black shopping bag. I had the pearls, now I just needed the girl.

Just around the corner I found a coin shop that stocked Trade Dollars. Locating a coin shop was on my list of things to find while on R&R and the timing was impeccable. In the shop I bought two coins for my friend and mentor, Lano Mosley. I wanted Mr. Mosley to know that it was because of his mentorship in aviation, that I was so deeply motivated and inspired to become a pilot. Among his many interests, Mr. Mosley was a coin collector. I had heard him once mention that he did not have a Trade Dollar in his collection, and they were only available in Hong Kong. I wanted to surprise him with the coins as a token of my appreciation for all that he had done for me.

The tour group took another sightseeing tour on Sunday and ate lunch on a floating restaurant while we were out. It happened to be the same restaurant that was shown in the movie, "*The World of Suzie Wong*" with William Holden and Nancy Kwan. I was in full tourist mode and enjoying the sights, sounds, and new experiences. The corn-fish soup at the floating restaurant was delicious and the experience was surreal.

Later that night we decided to eat dinner at the hotel restaurant since we had been out and about all day. While waiting to be seated I scanned the room and noticed a young American who was obviously sitting alone. I walked over to his table and started a conversation. He invited us to join him. As we sat there, I learned that he was a U.S. Navy A-4 pilot that was assigned to an aircraft carrier. He was about halfway through his tour of duty and was anxious to return home and see his wife. We enjoyed a good time swapping war stories while we were enjoying a meal exceptionally better than any mess hall. It was pleasant being away from combat.

I noticed that the Chinese entertainer at the restaurant sang the familiar song from Dr. Zhivago, "*Somewhere my Love.*" That was my favorite song at the time - I had sung and played that song on my guitar many times while winding down from a day in combat in Vietnam. Hearing that song made the dinner even more enjoyable. I was optimistic enough to believe that out there, somewhere, "My Someone" was waiting for me, and I had bought her the perfect string of pearls. It was an inspiring evening of hope and contentment.

On Monday, 24 April 1967, we went on a New Frontier Tour and peered into "Red China," at the border. The villagers at the border were selling expensive jade jewelry. On Tuesday, our tour bus traveled on a ferry from Kowloon to Hong Kong Island. The highlight of the tour was a visit to Tiger Balm Gardens. It was built by the Haw family from the vast proceeds made from selling Tiger Balm Oil, which was a deep heat rub. The garden was very impressive with a seven-story tall pagoda and many other statues and sculptures. It was one of the most interesting places that I had ever visited. We toured other historical sites on Hong Kong Island that same day and ate lunch at another excellent restaurant. I really took a liking to the Chinese food, especially the sweet and sour chicken.

Returning Back to An Khe after My R&R

On Wednesday, 26 April 1967, I woke up in plenty of time to check out from the hotel and board the bus that would drive us to the airport. The time had flown by fast and my money had run out. At least I had clothes and gifts to show for it. I was grateful for the gift of having such a memorable time in Hong Kong and it was a nice reprieve from being in Vietnam where people just kept trying to kill each other.

At the airport we went through customs and found the gate where our flight would board for the trip back to Cam Rahn Bay. I noticed that a little Chinese boy was crying frantically. It was clear to me what had happened. He had been separated from his mother. I wanted to help but I could not speak Chinese and the boy could not speak English. Thankfully, a lady that appeared to be his mother heard his cry and scurried in through a crowd of people and scooped him up to comfort him. Thankfully, compassion is not peculiar to any one race. We were all the same. I stood there momentarily thinking, "Why do we have to kill each other?" The flight back to Cam Rahn Bay on the DC-6 was pleasant. Enroute, I ate a steak dinner that was delicious, especially for inflight food. At Cam Rahn Bay I stayed overnight at the R&R Center enroute back to Vietnam. It was hot and uncomfortable which seemed an appropriate transition back to camp.

On Thursday, 27 April 1967, at 0530 hours we went to the airport. While in the terminal I ran into Warrant Officer Bob Donaghy my old roommate from flight school in Fort Wolters, Texas. At that time, we had been attending our preflight training. It was nice to see a familiar face. Bob was an accomplished career soldier and looked sharp in his tailored fatigues. He was a few years older than me and had already been in the U.S. Army for several years. When I had arrived directly from basic training at Fort Jackson, South Carolina, Bob had helped me get my uniforms tailored and offered pointers so that I would appear as a "Sharp Troop." Sadly, however, after preflight when our actual flight training began, he washed out. It was good seeing him now in the rank of Warrant Officer. After leaving Fort Wolters, he had returned to his Military Occupational Specialty (MOS) in food service. I was happy to hear that since he had completed the Warrant Officer preflight training he applied and got promoted to the rank of Warrant Officer. It was a pleasant surprise seeing him again. He was proud that I made it through flight school and that my uniform looked sharp with my wings and ribbons. I had learned a good deal from Bob and he was a tremendous encouragement during flight school. I will always have fond memories of Bob.

At 0900 hours we boarded a C-130 that was bound for An Khe. After an intermediate stop at Qui Nhon, the number one engine would not re-start. Consequently, we were delayed until 1400 hours. It was determined that C-130 replacement parts were not immediately available. The problem was isolated to the number one engine starter which would not properly disengage.

As an innovative solution, the maintenance personnel removed the starter altogether. The other three engines were started and our C-130 taxied behind another running C-130. The prop blast from the running C-130 that was positioned in front of our aircraft was used to motor our number one engine propeller. That cleverly-improvised action successfully started our number one engine, which permitted our aircraft to takeoff. From Qui Nhon it was only a short hop to An Khe. I noticed that after we landed at An Khe the number one engine was left running in the idle position. The C-130 needed to continue flying to at least one more destination before all the engines could be finally shutdown. It felt good to be back at An Khe. I caught a ride to our company area, and although our camp was still engaged in the Vietnam War, it felt good to see my friends again and to sleep in my own bed.

Getting Back into a Combat Flying Mode

I did not fly on Friday, 28 April 1967. There was much on my mind to think about as I mentally prepared myself to get back into the combat flying mode. I had heard from others that the last forty days in Vietnam are the worst. That night there was a "Hail and Farewell" party at the "O" Club and it crossed my mind that the next month it would be my turn. I enjoyed steak and lobster; and, the dinner and festivities were very pleasant. Several awards were presented and I was proud of their valor, honor and duty. It felt good talking to my friends through the perspective of winding down my tour of duty as I was excited at the prospect of going home soon and transitioning into a new civilian life.

I did not fly again on Saturday. I was experiencing a good deal of anxiety since returning from R&R. My mind was racing a million miles per minute considering all aspects of my life, past, present and future.

I didn't want to wish my life away, but at the same time I was ready to move on in life, hoping that some job prospect would soon turn up.

I woke up late on Sunday even though it was almost too miserably hot and uncomfortable to sleep. I focused on getting my gear together since I was scheduled to return to the field that afternoon for about three days. I only had about four more weeks of flying and then I would finalize my U.S. Army flying career. I only logged 0.5 hours.

It was good to be flying again on Monday, 1 May 1967 (May Day). The month of April had passed much more quickly than I would have anticipated. Flying among the clouds in my Chinook looking down, I felt content and comfortable knowing that it was always meant to be. That May Day we flew many kinds of routine missions on that first day of the new month logging 5.7 hours. The weather was hot and uncomfortable which led to my shirt becoming soaking wet from perspiration under the heavy chest protector. It would be a reprieve in the heat wave when the rain cycle began again. Tuesday, we flew 6.3 hours of routine missions.

On Wednesday, 3 May 1967, the hot weather persisted. We played our version of the "B-47 bomber" on a mission by dropping CS gas and napalm canisters in the An Lao Valley. I did not like dropping napalm because it was extremely dangerous in many regards. If one of the drums was hit by ground fire or was accidently ignited inflight then we would be finished. Gratefully, no problems were encountered. We logged 4.2 hours at the end of the day.

A Downed Chinook & the Loss of Eight Brave Souls

On Thursday we flew sorties all day and into the night. The weather was painfully hot and I had an uncomfortable headache from eye strain. The 1st Cavalry Division moved two artillery battalions to Ba

To. That was "bad guy" country and Two Step Vipers hung awaiting enemy prey. As far as I knew we were not shot at, which was extremely lucky. We logged another 8.4 hours that day.

The flying kept my mind occupied, but my goal at this point was to make it home in one piece so I could hug my mom, wear my new suits, and start the next chapter in my career. I continued to accrue flight time on every mission I was asked to fly, but I prayed that God would protect me in my final days in Vietnam from the coils of the python or the strike of the Two Step Viper.

On Friday, 5 May 1967, I spent all morning writing letters and preparing my thinking for heading back home. I had just been reflecting on the many times that I had been spared, when I heard that our Chinook battalion unexpectedly lost an armed ACH-47A "Guns-A-Go-Go" gunship 64-13145 named, "Cost of Living." The aircraft had crashed not far from Bong Son. It was another sad loss for all of us as the Grim Reaper snatched eight more valiant souls. That morning I had eaten breakfast in the same mess hall, with the aircrew. It was sobering and surreal to continue with such a terrible loss. Since I was on standby, another pilot and I had the sorrowful task of flying the accident investigation team to the crash site.

We arrived not long after the Chinook had struck the ground and burned. The wreckage was still smoldering after the ensuing fire. The ACH-47A had obviously come apart in the air and parts were scattered over a wide area. At first, we all thought the Chinook was taken down by enemy ground fire. The Chinook had struck the ground with a tremendous force. I had a lump in my throat and welling emotion as I considered that I was still alive while another brave Chinook crew had perished. It easily could have been any of us.

All eight persons of the crew were killed instantly. The main wreckage and the crew were completely charred. Several aircraft, including Chinooks and Slicks, had recently been lost in that dangerous area. I always feared more of getting hit by friendly artillery fire or aircraft component failures, than I did from the VC ground fire. The crash site area was an extremely dangerous place where we lost good and brave men and another CH-47A that day. We logged 1.8 heartbreaking hours after we returned to An Khe.

Sometime later more information was revealed about the circumstances of the crash. During the accident investigation, a portion of one of the forward rotor blades was found some distance away from the main wreckage with a large bullet hole right through a forward rotor spar. Part of the rotor blade had been shipped to the FBI Laboratory for ballistic analysis. After the lab analysis, it was determined that the round was a 20 mm high explosive (HE) round that had been fired from one of the Chinook's own 20 mm canons. That analysis had proven that the aircraft had shot itself down due to faulty aircraft maintenance and not by enemy ground fire. Below is an excerpt from the official explanation:

> *"On 5 May 1967 while on an attack run, a retention pin on the stub wing of 'Cost of Living' came loose and allowed the gun to elevate and fire into the forward rotors, causing the gunship to crash with the loss of all onboard."*

A defective retaining pin had been installed on the rear mount of one of the 20 mm canons. As the 20 mm canon was firing, the vibration had caused the aft mount securing pin to back out. Once the pin had migrated out of the aft 20 mm gun mount, the barrel of the canon had rotated upward around the forward mount and was pointed directly at the forward rotor disk as it was firing. Thus, unfortunately, a high explosive round struck a rotor spar and a portion of one of the forward rotor blades was hurled away by centrifugal force.

With the forward rotor system drastically out of balance, extreme "G" forces had ripped out the forward transmission with the forward rotor system. Those extreme "G" forces had probably rendered the aircrew immediately unconscious and the aircraft plummeted to the earth. I was very thankful that I was not onboard that Chinook and that God was not yet ready to greet me into the Great Beyond. It was always a painful and conflicting experience to lose good friends while also feeling relief and gratitude to have survived.

My Final Days in Vietnam

On Saturday, 6 May 1967, we conducted our annual Command Maintenance Management Inspection (CMMI). We were proud to have passed the inspection as our unit typically did well in some areas and poorly in others. I spent time painting a building in the company area until it rained. As I solemnly painted in the quiet of the day, I pondered the tragic aircraft loss the day prior while my mind drifted back to my own crash on, 18 December 1966. I was thankful to still be alive and even more thankful to be heading home.

The end of my tour in Vietnam was in sight. I checked with personnel and they were preparing my separation orders. I was to be out-processed and discharged at the Oakland Army Terminal in California. The next day I was to return to the field for two days which made the time pass quickly. I logged 0.3 hours when I dispersed a Chinook to the "Green Line." I knew that it would be a big day in the field the following day, so I went to bed early to ensure I was rested and was ready to begin with a clear mind.

Somewhere in that timeframe, I sent out job inquiry letters to Petroleum Helicopters in Louisiana and to Page Aircraft Maintenance Incorporated (PAMI) at Fort Rucker, Alabama. PAMI was the civilian maintenance contractor for all the aircraft at Fort Rucker. I provided my aircraft qualifications and my accumulated flying time. I was hoping for a positive job prospect in any response. My first choice was to return to Fort Rucker and to become a maintenance test pilot that way I could continue to fly Chinooks and UH-1 helicopters. I had cast my bread upon the waters and hoped that something would come of it.

On Sunday, 7 May 1967, we flew out to Hammond Field to replace another aircraft but there was little to do. We only flew 0.8 hours. On Monday I had a terrible head cold, so when I flew the pressure in my inner ears would not equalize and it was piercingly painful. Major Boles kindly filled in for me on some of the missions and that helped. He was an exceedingly kind man and I admired him. I logged 1.9 hours. I felt a little better that next morning, Tuesday, but the pressure in my ears were still slow to equalize. We flew back to An Khe logging 4.2 hours. I took a nap that afternoon and continued recuperating while I watched a movie that evening. I was excited at the thought of returning home and normalizing life.

On Wednesday, 10 May 1967, time was passing quickly. I was scheduled to drop off one Chinook at Saigon and then fly a new CH-47 back to An Khe. I had never been as far south as Saigon before and really didn't want to get stuck down there.

I started planning ahead in anticipation knowing that I would soon have to ship some of my personal belongings back home. I was ready to start preparing as much as I could ahead of time.

We finally got aircraft (917) off the ground about 1000 hours on

Wednesday. We experienced a bad fire detection unit on the number two engine that needed to be replaced. After taking off we made one fuel stop and flew to Saigon and landed. It ended up being a quick turn-around mission as we turned in the old worn-out aircraft and were assigned to a brand new one. We departed Saigon and spent the night at Vung Tau at the Pacific Hotel logging 3.6 hours.

After sleeping late, we performed a check out flight on aircraft (046) on Friday, 10 May 1967. It was a brand-new CH-47B helicopter, and it flew well and all the systems worked. At noon we completed the shake down flight to check out all the avionics and operating systems, and we returned to the hotel. We only logged 0.5 hours. I ate lunch and took a nap. Later I listened to a band at the "O" Club, ate dinner and went to bed early. The next day we were scheduled to fly to An Khe.

We got up early on Saturday, 13 May 1967, to eat breakfast at the hotel, and we were driven to the airfield. We took off and stopped at Nha Trang for lunch on the way to An Khe. Nha Trang was a beautiful French Colonial town and I imagined that it would be the perfect place to build a resort. It was located on the coast and the blue green sea was full of fish and the transparency of the water was a window into the spectacular marine life. After lunch in a beautiful and serene setting, we completed the flight to An Khe which turned out to be one of the most breathtakingly beautiful and memorable flights I'd ever flown along the Vietnam Coast. We logged 3.8 hours.

We were all awakened in the early morning on Sunday for enemy activities that had been reported in the area. A few hours later closer to sunrise, CWO-3 Leo Ellis and I flew out to LZ English. CWO Ellis was the head of our unit building program and he had not flown for a while. That day we flew many routine sorties resupplying various artillery fire bases. By sunset, we flew back to An Khe. It was an awfully long day and we both were tired logging 7.0 hours. I ate supper, watched part of a movie, and went back to the BOQ to go to bed. I was not scheduled to fly on Monday, so I slept in late. Once I got up I sat out on the patio and studied more instrument procedures. Going home and finding a job was consuming my mind.

All our flying on Tuesday, 16 May 1967, consisted of transporting a spare engine to LZ English. One of our Chinooks required an engine change. For the most part, the area around LZ English was relatively quiet with little recent contact with the VC. We logged another 2.5 hours. The days were hot and growing longer. We remained overnight at LZ English on RRF duty which required me to sleep in the cargo bay of our aircraft.

On Wednesday we flew general resupply missions to local LZs in the area. It was a long hot day, again. The flying was good, but for some reason it felt significantly more fatiguing. I sweated profusely which demanded that I consume significantly more water to ensure I didn't overheat. On flights we always carried an insulated water container with ice in it. To say the least, it was refreshing to have a cold drink in that intense heat. My "butt" felt like concrete permanently affixed to the seat. Standing up took great effort and I was worn out to say the least. We logged 6.8 hours. Gratefully, flying seemed to make the last few weeks pass quickly. I was antsy and restless as my thoughts focused on going home and seeing my family.

I was off on Thursday, 18 May 1967. Most of our building projects were completed so I sat out on our patio and studied instrument procedures. If I continued flying, then I would need to obtain an instrument rating. I was confident enough to get out of trouble if I inadvertently, ever, went into an instrument flight rule condition again. I had learned many survival skills from the older and more experienced Chief Warrant Officers. They had my best interest in mind. They were some of the best helicopter pilots in the world.

I noticed that my flying time had slacked off a little and I only had seven days remaining. At that point in one's tour of duty, the saying was, "I'm not short, I am next"; or, "I'm so short that I can take a bath in a saucer"; or, "I am so short I can sit on the edge of a rug and swing my feet." We had the same sayings when I left Korea. It would be good to go home.

I did not fly on Friday, 19 May 1967. I sat on our patio and studied instrument procedures. My going home anxiety jitters were compounding with each passing day. I remembered that I experienced the same feeling when I left Korea in August of 1965. This time the need to get home felt ever more intense.

We flew out to LZ English on Saturday, 20 May 1967. It was a good day of routine flights and I was happy to have logged 5.1 hours. The weather was very sultry and uncomfortable. Upon arriving back, it felt good when I took off my heavy chest protector to dry out my shirt. I was not scheduled to fly on Sunday. For lunch we conducted a "grill your own" steak buffet. It was always better than the usual mess hall food and I welcomed the variety of choices. I lay in the sun, on the patio, making a mental checklist of what I needed to accomplish before I departed Vietnam. I could feel my emotions churning inside as my life was transitioning. I knew there was a next adventure ahead and trusted God would lead with clarity. I believed, as a Christian, we don't always get what we think we want or ask for. Rather, God gives us what we really need, in His time, and on His terms. Even through my anxiety and worry, I was thankful that I was still alive, and knew that the unveiling of my next chapter was a good position to be in. I had become a better person, a better friend, a better family member and a better pilot than I was when I first had arrived in Vietnam. I was optimistically hopeful for a continuation in a fortunate future.

Officer of the Day Throwdown

I was scheduled as "Officer of the Day", the evening of Monday, 22 May 1967, and would not be flying. Everything was uneventful that night until several young "A" Alpha Company enlisted troops started to attack and beat up a "B" Bravo Company Private First Class (PFC). As I approached the scene, outside of the Enlisted Men's Club, I saw the PFC covering his neck with his head slumping down as he took punches to the arms and chest being repeatedly beaten. I assumed from where the assault was taking place, that it was probably an alcohol induced altercation. As I ran to the scene to assess the situation, I placed one hand on my holster as instinct. I approached the group and heard somebody yelling, "OD is on his way" to alert the others that the altercation had become an official incident. Clearly, the troops had been drinking heavily. When I came into view, the enlisted troops stopped the altercation realizing they could be court-marshalled for fighting. They could even have been imprisoned if anyone was severely injured. I strained to see if anyone had a weapon. Upon further evaluation no one was bleeding or appeared to be seriously injured. The group reeked of alcohol. No one appeared to have a knife or any other kind of weapon, so I relaxed my right hand momentarily off my side holster. Several in the group had already run away before I was on scene. I took command of the violent escapade, and the angry troops began to cool down and disperse. I hoped the evening's situation would not escalate into a "pack" mentality nor amp up in any way. The last thing I wanted to do was be forced to shoot one of our own, even in the cause of civil protection.

As the Commanding General's pilot, in Korea, I was required to carry a 45-caliber pistol side arm. During that tour I had become an expert pistol marksman. Adjacent to the landing pad at Camp Howze was a pistol range where we would often practice firing while waiting for the Generals before flying. Captain Chutter, the General's Aide-de-Camp, would give us a box or two of 45-caliber ammunition. We would "run up" the red range flag and would fire at targets until the barrels got hot and the ammunition was expended. Because of our time in the pistol range, we became outstanding marksmen having spent so much time as competitors with one another.

That night, in the worst-case scenario, I would have shot the most aggressive troop delivering those punches in one of his legs. At that short range I felt confident that I would not miss. As OD I never had any intention of killing anyone unless the unruly group had decided to attack me personally as an armed officer on duty, but they did not need to know that. The troops finally began to sober up and to return to their quarters. After the clubs closed it was quiet for the remainder of the night. I was glad to be relieved from OD duty on Tuesday. After debriefing the previous night's incident, I went to bed and slept until noon. I awoke with my heart racing, not because I was recounting the prior evening's altercation, but at the thought about going home. I tried to relax and to wind down my over-active nerves.

Final Days with "*The Second Team*"

On Wednesday, 24 May 1967, we flew aircraft (070) out to LZ English. We sling loaded a Quad 50 which was a mounted 50-caliber heavy machine gun with four barrels, to a pinnacle between LZ Glenn and Ba To. The Quad 50 was a very heavy weapon system, and the aircraft almost reached the aircraft's maximum gross weight just to lift it. The engine torque indicator needles were at maximum power levels as the sling load slowly lifted from the ground. "We could hover, so we could fly." It required some finesse on the flight controls to keep from bleeding off rotor RPM. With maximum loads like that, I would always beep the rotor RPM to just below the rotor speed indicator redline, for takeoffs and landings.

That technique provided additional inertia in the rotor system in case of an emergency. I certainly did not want to have to "punch off" that particularly important external load. All went well and the rotor system produced a cloud of dust as we landed with that heavy load. We returned to An Khe at the end of the day logging 5.7 hours. I was proud of what we had accomplished that day.

Captain Sines and I departed early for LZ English on Thursday, 25 May 1967. Captain Ken Sines was a slim high energy person and always uplifting and encouraging to be around. He was responsible for scheduling and coordinating most of our cargo load missions. That day we flew all types of missions. There was one humorous story that was circulating about Captain Ken Sines. As the story goes on one of the days when we were flying many long hours, we all became dog tired. One of the pilots keyed our unit FM radio frequency and emphatically said, "Give me liberty or give me death!" Captain Sines barked back, "Who said that"? The response came back, "Patrick Henry!" That broke the tension and, later, we frequently laughed about it.

Captain Sines was instrumental in putting my name up for a Bronze Star Medal for my extensive dangerous combat support missions. He based his recommendation on the fact that I always volunteered, and I never refused to fly on any of the assigned dangerous missions. I was proud of that and grateful for the recommendation.

Not long after, a Ground Troop Commander and a Major

requested that we sling load a grass shack from LZ Pony to LZ Sandra. I took a look at the load, and I tried to explain to the Major that the load was very light and it would be aerodynamically unstable in that configuration. I tried to explain to the Major that when the load was lifted, and any increased forward airspeed was applied, that the load would rise up and flail against the bottom of the aircraft. Regardless of my explanation, the Major insisted that we try. I was outranked, so we hooked up the load and started to move forward. As we went through the initial transitional lift, the crew chief said, "We have a problem, Sir." And just as I predicted, the hut was rising, the load was spinning, and it was banging against the belly of the aircraft. I slowed down to a hover, executed a pedal turn, we armed the cargo hook, and set down the load right where we had picked it up. From the look on his face, I believed the Major was embarrassed but he did not utter a word. He may have been a Major, but I was the Aircraft Commander. It was my decision and I had the authority to refuse to continue to fly the load, so I returned the grass shack to the pickup point and continued to fly the remainder of my routine resupply missions of the day.

Friday, 26 May 1967, was a happy day as I received my port call. This made it official that I was going home. I packed up my "hold baggage" which would be shipped home. I had eleven days left before departing Vietnam. I was undoubtedly a "short-timer." As my new all-consuming daily routine, I reflected on all my experiences and played them repeatedly in my head recounting all that I had learned in Vietnam. I was very thankful that I made it that far. Late in the afternoon I logged 0.3 hours when I dispersed a Chinook to the "Green Line."

I finished packing my "hold baggage" and sent it off on Saturday, 27 May 1967. Some of my clothes and belongings I sent through the mail. My going away party was held that night where I received a 228th Winged Warrior Plaque. I was also proud to have received my second Distinguished Flying Cross. As of that count I had been awarded a total of twenty-one Air Medals. If the citation was approved, I was also to receive a Bronze Star Medal.

I had mixed emotions about leaving Vietnam even though I had been counting down in anticipation for that very moment. I knew it was time for me to return home. I had arrived in Vietnam for a purpose, carried out that mission, and I knew that God also had a future planned for me. I had dutifully maintained my personal journal to remember the flying, the people, and the peculiarities of that war in Vietnam.

Saturday was another long day because there wasn't much going on. I read and imagined being back with my family and friends at home. On a sad note, I found out that an enlisted man from "B" Bravo Company was shot in the head the night before. One of his buddies was drunk and playing with a rifle. The rifle went off and the projectile struck his head and he died that same day. It was one thing to be killed by a Two Step Viper and left in the field like cattle by a vicious enemy, but another to be killed in the safety of camp by a friend. That was such a waste. The Grim Reaper had claimed another soldier by not-so-friendly fire.

On Monday, 29 May 1967, I was trying to find ways to keep busy as I found myself pacing as my anxiety level piqued. As part of the process for leaving, I was required to get a flight physical. On Tuesday I had my lab work done and an EKG. Nothing significant happened on Wednesday, 31 May 1967. Waiting caused time to pass painstakingly slowly. The month of May had officially come to an end.

On Thursday, 1 June 1967, I flew my last flight in the U.S. Army with "*The Second Team*." I flew with our company commander Major

McHaney to LZ English for him to pay the troops. We experienced a beep failure on the number two engine. As it turns out, I ended my U.S. Army flying career with a typical aircraft maintenance failure. On my last flight in the U.S. Army we logged 1.4 hours.

On Friday, 2 June 1967, had I sunburned my legs and it was rather uncomfortable. I needed lotion or aloe or anything I could get my hands on to sooth the burn, so I headed to the PX. I needed to go anyway to buy a few civilian clothes and white "T" shirts and underwear. No longer would I have a need to wear the required olive drab underclothes.

Saturday, 3 June 1967, I spent cooling down from my sunburn and organizing the rest of my belongings for shipping out. About that same time, I sold my small refrigerator, which was still in high demand. I supposed that someone else would be assigned as Mess Officer after I departed. That evening I headed to the "O" Club for one of my last dinners in Vietnam. That evening dinner was out of the ordinary as we barbequed venison. It was prepared to an optimal tenderness and seasoned to perfection. One of the guys had shot the deer around the outer perimeter of the compound not far from camp. I still can remember the smells, sights, and sounds as my chapter in Vietnam ended. I was officially a decorated U.S. Army combat pilot.

After dinner I somberly turned in my weapon and combat gear. I thought of an old west gunfighter who was hanging up his gun. I would no longer be part of the bloodletting. I had joined the U.S. Army as a boy from Florida that had a dream of flying. I felt accomplished. I felt I had outgrown that boy of trauma and I now had the freedom to be my own man. I was ready for the next cycle of my life, and I was excited for God to reveal the next chapter in my Providential path. I was ready to seek my fortune, back home.

My commander had asked me to extend my tour, but I had decided to return to my home in Florida. For me, the Vietnam War was over, and I wasn't looking back. That was my last Sunday in Vietnam and by the next Sunday I would begin attending church regularly with my family, once again.

Going Home and Life after Vietnam

By this time in my life, I was aware that a person's life evolves in cycles. I had experienced the toils of coming of age and spiritually evolving like many before me. In looking back on that period of my life, I had faithfully served my country as a soldier and as a combat pilot. That was a pivotal point in my life. I had completed another four year cycle in my growth to maturity. I entered the U.S. Army asking God for answers, knocking at His door, and seeking resolution for my past through His guidance and direction for my future.

> *Ask, and it will be given to you; seek. And you will find; knock, and it will opened to you. For everyone who asks receives, and the one who seeks finds, and to the one who knocks it will be opened.*
>
> *-Matthew 7:7-8*

During the time period of my life in the U.S. Army I found relief from my childhood trauma, discovered an open door as a pilot, received insight from my world travels, and began to understand my Providential purpose. One cycle had ended while another cycle of my life was beginning. I realized there was a time for everything "under the sun". My time as a combat pilot had ended with mixed emotions.

I will never forget the sight of fear on the faces of the brave young soldiers as they jumped out of our helicopter to face the enemy in hot landing zones, nor the relief on the face of each death-defying soldier we safely recovered. Sadness had become a part of me. Forevermore, I could not erase the ethereal experience of death scattered across a rice paddy field or bodies zipped in bags to be shipped off to mourning Gold Star Families.

Without sadness there would not be the sensation or experience of happiness. Happiness, too, was imbedded in my heart for the countless wounded soldiers that were rescued, for the bond of brotherhood, friendships that were forged, and for the most majestic scenes in nature that I have ever experienced. The depth and magnitude of my happiness came about through the wisdom and sorrow of struggle. Both experiences have offered me the understanding and wisdom to continue my days, living my version of a full life. I would never be the same person and forever I will carry a heavier and yet lighter burden knowing that it is all part of God's plan. Everything was His will, not mine.

A boy had joined the Army on 1 July 1963, but a proud man came back home on 14 June 1967. After my crash in December and the loss of my dear friend, Captain Bob Bradley, the following March, I had become a completely different person. I was content in heading home understanding the duality of my wartime experiences and was keenly aware that they would, for the rest of my life, weigh heavily on my mind. From that moment onward, I felt free to make my own decisions in life and that God would always chart the course of my destiny.

Traveling Back Home

My first stop after being discharged from the U.S. Army was in Eugene, Oregon. I had returned to visit my sister, Clara, brother-in-law,

Stan, and my nephew, Steven, on my way home to Florida. The timing was perfect as my sister, Harriett, happened to be in Oregon visiting at that time and I was excited to see her, too. My mind was once again in a state of high anxiety and filled with anticipation about leaving on Monday. After riding that "wild roller coaster" in Vietnam with "*The Second Team*" it would be a difficult transition back to a calm and more domestic civilian life. I hated the thought of having to face the Vietnam War protesters back home and to be viewed in such a negative light.

Tuesday, 6 June 1967, was an important day in American history to always be remembered. Our troops landed in Normandy on that day in 1944, "D" Day, when I was almost two years old. On that day I had received word that I would be departing one day earlier than expected. My departure day would be Wednesday, 7 June 1967, at 0700 hours. In anticipation, I did not sleep a wink that night. I arose early on Wednesday and ate breakfast for the last time in my mess hall. I chuckled at myself thinking, "After all that time, not only had I learned the difference between chicken crap and chicken salad, but I had also become a master chili maker."

After packing up my gear I headed out to the Jeep where I was then driven to An Khe Airfield. I spent most of the morning at the An Khe strip waiting to catch a hop to Pleiku. Rattled with nerves from this chapter changing in my life, I finally got on a C-123 that was bound for Pleiku. I bid a final farewell to my "*Second Team*" as I began my journey home. After landing in Pleiku I headed to the 526th Replacement Company, for final processing. I exchanged my MPC currency for U.S. "greenbacks." It was the rainy season and thick mud had formed on my jungle boots. I cleaned off what mud that I could and then I put a pair of socks over the boots and put them in a duffle bag for the trip back home. I had hoped and prayed that there would be no alerts or mortar attacks that night at Pleiku. My thoughts shifted as my emotions went from anxiety to that of excitement about leaving Vietnam. Of my three previous years as a Warrant Officer, I felt honored to have served, in the historic 1st Cavalry Division, in both Korea and in Vietnam.

The next morning, Thursday, 8 June 1967, I boarded a commercially contracted Boeing 727 at 0930 hours wearing my dress uniform and took off for Clark AFB in the Philippines. The next leg of my flight home would be on a Boeing 707 to Kadena AFB in Okinawa. After a fuel stop in Kadena we then flew non-stop to Travis AFB in California. I had watched the sun set and then then rise again, just four hours later. It was a pleasant trip home that transpired with ease, however, the travel caught up with me as I encountered severe jet lag.

Since I would be out-processing, I boarded a bus at Travis AFB in California bound for the Oakland Army Terminal. I found a place to stay and took a shower. After I cleaned up and settled in, I called home and talked to my incredibly happy mother. She wanted to talk my ear off because she hadn't heard my voice in many months, and I assured her I loved her and would see her soon. After that, a U.S. Army Lieutenant and I shared a cab and went to a restaurant at "The Wharf" where we enjoyed a wonderful lobster dinner, and we even drank real fresh cow's milk. It was a simple and satisfying luxury.

Early the following morning, Friday, 9 June 1967, I arrived at the Oakland Army Terminal for out-processing from the U.S. Army. I was there most of the day and attended various briefings. I especially remember the briefing about my newly earned Veterans Affairs (VA) benefits. The education and training benefits especially interested me. I could even use my VA benefits to complete my fixed wing flight training. After that long day of out-processing the last task would be to receive my final military pay. After receiving my cash pay in hand, I exhaled a breath of accomplishment and finality as I turned in my military ID card. I, then, was officially discharged. I was told that I could wear my uniform until I reached home and thus receive a military discount for an airline ticket. And just like that, the perils of my combat tour in Vietnam were over and my new civilian life had just begun in the United States of America. I was immensely proud of the time that I served as a pilot and as a soldier in the U.S. Army.

I continued my travels, heading to Oregon. I boarded a military bus that would take me to the San Francisco International Airport. I purchased a ticket to Portland, Oregon, and was looking forward to the first contact I would have with my family in almost a year. After landing in Portland in the late afternoon, I discovered that there were no flights available to Eugene until the next day. I didn't want to wait another day, so I rented a 1967 Chevrolet and drove the two hours' trip to Eugene. I felt a sense of freedom and belonging to be driving a car again and on a paved highway, nonetheless. As I pulled into the driveway, my sisters Harriet and Clara, my brother-in-law, Stan, and my nephew, Steven, all came out to greet me. Hugging family never felt better and I had an even deeper appreciation for our bond and the value of life. They looked happier than I had ever seen them, and I could feel the love they had for me beaming in every facial expression. I enjoyed an evening of catching up and resting after a long journey home.

The next day I turned in the rental car and just rode along with family while in Eugene. We enjoyed just being with one another again. It was fun shopping for clothes with a much bigger selection than the PX and eating Southern-style home cooking. We all drove to Crater Lake on Saturday and saw awe-inspiring places where the snow was ten feet deep. Crater Lake was a beautiful place to visit in the summertime. On Sunday we all went to church which was a real blessing. My sisters proudly shared that I was back from Vietnam and many in the congregation wished me well and thanked me for my service. I enjoyed the sermon and the familiarity of worshipping God. I cherished that moment of standing on American soil, with fellow Christian brothers and sisters, singing hymns and praising God. On Monday we did more shopping while visiting and catching up on the family news. I hated to learn that there was still trouble between my mother and father at home, although it was no surprise. I guess I was hoping they would mellow and have resolved things. Mainly, it was wonderful just seeing my family after such a long absence.

Arriving in St. Petersburg, Florida

On Tuesday, 13 June 1967, I departed Eugene about noon on a twin-engine high wing commuter airline. I landed back at the San Francisco airport an hour later. From there I purchased a half-fair ticket for a non-stop night flight, on Northwest Airlines, to Tampa International Airport. I made arrangements for family members to meet me at the airport early on the morning of 14 June 1967. My sister, Marilyn, and her boyfriend at the time picked me up at the airport and I hugged her tightly as she wiped away happy tears. She was my baby sister, and I was filled with delight to see her again. After landing, filled with excitement, we drove across familiar scenic Tampa Bay to St. Petersburg. The sights and sounds of home never felt better after experiencing the life-altering ordeal of Vietnam. It hit me that moment that I could exhale a sigh of relief as I was safely home and back in the USA. My mother swung opened the screened back porch door and with tears of joy in her eyes she grabbed me tightly and stood there hugging me, not wanting to let go. She placed her hands on my shoulder and through her deep genuine smile said, "Son, I'm proud of you and am glad that you made your way back home."

After returning home to St. Petersburg on 14 June 1967, all aspects of my life continued in an exciting state of flux. My baptism by fire in Vietnam was over and behind me. My mother was elated that her son had safely returned home, unharmed. She prepared some of my favorite meals filling the house with the aroma of fried chicken, yeast rolls, and chocolate pie. It was good being among the rest of my family and friends. I was anxious to see what the next cycle of life might bring. I began wearing the suits that I had tailor-made in Hong Kong, to church and to other important events feeling the satisfaction of the pride of ownership. One of the first things I did that first week home was to take my TR-3 out of the garage, buy a battery, get it back up and running, and purchasing car insurance.

My father had not been at home when I first arrived from Vietnam. He had been spending a good deal of time away in his camping trailer visiting his relatives and my brother, Harry, and family at their ranch in Brooksville, Florida. When he did finally come to St. Petersburg to visit, I was drawn into the unpleasant reality of my mother's and father's escalating domestic conflict. Over the course of the next few years my parents separated, bickered over property, and finally divorced. Those circumstances put a constant emotional strain on all of us; but, I understood from my time in Vietnam that even though the sun sets, so too, it rises again to a brighter dawn.

A short time after returning home I received my Armed Forces of the United States Report of Transfer or Discharge Document DD Form 214, in the mail. Not long after, I also received a medal and a Certificate for a Bronze Star Medal along with two additional certificates for two more Air Medals that were not listed in the DD Form 214. Captain Ken Sines' effort had paid off. Just as he had told me before I left Vietnam, he had written a citation for the Bronze Star Medal since he knew that I had always voluntarily flown more dangerous combat missions than any of the other pilots. He felt that I should be recognized for my dedication, courage, and valor. My awards for serving in Vietnam included two Distinguished Flying Crosses, one Bronze Star, twenty-one Air Medals, the National Defense Service Medal, the Vietnam Service Medal, and the Vietnam Campaign Medal. What I was proud of the most was serving my country, alongside, "The *Second Team*." I never wore a U.S. Army uniform again and I avoided the Vietnam protesters and dodged any talk of the war.

I had logged about two-thousand hours of total flight time and about six hundred and fifty-five of those were combat flying hours. The twenty-one Air Medals were calculated based on the total combat flying time. God had been merciful and generous to me and I have never lost sight of that. I moved on to the next cycle in my life and ceased posting daily entries in my U.S. Army journal.

In a state of waiting, I wondered what would transpire next. I anticipated moving ahead with any job opportunity my new civilian life might bring. Even though I was happy and relieved to be home, some of my Vietnam survival instincts occasionally flashed back. My sister, Marilyn, remembers that on some nights I was yelling at the top of my lungs, "Shoot back we are taking ground fire." Even weeks after being back home out of harm's way whenever I heard a loud clap of thunder, I had the spontaneous reflex to take cover.

Eventually the bad memories of the war in Vietnam began to fade and they were replaced by more pleasant ones as I moved forward as time went on.

Hoping for Providence Once Again

I prayed that Providence would continue guiding the choices that I would make in my life and that they would be obvious. I had saved most of my military pay from Vietnam and didn't have any current bills. I went down to our local bank and opened an account and deposited the money that I had saved in Vietnam.

I was virtually debt free and only had to spend money on things like car insurance and other minor living expenses. Because of my financial security, there was no urgency to immediately find a job. I knew I needed time to adjust to civilian life and to prepare for whatever opportunities the future might hold for me. I stayed busy helping my mother with the yard work and other tasks around the house that needed attention. I was always good at fixing things.

I first visited my friend Lano Mosley to surprise him with the Trade Dollars that I had purchased for him while I was in Hong Kong a few months earlier. He expressed admiration and pride for all that I had accomplished as a U.S. Army pilot. He insisted on listening to each story of how I earned my medals and he was appreciative of the two coins.

I also wanted to catch up on the local news and to discuss business opportunities for a returning Vietnam Veteran. I had always valued Mr. Mosley's opinion and knew he would provide sound advice. He seemed pleasantly surprised as I presented him with the two Trade Dollars from Hong Kong. During our discussion he even offered me a position in his thriving carpet business. I thanked him again for my first airplane ride and all that he had done to promote my aviation career. I still wanted to pursue aviation as a career. Over the years I was able to pursue my aviation career on my own and moved away. Slowly over time, as distance has a way of doing, our lives drifted apart. Much later in life I heard that Lano Mosley passed from this life on 21 November 2000, at the age of eighty. I always have fond memories of him and how he influenced and impacted my life.

On 16 June 1967, I enrolled in a science course at Saint Petersburg Junior College (SPJC). I only needed to complete three hours of a science course to graduate with an Associates of Arts Degree. Since I was looking for a job, I thought it would also be beneficial and timely to complete my Associates Degree and make it official.

Sometimes Pearls Come in Handy

That first Sunday after arriving in St. Petersburg, I started attending my local church. All my friends were glad that I had made it home safely and were genuinely excited to see me, as I was one of them. Ron and Lois Bastien were among my best friends a few years before I joined the U.S. Army. I was instrumental in bringing them to the Lord. They lived in the house behind us in St. Petersburg. We spent a good deal of time together cooking sweet and sour chicken, attending church services, and water-skiing frequently. They were like family. We became life-long friends and Ron eventually became an elder in the church. I was always proud of him.

While away in Vietnam and serving in the U.S. Army, my primary concern and focus had always been on flying and preparing for the future. I had not found "Miss Right" before leaving Vietnam, and while away I developed my own criteria for what I was looking for in a wife. Since I was out of the U.S. Army I thought it was the right time to consider seeking a wife and a job. I had longed for both while I was in Vietnam.

Just before I had departed for Vietnam, Bob and Louise Keammerer had just started attending our church congregation. They had relocated from Tennessee to Florida. Bob Keammerer was working for a local engineering firm and his job brought him to the St. Petersburg area. Bob and Louise had a married son, Rick, and two daughters, Carol and Vicki. Carol had caught my eye before I left for Vietnam, and I even thought about her a few times while away. I had taught Bible classes several times before my tour of duty and she attended my class, so I knew who she was. She came from a good Christian family, and I thought she was beautiful. At the time she had a boyfriend and that held me back from asking her on a date.

When I returned home from Vietnam, Carol was still there and this time, she did not have a current boyfriend. Many of the young members would gather and talk together after the church service to be social and to get to know one another. I was talking with some of the group when Carol walked up to join the conversation. I was telling stories about flying in Vietnam. While we were talking, I momentarily paused, looked at her and as cool and casual as possible asked, "Have you ever been flying?" She coyly responded that she hadn't ever been in an airplane. I knew there was something special about her, so the next day I called her and asked, “Who do you know that flies airplanes?” She replied, “Well that would be Sonny Downing, right?” She guessed it right and so I thought it was only fitting to ask her to go on a first date, flying. I was elated that Carol had accepted. In preparation for our first date, I updated my currency in a Cessna 172 at Albert Whitted Airport and flew around St. Petersburg solo for an hour or so. It was good to be back in the air over familiar surroundings where I had first learned to fly.

The next day I had reserved the Cessna 172 for a flying session. I picked Carol up at her home in my freshly washed TR-3, with the top down. I waved to her mom and dad, shook her dad's hand, and drove to Albert Whitted Airport in St. Petersburg. She looked classy and was sharply dressed in a knit top and slacks. She was stunning, I was on cloud nine, and we hadn't even taken off yet. My younger sister, Marilyn, and her boyfriend met us at the airport and joined us for a double date. They sat in the back two seats of the Cessna 172. It was a beautiful setting on Tampa Bay where I had experienced my own first airplane ride. This was where I learned to fly airplanes and where I had my first helicopter flying lesson. For me, that airport was a special place of new beginnings and wonderful life experiences. I was especially happy to be there that day, with Carol. It was interesting that my first flight was in a Cessna 172 and my first flight with Carol was also in a Cessna 172. I was confident that God was tipping His wing at me and giving me the thumbs up. That date with Carol Jean Keammerer sealed the deal and I knew that she, was forever, the love of my life. I knew those pearls had a purpose and that they would come in very handy. For me, Carol was one of God's greatest gifts and still is to this very day.

Timing is everything, and that day was perfect. I had always dreamed of having a pretty girl sitting beside me, cruising with the top down in my TR-3. I felt God's Providence as Carol rode beside me in both my TR-3 and in the airplane that day. It was a wonderful experience as things that I loved came together in that moment of perfection. That was her very first flight and based on her smile and comments, she was thoroughly impressed. The only downside was Marilyn's boyfriend got airsick and threw up in the back seat. I was so smitten with Carol and focused on flying that I didn't even know that until after we had landed. After that first flight we all continued the date and went out to lunch at Frisch's Big Boy restaurant on 34th Street.

We continued dating almost every day in my TR-3 the summer of '67 until I finished my college course at SPJC. After dating for most of the summer it was time to make an even bigger purchase than the pearls. I purchased a one-carat diamond engagement ring and proposed to Carol in my TR-3 overlooking the beach. We made our life-long commitment to each other in "our", TR-3. From that point on the focus of our lives was about, "us" and our newly forming family unit. After Carol had accepted my marriage proposal, I took her home and she showed the ring to her parents who were sitting in their family room. I don't think her mother was surprised at all. Sitting in that living room, I was seeking Bob and Louise Keammerer's, blessing. From their kindness and the looks of their faces, I think that they were happy that Carol had found someone that also met their standards. Her father did ask me how I planned to support her since I did not have a job at that time. I responded that I had good prospects for a job as soon as I completed my SPJC college course. I assured her father that we would not be married until I had a job and a suitable place for Carol to live. Her parents must have been in shock because they sat there, in silence, not knowing what else to say. I was relieved that Carol said, "Yes", and that there were no roadblocks to launching an enduring marriage. We had just made one of life's most important decisions.

Maintenance Test Pilot at Fort Rucker

While completing my Earth Science course at SPJC, I received a phone call from Bill Angle at Fort Rucker, Alabama. One of Bill Angle's responsibilities at Page Aircraft Maintenance Incorporated (PAMI) was to recruit maintenance test pilots. At that time PAMI was the civilian maintenance contractor for all the military aircraft at Fort Rucker. Bill Angle had received my letter that I had sent from Vietnam two months earlier and he had my home telephone number. He had knowledge that I would be discharged from the U.S. Army in the middle of June and return home. My previous Chinook experience in Vietnam was about to pay huge dividends. Bill indicated that PAMI was in desperate need of qualified Chinook maintenance test pilots. I felt that Providence was still active and at work in my life.

When I left Vietnam, I had accrued over five hundred and sixty hours of Chinook flying time and about two thousand flying hours altogether. I was already qualified to fly all the helicopters that would require test flight for PAMI, at Fort Rucker. Due to my vast experience with helicopter maintenance problems in Vietnam, my experiences were a perfect fit for employment with PAMI. I promised Bill that as soon as I had completed my college course that I would drive to Fort Rucker for an interview. I kept my word and after I had taken my final exam and completed the course, early in September of 1967, I drove my TR-3 to Fort Rucker for the interview with Bill Angle. With the wind flowing through my hair, I was filled with hope and anticipation as I drove the 325 miles to Fort Rucker.

I checked into a local motel then I visited with my good friend, John Moats. I knew John and his family from the church in Ozark. John also worked as a supervisor with PAMI. John and his family were awfully glad to see me. When I told John that I had an interview with Bill Angle the next day he was even more excited. John said that he knew Bill Angle well and would give him a call that evening. He followed through with his word and called Bill Angle and gave me a glowing personal recommendation.

I would be interviewing for my first civilian flying job after separating from the U.S. Army. I had hoped that my anxieties of life after Vietnam would continue to wane as the next cycle in life for me, started coming together.

The next day after I had arrived at Fort Rucker, I was interviewed by Bill Angle. I presented my military flight records and my FAA Commercial Helicopter Certificate for Bill Angle to review. He said, "James, you come highly recommended, and I'd like to hire you." I gratefully accepted the position and was thankful to be hired on the spot. I filled out all the employment forms and began working immediately. After leaving the interview, I was so elated that I went straight back to the hotel and called Carol with the good news. She and I both knew that it signified that we could start making wedding plans.

As part of the employment agreement, I would take a week off without pay in order to get married November 10, 1967. I was assigned to Hanchey Field, which was the largest permanent heliport at Fort Rucker where the CH-47 Chinooks were based. I had come full circle as it was where I had received my Chinook training a year earlier. I was so familiar with the surroundings that I simply felt Providence played a part and I was at home. God had smiled on our relationship and it was exhilarating to be alive.

I was assigned the maintenance test pilot identification, "PAMI 42" and issued PAMI dog tags in case of a crash. When conducting local area maintenance test flights, I was only required to use my "PAMI 42" call sign, instead of an aircraft tail number. I would say, "Hanchey tower this is PAMI 42 ready for takeoff." My first flight as PAMI 42 was in a UH-1A on 6 September 1967. Merton Fine was the PAMI pilot supervisor at Hanchey Field but the pilots called him "Pappy Fine." He was the one who officially checked out all the pilots on all the helicopters. On that first flight with "Pappy Fine", my memory took me back to my first checkout ride, flying Slicks, in Vietnam. It was an easy checkout.

It was wonderful flying U.S. Army helicopters again and the only difference was, I had become a civilian test pilot. That flight was followed by another checkout flight with "Pappy Fine", this time in a CH-47A and a CH-47B on that very same day. With great success, I was additionally signed off on both CH-47 Chinook models. Soon after that I was checked out in a Bell TH-13T. I discovered that I was one of the most experienced CH-47 Chinook pilots at PAMI. The flying at Fort Rucker was rewarding and I was simply relieved that nobody was shooting at me. I began my first civilian, dream job.

A New Life Together

I continued building flight time and gaining aircraft maintenance experience. Immediately after being hired by PAMI I started to make some domestic living arrangements and established a local bank account in Ozark, Alabama. I was more than ready to start building a new life together with Miss Carol Jean.

Around that timeframe my good friend CWO John Greene, "The Chili Guy", had returned to Fort Rucker. I visited his home and met his wife, thanking her profusely for sending John the ingredients for his signature chili. I shared several stories about our invitation-only chili cookouts and we laughed together sharing the time when it came out a bit too spicy. It was great to see CWO Greene and meet his wife, on American soil.

Not long after that, I crossed paths with Captain Carl Dunn. Occasionally, I would see some of my other U.S. Army friends on the flight line and it felt good being back at Fort Rucker. I ended up spending a total of six years of my life there. My first civilian job was a pleasant transition from military to civilian aviation and it continued to fulfill my love of flying. I loved flying, I loved my new job, but I loved Carol even more, and was eager to be married to her. I was "living a pilot's dream." I was very thankful to still be alive and able to enjoy those wonderful experiences.

I was placed on a waiting list for a small furnished apartment in Ozark, Alabama. I had many good friends that I had gotten to know both stateside and abroad. I also had attended the church in Ozark since I first attended flight school in 1964. I stayed with my wonderful friends, Don and Thelda Henderson, for a few weeks until I could move in to my first furnished apartment. Nearly every weekend, I drove the 325 miles to St. Petersburg until we were married. On those trips home we visited our friends, the places that we liked on the beach, planned our wedding and prepared for married life together in Alabama. It was an incredibly happy time for us.

I knew that as a married man I would need a larger car. On one of my first trips home from Fort Rucker, I stopped by my local bank to transfer some money to my bank account in Ozark. I also mentioned to the bank official that I might apply for a loan to purchase a new automobile. That happened to be my lucky day because the bank had just repossessed a sporty white 1967 Pontiac Sprint Tempest. I test drove the car and then agreed to purchase it. The bank financed the loan on the spot, and I was the new proud owner of the car. From that time on I traveled from Alabama to Florida in the Pontiac Sprint Tempest. I left my TR-3 parked at my parent's home and Carol drove it occasionally. I moved into my new apartment in Ozark and took time off for the wedding.

Wedding Bells

Life had seemed to come full circle as Harry Payne Sr., the minister who baptized me, would conduct our wedding ceremony in the same building where I had grown up and first met Carol. I presented Carol with the string of pearls the evening before our wedding. Carol was a beautiful bride. It was a very happy day for all of us as we officially began our life together. Even my father attended the wedding.

Immediately following our wedding our reception was held at the Women's Club on Snell Isle. Our families and close friends, who all shared the same common religious beliefs, joined us and wished us much happiness in our marriage together. As all young married people, we hoped to blend our lives' and live, happily ever after. Our wedding day truly was a perfect moment in time. I was a very happy and a proud man on that day. I was grateful that I had received the blessings that I had prayed for, in Vietnam.

Happily Ever After

Of course, the reality of living "happily ever after" cannot be seen when two hopelessly in love young people first take their wedding vows and become one. After our wonderful honeymoon in the Bahamas we packed up Carol's clothes and our wedding gifts in the Sprint Tempest for our trip to our first apartment in Ozark, Alabama. Carol had inherited the family poodle, named Penny, who came along also. That was our first road trip as a married couple. Flying and our first years of marriage at Fort Rucker were wonderful. We often visited our families and friends in St. Petersburg.

During that timeframe I was checked out in the new CH-47C Chinook. The amazing CH-47C "Super 'C'" was capable of lifting a sling load of 20,000 pounds on the cargo hook. That was more than twice the lifting capacity of the Chinooks in Vietnam. That was one powerful and high-performance helicopter and I loved flying it. My Providential "happily ever after" incorporated faith, freedom, flying, and a wonderful new wife. What more could I ask for?

Our Spiritual Quest

It was a few months into our marriage, in 1968, that we began our personal quest to understand and fulfill our spiritual mission in life. God had spared my life for a greater purpose and I owed it to Him to understand what that was. As my new wife and I began to study the Bible together with open minds, a new and a profound understanding of the Bible Scriptures began to emerge. As we studied early church history, it was becoming obvious that Christendom had drifted away from the early first century teachings. As our understanding of the Bible increased, it became a shocking reality that some of the traditions that we had grown up in were not well-founded in Biblical Scripture. Thus, seeking truth in spiritual matters, became the guiding prime objective for the rest of our spiritual lives together.

The Later Years

I am constantly reminded that it was God who spared my life for a greater purpose. By God's grace, the Angel of Death had passed over our truck at age eleven and again over our aircraft that tragic night in the Phu Cat Valley. Others were not as fortunate and were claimed by the Grim Reaper. Those experiences both evoked purpose and were catalysts for my life-long mission.

Throughout my life, the tragic death of my dear friend, Captain Robert Neal Bradley, has always reminded me of who I needed to be. He was the perfect example of the good American Soldier that I idolized as a child. To me, Bob was like Nathanael.

> *Jesus saw Nathanael coming to him and said of him, "Behold, an Israelite indeed, in whom there is no deceit!"*
>
> *-John 1:47*

Bob loved God, he loved his wife and family, and he loved his country He died trying to save the wounded and I will always honor Bob's memory. America should always honor the fallen and we all must try to do better in the future. We all have something good in us that we need to share with others, while we are still alive.

Over half of my classmates died in the war in Vietnam. Many more have passed on since then. There are not many of us still living. I honor God and my fallen comrades. The 1st Cavalry Division "First Team" bravely fought the Battle of LZ X-Ray. As part of "*The Second Team*", we proudly defended LZ Bird. We pioneered the art of helicopter warfare, were good soldiers, and we proudly served our country in Vietnam as did the teams that continued in our footsteps.

The poem, "High Flight", still crosses my mind frequently and encapsulates my life in aviation and my personal walk with God.

High Flight

Oh, I have slipped the surly bonds of earth,
And danced the skies on laughter-silvered wings;
Sunward I've climbed and joined the tumbling mirth
Of sun-split clouds — and done a hundred things
You have not dreamed of — wheeled and soared and swung
High in the sunlit silence. Hov'ring there
I've chased the shouting wind along and flung
My eager craft through footless halls of air.
Up, up the long delirious burning blue
I've topped the wind-swept heights with easy grace,
Where never lark, or even eagle, flew;
And, while with silent, lifting mind I've trod
The high untrespassed sanctity of space,

Put out my hand, and touched the face of God.
-John Gillespie Magee

Over fifty-three years later, on 20 August 2020, my daughter, Rebecca, and her children visited Carol and I in Fort Worth, Texas. We all made the short trip to the National Vietnam Museum in Mineral Wells, Texas, and drove by Camp Wolters where I had first trained. I enjoyed telling stories and sharing my love of flying with my wife, daughter and grandchildren, knowing that, some of my best and worst experiences of war led to my Providential encounters and spiritual growth. My life had purpose and meaning and now I pass my learning and experiences on to future generations for their encouragement.

Seeing that UH-1D poised on the pedestal above the earth brought to mind a flood of intense emotional memories of the war in Vietnam. I am happy to say that after my Chinook crash in Vietnam on 18 December 1966, I never experienced another major mishap in my long aviation career. I had been delivered from death to tell my personal story of faith, to share my personal journal account of those who paid the ultimate cost for freedom, and what it was like to experience the pure joy of flying. My wish, now, is for you to also experience the majesty of knowing God and the beautiful blessings of Providence that He has planned for you.

> *Finally, brothers and sisters, whatever is true, whatever is noble, whatever is right, whatever is pure, whatever is lovely, whatever is admirable; if anything is excellent or praiseworthy; think about such things. Whatever you have learned or received or heard from me, or seen in me, put into practice; and the God of peace will be with you.*
>
> *-Phillipians 4:8*

About the Author

James C. Downing Jr. was born in 1942 in High Springs, Florida. He had an insatiable love of aviation from a young age. While attending Saint Petersburg Junior College and working as an engineering draftsman, he took flying lesson at Albert Whitted Airport in St. Petersburg, Florida. His first training flight was in a Cessna 150 in 1962 and obtained his Private Pilot Certificate in 1963. After completing the qualifying testing, he enlisted in the U.S. Army for the Warrant Officer Helicopter Flight Training Program. Following Downing's tour in Korea and Vietnam, he continued his entire career as a leader in aviation. His aviation career is as follows:

- In 1971 he was employed by Boeing Vertol in Philadelphia for a one-year Chinook assignment for the Government of Iran.
- In 1972 he was employed by Agusta Bell for another year in Iran.
- From March 1974 to March of 1976, he was employed by Bell Helicopter International as the Ch-47C Program Manager in Iran. He flew his last CH-47C Chinook flight on 9 June 1975.

- In 1974 the new F-16 Program was in the very early stages of development and Downing was employed by General Dynamics on the F-16 Program, in 1977, as a Field Service Engineer in Fort Worth, Texas.
- In 1993 Lockheed Martin acquired the General Dynamics Fort Worth Division. He was assigned to various field assignments that moved him to Edwards AFB, California; Hill AFB, Utah; the Lockheed Martin Factory, Fort Worth, Texas; Eglin AFB, Florida; Luke AFB, Arizona; and his last assignment was at the Lockheed Martin Factory in Fort Worth, Texas, as a Senior Analyst in the Global Sustainment Support Center (GSSC) where he also witnessed the launch of the F-35 Program.

Along the way he completed his dream of finishing his education. He received a Bachelor of Science Degree in Logistics from Weber State College in Utah. During that period, he also joined the "Society of Logistics Engineers (SOLE)." In 1984 he completed the requirements for the "Certified Professional Logistics (CPL) Certification". During his General Dynamics assignment at Eglin AFB, Florida, he earned a Master of Aeronautical Science (MAS) Degree from Embry-Riddle Aeronautical University (ERAU).

Upon graduation in 1994 he was invited to be an Adjunct Professor in the ERAU Eglin AFB Center. He continued to instruct at various locations for the next 20 years. He was one of the first instructors that taught ERAU courses on the Internet. He taught his last course in Texas in 2014.

After 38 years of service in the field of aviation, he retired in Fort Worth, Texas, on his birthday, 19 August 2016. Since his retirement he has worked on this manuscript, "*The Second Team*", transcribing his journal from Korea and Iran, and even anticipating writing his first fictional novel. He and Carol are actively engaged in their lives at church and continue to seek truth through their Biblical research and studies. Downing is a serious religious student of ancient history and the Scriptures and enjoys sharing his in-depth articles with family and close friends.

For more information, additional pictures, and updates visit:

www.jamescdowningjr.com

www.encodableimpact.com

Made in the USA
Columbia, SC
22 October 2021